Introduction to Teaching

The expectati   to Teaching,
which is the s   , provides a
fully up-to-da   ersonal and
professional s

This compre   ith Teacher
Training Ass   e of all the
modules incl

Taking into ac   ave incorporated new m   proaches to
planning, ta   ements and
continuing p

The book inc

- The
- Chile
- The
- Plan
- Teach
- Speci
- Worki

An Introduction to Teaching will be an indispensable textbook and resource for all students training to be teachers and NQTs whether at primary or secondary level. It is the generic textbook of the Teaching series, which features a range of subject-based and issues-based textbooks.

Professor Gill Nicholls has taught in secondary schools for a number of years and is now Director of King's Institute of Learning and Teaching at King's College London.

An Introduction to Teaching

Second Edition

A handbook for primary and secondary school teachers

Edited by Gill Nicholls

RoutledgeFalmer
Taylor & Francis Group

LONDON AND NEW YORK

First published 1999
by Kogan Page Ltd
120 Pentonville Road
London N1 9JN
Reprinted 2000

Second edition published 2004
by RoutledgeFalmer
11 New Fetter Lane
London EC4P 4EE

Simultaneously published in the USA and Canada
by RoutledgeFalmer
29 West 35th Street, New York, NY 10001

RoutledgeFalmer is an imprint of the Taylor & Francis Group

© 1999 Gill Nicholls
© 2004 Gill Nicholls for editorial material and selection and the contributors for individual chapters

Typeset by Saxon Graphics Ltd, Derby
Printed and bound in Great Britain by St Edmundsbury Press, Bury St Edmunds, Suffolk

British Library Cataloguing in Publication Data
A catalogue record for this book is available from the British Library

Library of Congress Cataloging in Publication Data
A catalog record for this book has been requested

ISBN 0–415–33531–0

Contents

CONTENTS

Introduction

Gill Nicholls

Teacher training continues to go through significant changes, the most recent of which has been the response to *Qualifying to Teach: Professional standards for Qualified Teacher Status and requirements for initial teacher training* [TTA 2002]. This document has increased the expectations of what it is to be a teacher, and have also set the standards by which future teachers are to be assessed. School-based training has not changed: trainees are still expected to spend the majority of their training time in schools with their mentors. However, the TTA 2002 document gives clear categories and standards under which trainees have to demonstrate their abilities; these include:

- knowledge and understanding;
- planning, teaching and class management;
- monitoring, assessment, reporting and accountability;
- other professional requirements.

This book aims to help guide the trainee through each category, with the anticipated help of their mentor. The underlying principle of the book is that teaching is an art as well as a science. Teaching is one of the most creative and satisfying professions to be involved in. Yet as in any profession there are key elements, skills, practices and standards that have to be achieved, if effective and efficient practitioners are to be developed. This book addresses all the key areas of the TTA 2002. In some chapters this is made more explicit than others; however, throughout it is assumed that trainees will have their own copy of the circular and gain, with the help of the book, a good working knowledge and understanding of the standards required to gain qualified teacher status (QTS).

The book through its tasks and overall design is aimed at helping trainees develop their skills, knowledge and pedagogic practice so that they not only meet the demands of TTA 2002 but also develop and nurture their own philosophy of teaching.

Every teacher-training course starts trainees on their way. Learning the art and craft of teaching is a process, one that lasts a career – from trainee to newly qualified teacher (NQT) to very experienced teacher. The book attempts to address this learning process by involving the mentor in the trainee's learning. It also shows in later chapters the need to understand what it is to be professional and be involved in continual professional development. The final chapter is specifically aimed at the NQT – taking the trainee from 'trainee' to 'newly qualified teacher'. It allows the NQT to have confidence in what they can do as well as prepare them for the challenges ahead.

Structure of the book

The book is specifically designed to direct trainees at each stage of their learning. Each chapter is designated to a specific task aimed at focusing the trainee on key areas of development. The book is generic in its approach, but all areas and phases of education are catered for through the tasks.

Trainees are expected to use the text as a means of facilitating their learning, within their chosen phase of training. The text highlights key development areas and issues that need to be addressed in order to gain QTS. As such the book can be used as a whole, working through from start to finish, or as a resource that can be dipped in and out of as appropriate to the trainee's learning and development needs. The objectives set in each chapter reflect the demands set in TTA 2002 as a means of achieving QTS.

The various authors of this text feel that the way the book has been devised allows creativity, motivation and self-development to thrive, while also meeting the highly defined legislative standards required of those wishing to join the teaching profession.

1 An Introduction to Teaching

James Williams

> Education... is the greatest work of all those which lie ready to a man's hand just at present. (T H Huxley, 'A liberal education and where to find it', address to the South London Working Men's College, 4 January 1869)

Your vision of what it is like to be a teacher is probably a composite one made up of memories of your own teachers and the media representation of teachers, with a little bit of you thrown in. What it takes to be a teacher is dedication, professionalism, intelligence, commitment, energy and above all else intuition: knowing what is the right thing to do in any given situation. This chapter is an overview of teaching and introduces you to the concepts related to effective teaching and learning. In reaching Qualified Teacher Status (QTS) you will need to demonstrate various skills and attributes, over and above those listed above.

The Teacher Training Agency (TTA) specifies the standards that all trainees must reach in order to be awarded QTS. They are set out in *Qualifying to Teach: Professional standards for Qualified Teacher Status and requirements for initial teacher training* (TTA, 2002a). These standards came into effect on 1 September 2002. Your training is designed to enable you to reach those standards; this book is intended to help to achieve this.

Objectives

By the end of this chapter you should be able to:

- understand the historical context of education in England and Wales;
- identify the key areas you are required to meet to gain QTS;
- understand the relationship between the statutory requirements and your personal development as a teacher;
- identify the characteristics of good teaching and of effective teachers.

A brief historical context of education in England and Wales

The 1870 Elementary Education Act, recognized as the first Act to regulate schools and teachers, resulted from a realization that teachers and teaching can only be successful if carefully structured and regulated. The Act prescribed what should be done in those institutions designated as 'schools'. A main feature of the Act was the establishment of the first education authorities, referred to as school boards, and it set up a countrywide system of schools that all children could attend. Thomas Henry Huxley (1825–1895) was a prime mover in the world of Victorian education. When the London School Board was established, it was charged with setting the education agenda of the day. Huxley campaigned for a place on the Marylebone ward of the board with, among others, Elizabeth Garrett, the first woman doctor. His influence on education in London and nationally was profound, especially in establishing science in the education framework, or curriculum of the day.

Since that first Act, education has been the central plank of political parties of all persuasions, and the inaugural 1870 Act has given way to many others, notably the 1944 Act that remained the main legislation governing schools for over 50 years. The next major Act, the 1988 Education Act, established the introduction of a National Curriculum. It was soon realized that the legislation governing schools needed to be simplified and consolidated. This led to the introduction of two consolidating Acts of parliament to draw all of the now widespread school legislation together – the 1996 Education Act and the 1996 Schools Inspections Act. The 1997 Act established long needed principles with respect to the physical restraint of pupils. Since then, there have been two major legislative Acts that have brought about major reforms to the school education system in England and Wales. First, there was the 1998 School Standards and Framework Act that created new categories of schools, namely community schools, foundation schools and voluntary schools, thereby ending the experimental and somewhat controversial Grant Maintained schools. In addition, the passing of the Teaching and Higher Education Act 1998 made new provisions with respect to teacher training, introducing standards for QTS, along with student fees, grants and loans.

In 2001, the DfES published a White Paper, *Schools Achieving Success* (DfES, 2001), which outlined the government's plans for education reform. The key features of the White Paper are:

- a more flexible curriculum;
- measures to support a less rigid framework for the staffing of schools;
- enhanced provisions to tackle poor performance;
- greater flexibility for school governance; and
- greater transparency for school finance.

In 2002, a Green Paper outlined the government's proposed reforms for 14–19 education, including ideas for creating a more flexible curriculum and improving technical and vocational education and its status in society.

Table 1.1 The Main Education Acts of England and Wales and their principal provisions. (This is not a comprehensive list of all Acts relating to education provision in England and Wales)

Date and Act	Main Provisions
1870 Elementary Education Act	Establishment of School Boards Allows for Boards to create and enforce by-laws for compulsory school attendance
1902 Education Act	Established the provision of Local Education Authorities (LEAs) Established the provision of county secondary schools
1944 Education Act	The basis of current law on education (repealed and largely replaced by the 1996 Act)
1980 Education Act	Established school governors for primary schools Established the right of parental choice of schools and the right of appeal if a child fails to gain a place at the school of first choice
1981 Education Act	Major changes introduced over the education of children with Special Educational Needs (SENs)
1986 Education (No 2) Act	Reform of school governing bodies
1988 Education Reform Act	Establishment of the National Curriculum Provision for schools to obtain Grant Maintained Status (GMS) Introduction of Local Management for Schools (LMS) Creation of a Standing Advisory Council on Religious Education (SACRE) required of all Local Education Authorities (LEAs) Provision for the establishment of City Technology Colleges (CTCs) Requirement for all pupils in maintained schools to attend a daily act of worship
1992 Education (Schools) Act	Establishment of new provisions for the inspection of schools Creation of Registered Inspectors (for the Office for Standards in Education: Ofsted) Outlined the functions and powers of Her Majesty's Chief Inspector of Schools
1993 Education Act	Creation of the Funding Agency for Schools (FAS) Creation of the School Curriculum and Assessment Authority (now part of the Qualifications and Curriculum Authority) Creation of a Special Educational Needs (SENs) tribunal and Code of Practice The Act was repealed in 1996 and replaced with the 1996 Education Act and the School Inspections Act
1994 Education Act	Established the Teacher Training Agency (TTA)

1996 Education Act	A consolidation Act, allowing for regulations and laws relating to schools set up by previous Acts to be covered in one statute. Although many laws have not been altered from earlier Acts those Acts have been repealed, including the 1944 Act which was the basis of much legislation relating to primary and secondary schools for over 50 years
1997 Education Act	Established the position over the physical restraint of pupils and detention of pupils in schools. The 1997 Education (Schools) Act also abolished the assisted places scheme
1998 School Standards and Framework Act	Limited class sizes for 5–7-year olds Established education action zones (EAZs) Required local education authorities (LEAs) to prepare educational development plans (EDPs) Abolished Grant Maintained schools Revised school admissions legislation Introduced new financial arrangements for school budgets Provided for early years education
2000 Learning and Skills Act	Primarily concerned with post-compulsory education (PCE) and the organizations involved in PCE, but also impacted on schools that provided PCE
2002 Education Act	This legislated for the proposals outlined in the government white paper *Schools Achieving Success*. The main provisions are:

- granting schools variance from the national curriculum requirements in order to innovate in the curriculum;
- good schools allowed more autonomy and flexibility over their National Curriculum provision;
- ability for schools to form companies to procure or provide services;
- greater flexibility in school governance;
- the incorporation of a foundation stage into the National Curriculum framework (for reception pupils aged from 3 to 5);
- power for the Secretary of State to set a minimum level of budget for any LEA;
- consolidation of legislation on teaching and support staff employment.

The legal status of schools

A school is simply an educational institution which is outside the further education sector and the higher education sector and which provides any one or more of the following:

- primary education, ie up to age 11;
- secondary education, ie from age 11–16
- full-time education for those who are over compulsory school age (16) but under the age of 19.

In essence there are two types of schools: maintained and non-maintained. The maintained schools are those funded by central government and the non-maintained are funded by private subscription.

Maintained schools

The School Standards and Framework Act 1998 created a new legal framework of maintained schools.

Community schools are mostly set up by Local Education Authorities; the LEA owns the school premises and the schools are fully funded by LEAs for both revenue and capital expenditure. The LEA employs staff and is the admissions authority, ie it controls the admissions policy and procedure.

Foundation schools (many of which were formerly known as grant-maintained schools) are owned either by the school governing body or by trustees of the school, but LEAs fund them in a similar way to community schools. The governing body is the admissions authority and employs the staff.

Voluntary controlled schools and voluntary aided schools include former special agreement schools and those grant-maintained schools that originally had voluntary aided status. They are owned either by school trustees or by the founding body of the school (such as the Church of England or the Catholic Church). Both types of school receive full funding for revenue expenditure, but voluntary aided schools are expected to contribute 15 per cent of capital costs. The LEA employs the staff and is the admissions authority in voluntary controlled schools, while the governing body performs these functions in voluntary aided schools.

A common misconception when using terminology relating to the status of schools arises over the term 'independent'. It is usually applied to fee-paying schools, but this is strictly incorrect. Non-fee-paying schools (ie maintained schools) can have independent status. The term refers to independence from the legal requirements to teach the National Curriculum, not independence from funding by central government. The following schools are technically independent schools, though they are not fee-paying.

City Technology Colleges (CTCs) and *City Colleges for the Technology of the Arts* (CCTAs) were established by the Education Reform Act 1988. Although they are largely publicly funded with additional funding from private sponsors, they have been designated as independent schools. They must be in urban areas, provide education for pupils of different abilities from the age of 11 who are wholly, or mainly, drawn from the area in which the school is situated, and they must provide a broad curriculum with an emphasis on science and technology, or, in the case of a CCTA, on the application of technology to the creative and performing arts. They are not allowed to charge fees.

City Academies are a new type of independent school in England; the first schools became operational in September 2001. These academies will replace seriously failing secondary maintained schools in urban areas. They are built and managed by partnerships involving the government and sponsors from the voluntary sector, churches and business and are registered as independent schools, subject to inspection by OFSTED, but charge no fees. They must cater for all ability 11 to 16/18-year olds, according to the pattern of local provision. They have advantages in that they will have state of the art facilities (whether in newly built or refurbished premises), offer a broad curriculum, but with a special emphasis on one area of the curriculum such as science and technology, and an emphasis on the needs of the individual pupil. They are charged with developing in their pupils the qualities of enterprise, self-reliance and responsibility that young people need for adult life.

Non-maintained schools

Non-maintained schools are known as private schools, but are often referred to as 'independent schools'. Some long-established private schools are known as 'public schools'. Private schools do not receive direct government funding and most private schools have charitable status and, as such, benefit from tax relief. They may also apply for some public support, for example, through the National Lottery. They charge fees that can vary from £3,000 per year to over £20,000 for a top secondary school.

Routes into teaching

Teaching has been a graduate profession since 1983. Prior to 1983 non-graduates were offered a route into teaching via a certificate in education (Cert Ed). Many who came through this route subsequently undertook an enhancement course to upgrade their teaching qualification to degree status as a bachelor in education (BEd), though many excellent Cert Ed teachers are still teaching today.

In 1992 the then government set out the first framework for initial teacher training, referred to as competencies, in Circular 9/92. The competencies covered the following areas:

- subject knowledge;
- subject application;
- class management;
- assessment and recording of pupil progress;
- further professional development.

In 1994 the Teacher Training Agency was established to manage initial teacher training (ITT) and it devised the first 'standards' in 1998 in Circular 04/98. There was also a national curriculum for ITT that set out the expectations of trainees with respect to subject knowledge. It is these standards that form the basis of QTT, the current standards for QTS that all trainees must reach.

In 1990 the first employment-based routes into teaching were introduced – articled and licensed teachers – but these were soon discontinued. The idea of employment-based routes was revived with first, the introduction of SCITT (School Centred Initial Teacher Training) where schools were able to take responsibility for the complete training of teachers, without any formal university input; although the trainees were not formally employees of the school many did end up employed by their schools as vacancies arose. Then the Graduate and Registered Teacher Programmes (GTP and RTP) were introduced by the TTA as a fully employed route. Initially, trainees are employed as non-qualified teachers and receive their training 'on the job'. This often results in conferment of QTS, but not the academic award of a Post Graduate Certificate in Education (PGCE).

Many teachers and trainees are confused about the status of the PGCE and QTS. The former is an academic award conferred by an institution, for example a university or higher education institute, while the latter is the licence to teach awarded by the DfES through the General Teaching Council for England or Wales (GTCE/GTCW). It is this status, not a PGCE, which means that you are paid on the qualified teacher pay scale. It is possible to have a PGCE without QTS, for example a PGCE in adult and further education. Likewise it is possible to have QTS without a PGCE, as is the case with the majority of GTP trainees. The registered teacher programme is for those who do not yet have first degree status and who wish to complete their study for degree status alongside their teacher training. This normally takes place over two years and is probably the least popular route into teaching.

For those wishing to be primary teachers, a four-year undergraduate degree (BA, BEd or BSc with QTS) is the most common and competitive entry into teaching. It is also possible to train for primary teaching via a full-time one-year PGCE, having previously studied for a first degree. For secondary education, the traditional route is via a first degree followed by a one-year full-time PGCE. Recently, however, new routes for gaining a PGCE have been introduced. These include part-time two-year PGCEs, flexible PGCEs that are modular and may be completed either full time over one year or less, or part time up to two years.

All trainees have to meet minimum entry qualifications. These include grade A* – C (or its equivalent) in the GCSE examination in English and mathematics and, for those wishing to do primary teaching, a GCSE grade A* – C in science if they were born after 1979. As has been stated, all qualified teachers must now hold a degree from a UK higher education institution or an equivalent qualification.

All entrants must have met the Secretary of State's requirements for physical and mental fitness to teach. An enhanced criminal background check is carried out in addition to ensuring that entrants have not previously been excluded from teaching or working with children by checking a central government list called list 99. In order to gain entry to ITT it is now a requirement that admissions tutors check that potential entrants can read effectively, and are able to communicate clearly and accurately in spoken and written Standard English. This is normally done during the interview stage: all candidates admitted for training must have taken part in a group or individual interview.

The standards for Qualified Teacher Status

The standards for the award of QTS are outcome statements that set out what a trainee teacher must know, understand and be able to do. The standards are organized in three inter-related sections that describe the criteria for the award:

1. Professional values and practice.
2. Knowledge and understanding.
3. Teaching.

It would be a mistake to look at the standards for QTS and any requirements for subject knowledge and understanding and assume in a rather simplistic way that these will necessarily lead to quality teaching. Stones (1992) confirms that this view is inadequate. He rightly denigrates this surprisingly widely held thesis and contends that insufficient attention is paid to knowledge and understanding of the theories behind teaching. Although the standards do not explicitly refer to these theories, they are implicit in meeting the standards. Many trainees and experienced teachers believe that the theoretical approach to teaching is actually a waste of time and the legendary 'Monday morning theory' lectures were of little value to them. Try not to fall into this trap. Understanding how you teach, how children learn and acquire knowledge, understanding and skills is essential to good teaching. Your course, despite being labelled a 'training' course, is much more. It is also an education, and educated teachers understand not just what they teach but also how to teach and how children learn.

Much of what is implicit in the standards is grounded in sound theory.

1. Professional values and practice

These standards outline the attitudes and commitment to be expected of anyone qualifying to be a teacher, and are derived from the professional code of the General Teaching Council for England (GTCE). This revolves around the notion of professionalism and the expectation that teachers should have a commitment to raising the educational achievement of all their pupils, regardless of their background or current level of attainment. As a teacher you will need to develop awareness of your pupils' social, cultural, linguistic and ethnic backgrounds and their individual needs. With this awareness your teaching should be planned to engage pupils and to challenge them. This does not mean that you are required to have an intimate knowledge of the backgrounds of all the pupils you teach: it is more about the attitude you have towards teaching pupils from diverse backgrounds with diverse needs.

Gaining the respect of your pupils is also a key to good teaching and this set of standards includes the requirement to treat pupils with respect and consideration as this will in turn lead to respect for the teacher. As a teacher you will be role models for your pupils and, as you would expect, that role model must be a positive one. You will be expected as a teacher to demonstrate this by respecting others, adopting appropriate attitudes and values, respecting cultural diversity and exercising a degree of social responsibility.

As a teacher, a key skill is that of communication; not just communication of ideas to pupils but also general communication with other audiences, such as other teachers and, in particular, parents and carers. Trainee teachers are expected to know the statutory rights of parents and carers regarding the information given about their child's progress in school. Giving feedback to parents and carers that is both informative and supportive, for example giving suggestions as to how they can support their child's education, calls for care and skill. As a trainee, you will not be required to do this without help and support from other, qualified staff, but it is, nevertheless and important skill that needs to be developed right from the start.

A school is a community, set within the wider community and, as such, you will be expected to contribute to the community as a whole. No teacher should work in isolation and the days of teachers working behind closed doors with little or no accountability for what is happening in their classrooms are long gone. School life is rich and varied. Teachers regularly share with pupils personal hobbies, setting up clubs for example, or simply having fun at the end of term in concerts and school productions. Some unlikely teachers can display hidden talents: the science teacher with a good singing voice, the art teacher who plays the flute, even the occasional staff room rock band, have made pupils sit up and take notice. Sharing these things in schools is a positive contribution to the school community and, when shared with the local residents via a school production, shows a commitment to the wider community. Not every trainee has a hidden talent, but even joining in events as an usher or box office assistant is a positive enrichment activity.

Teachers who work in isolation from their peers are often less effective than those who actively seek teamwork. In addition to other teachers there is a variety of staff who contribute towards effective schooling, from administrative staff to classroom assistants and technical staff. Trainees' skills in collaborative working and managing the work of others in the classroom are also covered in the standards.

Training for and gaining QTS is not the end of your professional development. Just as learner drivers continue to learn and, hopefully, improve their driving skills as they encounter new and different road situations, so too should you be concerned with your professional development as a teacher after qualifying. During ITT you will come across the term 'reflective practitioner'. This is not an empty phrase to be bandied about in academic essays and assignments. It is something that is critical to your development as a teacher. The ability to reflect on your teaching and to learn from your mistakes and successes is central to high quality teaching. You will be asked to comment critically on your teaching and from that to make informed judgements about how you could improve and how effective you are as a teacher. Once you are qualified you are expected to continue to reflect and develop your teaching skills. Schools should provide opportunities for your development, which may include sending you on In Service Training (INSET) courses run by local authorities, universities or commercial companies. Likewise you have an obligation to identify needs for yourself and request specific training in areas you have identified as necessary for your professional development or to enable you to climb the promotion ladder.

You will also need to show an awareness of the major legislation that applies to schools and teachers, such as the duty of care teachers must have for pupils' health and safety at work; your pay and employment conditions; and the statutory requirements for teaching your subject(s). The legislation is comprehensive and you are not required to have detailed knowledge, but it is a requirement that you at least are aware of the main legislation covering your work as a teacher and where to find help and advice when necessary. It is a good idea to join one of the main teaching unions or professional subject associations as they can offer advice and support of a specialist nature.

2. Knowledge and understanding

'Of course, teachers should know everything.' This is often hinted at, but is it true? Can you really be the fount of all knowledge? Can a primary teacher really be an expert in all subjects? The simple answer is no, but it is not unreasonable to suggest that a teacher should have a basic level of expertise. This will vary according to your subject and the phase of education that you are teaching or plan to teach in. Having a highly qualified scientist teach German, with no working knowledge of the language, is a recipe for disaster. This area of the standards requires NQTs to be confident and authoritative in the subjects they teach and to have a clear understanding of how all pupils should progress and what teachers should expect them to achieve.

The basic requirement is that you have secure subject knowledge for the subject(s) you are trained to teach. There is no doubt that having a well-qualified teacher who has secure subject knowledge and the ability to learn new subjects (which is essential in primary teaching where individual subject teaching by specialists is not the norm) is a distinct advantage. As the TTA states, 'Secure subject knowledge enables teachers to judge how ideas and concepts can be broken down and sequenced logically so they can support pupils' learning' (TTA, 2002b, p18). In an attempt to raise the standards of those training to teach, in 1998 the TTA introduced national curricula for primary and secondary courses of ITT in English, mathematics and science. These specified the core of knowledge, understanding and skills that trainees need in order to teach the various Key Stages and post-16. While these curricula are no longer in force, they are still a useful guide to the range and level of knowledge and understanding needed (DfEE, 1998).

How teachers teach – their pedagogy, and what teachers teach – their subject knowledge, cannot easily be split. Moon and Mayes (1994) observed that only 100 years ago a central characteristic of pedagogical accomplishment was knowledge of content. They argue that research in the 1990s on teaching exposed a lack of emphasis on subject knowledge:

> The emphasis is on how teachers manage their classrooms, organize activities, allocate time and turns, structure assignments, ascribe praise and blame, formulate levels of their questions, plan lessons and judge general student understanding. What we miss are questions about the content of the lessons taught, the questions asked and the explanations offered. (p127)

No longer is this the case. Subject knowledge is a key requisite for teaching. The question is, how do you transfer your knowledge into a form that pupils can understand? Shulman (1996) categorized knowledge in three ways:

a. Content knowledge: the subject specific knowledge that a teacher possesses.
b. Pedagogic knowledge: how that subject knowledge can be used during teaching.
c. Curricular knowledge: knowledge of the whole curriculum, its structure and the materials used.

Given that the role of a teacher is to develop knowledge, understanding and skills in children, how these three interact is important. A teacher must be aware of the relationship between them in order to be effective. A successful teacher has the right balance and provides pupils with opportunities to increase their competence in all three areas. The result is pupil learning. But what is the relationship between a trainee's knowledge and pupil learning? Alexander *et al* (1992) say of the teacher's subject knowledge: '(it) is a critical factor at every point in the teaching process: in planning, assessing and diagnosing, task setting, questioning, explaining and giving feedback'. It is, therefore central to teaching.

The standards for QTS specify the scope of the knowledge and understanding required for teaching at each of the Key Stages. It also requires trainees to understand the broad aims and guidelines of the National Curriculum as taught in maintained schools. The National Curriculum is more than just a set of guidelines for subjects: it is founded on a set of values and principles that also aim to prepare pupils for life outside school. The National Curriculum is divided into Key Stages. These reflect defined periods of schooling and the issue of continuity and progression across these Key Stages is also addressed within the standards. Taking account of pupils' prior learning is central to effective continuity and progression as is an awareness of how pupils' physical and mental development affects learning. Theories of learning, child development and behaviour are essential to meeting this aspect of the standards.

The use of technology in schools to enhance learning experiences has been a feature of government investment for a number of years. Schools with hi-tech learning and teaching tools, high speed access to the Internet from a variety of locations and the use of interactive whiteboards, digital projectors, digital cameras, scanners, video, and control, sensing and data capture are a common feature of teaching. How trainees use Information and Communications Technology (ICT) effectively in teaching and in support of their own work (such as recording data, analysing pupil data, reporting to others on pupil progress) is also a feature of this section on knowledge and understanding. You are not required to be an advanced user or expert, but your training will encompass aspects of personal and professional use of ICT. All trainees are required to pass three government tests in order to be awarded QTS: literacy, numeracy and ICT. These tests measure whether trainees have acquired the basic and necessary skills in these three crucial areas of knowledge and understanding.

In becoming a professional teacher you have a duty to educate all pupils, regardless of ability. Your knowledge and understanding of the area of Special Educational Needs (SEN) will also be the subject of attention during and after your training. Knowledge of the range of learning and behavioural difficulties you may encounter as well as how to provide for a child's special educational needs is required.

3. Teaching

These standards relate to skills of planning, monitoring and assessment, and teaching and class management. They are underpinned by the values and knowledge covered in the first two sections. The section on teaching is the broadest and is subdivided into:

- planning, expectations and targets;
- monitoring and assessment;
- teaching and class management.

Planning, expectations and targets

Although these three subsections must not be treated in isolation as they are all interrelated and interdependent, it is necessary to tease out what is actually meant by the terms used.

There are four stages involved in planning and delivering a successful lesson:

a   *Preparing.* Thorough preparation will involve getting to grips with the subject knowledge required for the lesson or series of lessons and determination of the lesson objectives and learning outcomes (what you want to teach and what you want the pupils to learn). It will involve researching activities that are appropriate for fulfilling the objectives and outcomes and the required links to the National Curriculum and the school/national scheme of work that guide the delivery of the curriculum.

b. *Designing.* The design of a lesson is critical to its success. There must be variety in teaching styles and activities and the lessons must motivate the pupils and maintain their interest. The lesson must take into account evidence of pupils' past and current achievements, the expected standards for pupils within the age range being taught and the range and content of work that is relevant to pupils in that age range.

c. *Presenting.* The delivery of the lesson, its timing, and the way in which you execute your plan will be key contributory factors in its success.

d. *Evaluating.* An often forgotten part of successful planning is the incorporation of lessons learnt from previous experiences. Evaluating the success of lessons, or the reasons for failure, provides many pointers when designing future lessons. The notion of teachers as reflective practitioners is sometimes derided as to be so obvious that it is not worth pointing out. The importance of reflection should not be undervalued.

Before deciding the activities that pupils will attempt in the classroom, teachers must be clear about the purpose of the lesson. Clear learning objectives and learning outcomes are needed. It may well be that the lesson being planned is one in a series of lessons that form part or the whole of a scheme of work for a topic. In a primary setting it may be part of a multidisciplinary approach to a theme. In the secondary setting it is more likely to form part of a teaching scheme for Key Stage 3 or a GCSE specification (formerly known as a syllabus). As well as the purpose of the lesson, the planning must also take into account the context in which that lesson will be taught, for example as a practical lesson in science, art or music, as part of a specification in order to assess pupils against published criteria, or as a theoretical lesson delivering subject knowledge. Lesson planning takes place within the agreed curriculum and schemes of work delivered in schools (see Figure 1.1).

Planning must also have short, medium and long-term objectives linked to them. Short-term objectives for lessons, parts of lessons or short sequences of lessons will be much of the day-to-day work of the teacher. This must take place within a framework of medium and long-term planning. The medium term may be a topic or unit of work that will last for part or the whole of a teaching term. This, in

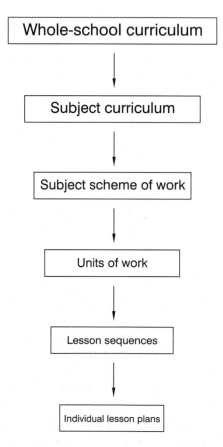

Figure 1.1   The place of lesson plans in the whole-school curriculum

turn, will be subsumed in a long-term plan that may be based on a Key Stage within the National Curriculum or an academic year. In secondary schools it may be part of the specification that leads towards a recognized certificate or award.

The care taken in planning lessons is more often than not reflected in their success in practice. A poorly planned lesson is rarely successful. It may take place without incident and the pupils may not necessarily run riot in the classroom, but the learning experience for the children will almost certainly be limited and narrowly focused.

Monitoring and assessment

The marking of pupil work is a core activity of teaching. There are many stereo-typical views of teachers marking – scores out of 10, grading by letter, any combi-nation of letters and numbers and the now legendary 'must do better' comment written in red. Teachers need to know how well pupils have learnt and under-stood what was intended so that they know what and how much progress has been made.

Marking is just one form of monitoring and assessment, and effective teachers utilize a range of strategies. Immediate feedback to pupils about their progress makes it more likely that pupils will progress in their learning. For this to happen, the monitoring and assessment of pupils should be integrated into day-to-day teaching. Day-to-day monitoring allows you to recognize when pupils are encoun-tering difficulties with concepts or skills: the job of the teacher is to address these difficulties and allow pupils to play an active part in their learning.

The day-to-day monitoring and assessment is just one facet. Assessment must also take place within nationally agreed frameworks and national benchmarks. To begin with, you will need expert guidance in how to mark and assess against national criteria; the goal is to be able to do this with minimal support.

It is vital at the start of your teaching career that you get into the habit of systematically recording pupil progress. During training, many trainees are advised to shadow experienced teachers as they mark, monitor and record pupil attainment. This is vital for continuity and progression in pupils' learning. Often comparisons with prior achievement will produce useful information that can aid planning and target setting for pupil progress. The information that a teacher has on individual progress is also needed for reporting to parents and for informing other teachers who may take on responsibility for that pupil's learning in subsequent years.

Parents and carers have a legal right to be informed of their children's progress in schools. As a trainee you are not required to provide those reports to parents, but experience of attending parent consultations is a key part of the process of understanding how good quality, accurate reports are produced and communicated home.

Teaching and class management

This is the aspect that trainee teachers often consider to be the most important. Teaching can be defined as 'the art or profession of a teacher'. As a strict definition it is not particularly useful: it gives no clue as to the actual process. Claxton (1984, p211) defines teaching as 'what one person does to try and help another to learn', a broad definition that includes a number of the activities that most people associate with the act of teaching:

- demonstrating skills;
- giving friendly advice;
- explaining things;
- dictating homework.

Claxton goes on to maintain that a prime consideration for teachers is how learners learn: 'If teachers do not understand what learning is and how it happens, they are as likely to hinder as to help' (p212). Kyriacou (1997) defines effective teaching as '(that) which successfully achieves learning by pupils intended by the teacher'. Again this makes the common sense link between learning and teaching. For learning to occur there must be order in the classroom and this is where the notion of sound classroom management comes in to play. The standards recognize this and place an emphasis on building successful relationships with pupils centred on teaching and learning. Many behavioural problems teachers come across may be related to boredom. Pupils will often complain of being bored during lessons, which may result from the repetition of work or because the pupil is unable to do the work. If the issue is a failure of engagement due to a lack of interest, teachers must be aware of this and employ strategies and teaching that are varied and stimulate interest.

Developing an arsenal of teaching strategies, methods and styles is essential if you are to become an effective teacher. In short, the motto is: 'Teach for 20 years; do not teach one year 20 times.'

The characteristics of a good teacher

What makes a good teacher and what good teaching is, are a source of endless debate. In reality there is no one correct answer to these two questions. Kyriacou (1997) cites a survey conducted in 1931 designed to ascertain the most important qualities of a good teacher. Teachers, pupils, teacher trainers and others reported the following qualities in order of frequency:

- personality and will;
- intelligence;

- sympathy and tact;
- open-mindedness;
- a sense of humour.

This view of the characteristics of good teachers is in itself not helpful. Someone with a strong personality and all of the above characteristics will not necessarily make a good teacher. The limitations of such a simplistic characterization was also recognized in the 1930s:

> Education is not so simple a business as is often supposed. It is not enough for the teacher to collect together a mass of knowledge, and retail it to his class. Nor is it enough for his personality to be strong enough to make the children do what he wants them to do... Education in fact depends both on the school environment and on the response of the children to the teaching as well as on the subject and the teacher. (Board of Education, 1937)

It was clearly recognized that the complex nature of teaching and education could not be unravelled by a simple categorization of qualities, skills and knowledge. Yet that is what we have in the standards for QTS. Stones (1992) confirms that despite attempts to come to a consensus on the nature of quality teaching, there is none. Just how far the standards define what good teaching and a good teacher are, and how they can assist in the development of quality teaching and teachers, are the subject of this book.

The education of children is a multifaceted process that has a crucial aspect that cannot be ignored: teacher/pupil interaction and the structure and delivery of activities within the classroom. This is the one aspect that legislation cannot prescribe – what actually happens in the classroom. Black (1995) states that 'teaching is both an art and a craft that can be learned through hard work'. There is no doubting that teaching is hard work and learning to teach is not a simple process, but recent moves to clarify the requirements have identified the areas in which trainees need to be accomplished in order to qualify as teachers.

Task 1.1: The characteristics of a good teacher

Describing the perfect teacher is not easy and, indeed, it may not be desirable for reasons made clear earlier. For this task you need to have in mind teachers and lessons from your own experience. Think about lessons you attended as a pupil or about lessons run by teachers you have observed. Make two lists of notes: one for those things that you believe made the teacher memorable and/or successful and that made the lesson a positive experience, and the other for a lesson that was not successful. List those features that can be ascribed to one of the three categories of influence: the teacher, the pupil and the subject. Now think about the following:

- Who/what has the greatest influence in the classroom?
- How could the proportion of each of the influences (teacher, pupil subject) in a lesson impact on its outcome?
- Is a totally teacher-dominated lesson always successful?
- Does giving pupils autonomy in their learning lead to more highly motivated pupils?

References

Alexander, R et al (1992) *Curriculum Organization and Classroom Practice in Primary Schools: A discussion paper*, DES, London

Black, P (1995) Curriculum and assessment in science education: the policy interface, *International Journal of Science Education*, **17** (4), pp453–69

Board of Education (1937) *Handbook of Suggestions for Teachers*, TSO, Norwich

Claxton, G (1984) *Live and Learn: An introduction to the psychology of growth and change in everyday life*, Harper and Row, London

DfEE (1998) *Requirements for Courses of Initial Teacher Training*, Circular 04/98

DfES (2001) *Schools Achieving Success*, White Paper, DfES, London

Kyriacou, C (1997) *Effective Teaching in Schools*, 2nd edn, Stanley Thornes, Cheltenham

Moon, B and Mayes, A (1994) *Teaching and Learning in the Secondary School*, Routledge, London

Shulman, L S (1986) Those who understand: knowledge and growth in teaching, *Educational Researcher*, **15**, pp4–14

Stones, E (1992) *Quality Teaching: A sample of cases*, Routledge, London

TTA (2002a) *Qualifying to Teach: Professional standards for Qualified Teacher Status and requirements for initial teacher training*, TTA Publication Number TPU 0803/02–02

TTA (2002b) *Qualifying to Teach: Handbook of guidance*, TTA Publication Number TPU 0934/10–02

2 The National Curriculum – 15 years of reform

Steve Alsop, Graham Dock and Lyn Leversa

The aim of this chapter is to help the trainee become familiar with the National Curriculum – the compulsory curriculum for all pupils aged 5–16 in state schools in England and Wales.

Objectives

By the end of this chapter the trainee should be able to:

- understand the structure and terminology of the National Curriculum;
- explore key issues in the implementation of the curriculum;
- recognize the role that their specialist subject has in the curriculum;
- appreciate the classroom experiences of school pupils;
- appreciate the role the curriculum has in what is taught.

Introduction

The school curriculum has been a topic of intense debate for many years; in the last 15 years, in England and Wales, the debate has firmly focused on the National Curriculum. In 1988, in over 20,000 UK schools the curriculum changed – this magnitude and type of state intervention in education is unprecedented. It is now 15 years since the Educational Reform Act (ERA) and during these years the curriculum has undergone both major and minor revisions. The implementation of the original proposals was swift: four years after the ERA most significant features were in place. In all state schools in England and Wales, for example, it was possible to identify the subjects and content that all pupils were entitled to receive (ages 5 to 16). Further modifications were made in 1995 and extensive consultation has led to the implementation of a revised National Curriculum and new GCSE syllabuses in 2000 and the introduction of Key Stage 3 strategies.

What is a curriculum?

It is difficult to reach a consensus over the definition of the term 'curriculum'. *The Collins Dictionary,* for example, defines a curriculum as 'a list of all the courses of study offered by a school or college'. This would seem to place an emphasis on school subjects and, presumably, more specifically the content of these subjects. In this regard, the 'curriculum' contains what should be taught and could look like a syllabus or a list of content – much like a type of revision guideline used for a final examination. A list of what content should be taught in schools is clearly important and in the following discussion we refer to this as 'the subject curriculum'. However, some may argue that a curriculum is more than this and that to restrict a curriculum to a list of subject content would fail to embrace significant considerations such as how courses are taught or the amount of time spent in school or on a particular subject. These are also defining components of school experience – for example, the amount of time spent on a subject carries messages about its importance or perceived intellectual difficulty.

Alternatively, it could be argued that a 'curriculum' should be defined as a product: a description of what is learnt rather than what is taught. In this case it would place greater emphasis on experiences, learning goals, objectives and assessment. Of course, what is taught by a teacher can be quite different to what is learnt by a pupil. As we will indicate, the National Curriculum specifies both the taught content as well as content that should be assessed.

So far, the discussion has considered the assessed subject curriculum; however, a school curriculum will also contain social, personal and health elements – these are commonly referred to as 'the pastoral curriculum'. Furthermore, a balanced curriculum will cover cross-curriculum issues of, for instance, equal opportunities and key life skills, including communication, study, problem solving and information technology. A 'whole-school' curriculum is, at least, comprised of these three areas.

In this chapter, the National Curriculum is outlined – the statutory component of the 'whole curriculum' for state schools in England and Wales. This curriculum has evolved and continues to evolve and as a consequence we outline the curriculum in its current phase. Before outlining this curriculum, a brief historical background to the current legislation is provided.

Background to the National Curriculum

The National Curriculum for England and Wales was just one of a raft of major changes to education brought about by the 1988 Education Reform Act, including Local Management of Schools and the introduction of Grant Maintained Schools and City Technology Colleges. In order to understand the present form of the National Curriculum, it is useful to have some knowledge of the background that led up to what was, in British terms, a revolution. Some of the main political events, ideas and personalities are identified as a means of encouraging further reading.

Considering state education from its inception, say the Forster Act of 1870, it becomes apparent that education in Britain has existed for a long time without anything resembling a National Curriculum. Indeed, for a large part of the 20th century the control of the curriculum by the individual classroom teacher was regarded by some as a pillar of democracy. The important 1944 Education Act, which established secondary education for all as an integral part of the system, paid little attention to the curriculum other than the requirement that: 'it shall be the duty of the local education authority for every area, so far as their powers extend, to contribute towards the spiritual, moral, mental and physical development of the community' (Section 7).

There is not an obvious starting date but certainly the origins of the National Curriculum can be traced to before the Conservative Government of 1988. Furthermore, the events and influences are not confined to a single political party. To justify these last two statements, it is necessary to look at what was being said and written about education during the two decades which led up to the ERA. For the first four years of the 1970s, the Conservatives were in power and Margaret Thatcher was Secretary of State for Education. Raising of the school-leaving age aside, there was little that was revolutionary about government education policy during this period. On the contrary, it continued to maintain and develop policies that had been developed in the 1960s. The rapid growth of comprehensive schools continued. Simon (1988) points out that more schools went comprehensive between 1970 and 1974 than either before or after. The major policy statement of the period took the form of a White Paper in 1972: *Education: A framework for expansion,* that set out a ten-year programme for educational advance involving substantially increased expenditure in five directions: a new nursery programme; a larger building programme for the renewal of secondary, special and primary schools; a larger teaching force to improve staffing levels in schools; a new initiative to improve the pre-service and in-service training of teachers; and the development of a wider range of opportunities in higher education. It is difficult to find the roots of the 1988 Education Reform Act here. Certainly, a National Curriculum and a system of assessment were not part of this 10-year plan.

Within Conservative ranks as a whole, however, there were many who were not happy with the comprehensive 'roller coaster'. One of the most visible manifestations of this dissatisfaction was the series of Black Papers which appeared between 1969 and 1977. Each of the papers consisted of a collection of essays from a wide range of contributors including academics, teachers, MPs and various celebrities. A number of connected themes can be seen running through the publications. There was a conviction that educational *values* and *standards* were threatened by what the authors saw as a growing orthodoxy of progressive education. They argued that the advance of comprehensive schools should be slowed and grammar schools retained to help preserve standards and to provide *choice*. This debate is still very much alive today.

Rhodes Boyson replaced Dyson as co-editor of the Black Papers and, with Cox in 1975, started to advance alternative policies, rather than recommending moderation of prevailing ones. In the final Black Paper, under the heading: 'Letters to Members of Parliament: School Standards' the editors suggest:

> a return of the national inspectorate of HMIs to their original task of the inspection of schools. At the same time the national monitoring of basic standards by examinations for all children at the ages of 7, 11 and 14 or 15 should be introduced. . . The school results of these tests should be available to parents, school governors and the local community. Names of children should not be published, but parents have a right to know the comparative achievement of schools.

There is much in this passage that is similar to aspects of the ERA; particularly striking is the reference to testing at ages 7, 11 and 14 or 15. If this is not a direct antecedent of assessment in the Act, then it can at least be acknowledged that the writing of the Black Papers and the appearance of extracts from them in the popular press helped fuel a growing concern with standards and accountability in schools. In doing so, they were helping to produce a climate that made possible the relatively smooth passage of the 1988 Act.

In both the academic world and in the media, there was, by the mid-1970s, a fierce argument in progress over whether educational standards were in decline. Whether this concern was well-founded or not is not material to the argument here; that the concern existed is very pertinent.

The year 1976 can be regarded as an important watershed. It was the year in which Thameside local authority won its case against the government not to implement comprehensive reorganization and also the year when Fred Mulley, Secretary of State for Education, furnished Prime Minister Callaghan with the HMI 'Yellow Book' that voiced concern about standards in comprehensive schools. It was this document that provided the basis for Callaghan's speech at Ruskin

College, Oxford, later that same year. This speech was announced to the media well in advance (CCCS, 1981) and in it the Prime Minister proposed a national debate around several themes:

> There is a challenge to us all in these days and a challenge to education is to examine its priorities and to secure as high efficiency as you can by the skilful use of the £6 billion of existing resources. Let me repeat some of the fields that need study because they cause concern. There are the methods and aims of informal instruction. The strong case for the so-called *core curriculum of basic knowledge*. What is the proper way of monitoring the use of resources in order to maintain a proper national standard of performance? What is the role of the inspectorate in relation to national standards and their maintenance? And there is a need to improve relations between industry and education.

Following the Ruskin speech, the Department of Education and Science organized eight regional one-day conferences under the heading 'Educating our Children' and set in motion what became known as the Great Debate. Discussion centred around the school curriculum 5–16, including the composition of a core curriculum, the assessment of standards, the education and training of teachers and the relation of school to work. Although the concerns are not dissimilar to those addressed by a different government a decade later, the solutions proposed in the subsequent Green Paper (DES, 1977) are different in kind and attention to detail.

The Green Paper points to the need for a 'core' or 'protected' part of the curriculum but seeks to establish a 'broad agreement' with the local education authorities and others on a framework for this. At the same time, it recognizes that a growing need 'for schools to demonstrate their accountability to the society which they serve requires a coherent and soundly based means of assessment for the educational system as a whole, for schools, and for individual pupils'.

The Green Paper did not, of course, bring about immediate tangible changes in schools or in the education system. It did enable and promote the continued discussion about the curriculum and during the next 10 years there appeared a steady stream of documents on the subject from the DES, culminating in *The National Curriculum 5–16: A Consultation Document*, in July of 1987. The Green Paper and the Ruskin speech also brought into open discussion within the education world and in the wider public domain topics which previously appeared to be the sole concern of the educational fringe, such as those writing for the Black Papers. Prominent among these topics were *accountability* and *evaluation*. It is these two topics, together with an increase in parental choice, that form the main political aims of the educational reforms of the 1980s, culminating in the 1988 ERA and the introduction of the National Curriculum.

The plan was to phase in the National Curriculum for the different Key Stages over a four-year period beginning in 1989. It soon became clear that the very detailed curriculum and assessment framework was running into manageability problems within schools. The teaching profession showed their opposition to the nature of this testing and the additional workload it involved by taking strike action. Significant modifications to the design and level of detail of the curriculum and to the approach to assessment were made in 1991. However, these changes were to prove insufficient and in 1993 the Government invited Sir Ron Dearing, Chairman of the National Curriculum Council and of the School Examinations and Assessment Council to carry out a review of the National Curriculum in England. A parallel review was carried out by the Curriculum Council for Wales. The new orders introduced in 1995 retained the range of subjects but reduced what must be taught outside the core. Broader choice was available at Key Stage 4, with the introduction of GNVQ and GCSE short courses, and in place of the 10-level scale assessment was to be made using the GCSE A* – G grades.

Despite Dearing's recommendation that this version of the National Curriculum should have a shelf life of five years the reviews continued, leading to the introduction of the literacy hour in 1998 and the numeracy hour in 1999. On 9 September 1999 the Secretary of State announced the revised National Curriculum that was to be introduced from August 2000 and the plans for its implementation (QCA, 1999a).

Programmes of Study were re-designed and produced in 'user-friendly' handbooks (DfES and QCA, 1999 b and c) and a rationale for the curriculum was included along with general teaching requirements on inclusion, use of language, use of ICT and health and safety. New frameworks for Personal, Social and Health Education (PSHE) at all Key Stages were published and Citizenship became compulsory at Key Stages 3 and 4 from 2002. At Key Stage 4 revised GCSE syllabuses were made available with a wider range of vocational qualifications. New Section 363 regulations permitted disapplication of design and technology and/or modern foreign languages to allow 'pupils making significantly less progress than their peers to study fewer National Curriculum subjects' or to permit 'pupils, in response to their individual strengths and talents, to emphasise a particular curriculum area' (QCA, 1999a, p10).

Task 2.1: The evolution of your subject

Research what happened to your subject from the introduction of the National Curriculum in 1989 to the 1995 orders and now to the description in the 1999 handbook. For example, what happened to the content and the number of attainment targets?

An outline of the National Curriculum

The school curriculum should aim:

- to provide opportunities for all pupils to learn and to achieve;
- to promote pupils' spiritual, moral, social and cultural development and prepare all pupils for the opportunities, responsibilities and experiences of life. (DfEE and QCA, 1999c, p11)

In the revisions in 2000 a rationale or four main purposes have been included as an introduction to the National Curriculum:

1. to establish an entitlement;
2. to establish standards;
3. to promote continuity and coherence;
4. to promote public understanding.

The Curriculum is composed of 12 subjects that are studied by all 5–16-year-old pupils. These subjects are well known and have featured in the school curriculum for many years. They are divided into *core* and *foundation* subjects. The *core* comprises English, mathematics, science (and Welsh where the medium of instruction in the school is Welsh); the *foundation* comprises art, geography, history, modern language (for 11–16-year-olds), music, physical education, ICT, design and technology and citizenship (and Welsh where the medium of instruction in the school is Welsh). These subjects form the statutory curriculum (the minimum entitlement) but schools can extend the curriculum to meet their particular needs and circumstances.

The content of National Curriculum subjects is described using a series of generic terms, namely:

- Key Stages (KS);
- Programmes of Study (PoS); and
- Attainment Targets plus Level Descriptors (ATs).

You need to be familiar with these terms as they are in common use in schools. They are briefly outlined in the following sections.

Key Stages

The National Curriculum classifies school years (ages 5–6) into four Key Stages. A Key Stage corresponds to either two or three years of schooling. Details of these Key Stages, with the addition of the school reception year, are provided in Table 2.1.

Table 2.1 The Key Stages and years of the National Curriculum

Age	Description	School year
3–5	Foundation Stage	Reception
5–7	Key Stage 1	Years 1–2
7–11	Key Stage 2	Years 3–6
11–14	Key Stage 3	Years 7–9
14–16	Key Stage 4	Years 10–11

In this manner, Key Stages are defined by the age of the majority of children in a particular school year group. KS1 starts at the beginning of the term after a pupil's fifth birthday. Secondary school classes start at year 7 (the beginning of KS3), and finish at year 11, the year of GCSE examinations and the end of KS4. The sixth form, post-16, is now commonly referred to as year 12 or 13 – or in some cases, KS5. School years labelled in this way emphasize continuity and progression from one year to the next.

Programmes of Study

The Programmes of Study specify the compulsory teaching within each subject. In other words, they describe what content, skills and processes should be taught. In each subject, the PoS are separately documented in Key Stages (ie the content for KS1 is followed by the content for KS2, etc). The content is divided into a series of subject *areas* and each area directly matches an assessment attainment target (see the following section). The number of areas differs from subject to subject; as an example, the areas for the core curriculum subjects (English, Welsh, mathematics and science) are listed in Table 2.2.

In some subjects, the content is further divided into sections – a section describing a series of related ideas progressing through the programme of studies. For example: in science, the area 'Life Processes and Living Things' is divided into five sections:

1. life processes;
2. humans as organisms;
3. green plants;
4. variation and classification;
5. living things in their environment.

However, this subdivision is not clear in all subject areas.

Table 2.2   Areas in the Programmes of Study of the core curriculum

English	Welsh	Mathematics	Science
Speaking and listening	Oracy	Using and applying mathematics	Scientific enquiry
Reading	Reading	Number and algebra	Life processes and living things
Writing	Writing	Shape, space and measures	Materials and their properties
		Handling data	Physical processes

Attainment targets

As well as PoS, each subject in the National Curriculum has one or more attainment targets or ATs (see Table 2.3). These set out the standards of performance which are used as a basis for making judgements about pupils' attainment on particular aspects of the PoS. They do this in terms of either 'level descriptors' or 'end of Key Stage descriptors'.

ATs define the assessment agenda of the National Curriculum (what should be assessed) whereas the PoS define the content agenda (what should be taught).

Level descriptors

Level descriptors exist for ATs in all subjects. Each AT contains eight level descriptors of increasing difficulty. Teachers use their professional judgement to decide which of the descriptors best fits their knowledge of a pupil's performance in the subject over a period of time. The expected range of levels of attainment for the great majority of pupils at the end of a particular Key Stage is shown in Table 2.3

Table 2.3   The National Curriculum attainment targets (Source: DfEE and QCA, 1999c, p1)

Range of levels within which the great majority of pupils are expected to work		Expected attainment for the majority of pupils at the end of the key stage	
Key Stage 1	1–3	at age 7	2
Key Stage 2	2–5	at age 11	4
Key Stage 3	3–7	at age 14	5/6

Level 8 is available to cater for very able pupils at the end of KS3 and a further descriptor above Level 8 is provided to allow teachers to indicate exceptional performance. Note that the level descriptors do not apply to KS4 where GCSE examinations are the main means of assessing attainment in the National Curriculum.

Table 2.4   The National Curriculum attainment targets (Source: DfEE and QCA, 1999a and b)

Subject	Attainment targets			
English	Speaking and listening	Reading	Writing	
Welsh	Oracy	Reading	Writing	
Mathematics	Using and applying mathematics	Numbers and algebra	Shape, space and measures	Handling data
Science	Scientific enquiry	Life processes and living things	Materials and their properties	Physical processes
Design and technology	Design and Technology	Making		
Information and Communication Technology	Information and Communication Technology capability			
History	History			
Geography	Geography			
Modern Foreign Languages	Listening and responding	Speaking	Reading and responding	Writing
Art	Art			
Music	Music			
Physical Education	Physical Education			
Citizenship (Key Stages 3 and 4)	Becoming informed citizens	Developing skills of enquiry and communication	Developing skills of participation and responsible action	

Task **2.2:** Familiarize yourself with the National Curriculum

Observe a class being taught and identify the content of the lesson. Then use the relevant subject National Curriculum subject booklet to consider the following questions:

- Where does the content appear in the subject's Programme of Study?
- Does the content appear within a given Attainment Target? If so, where?
- Does the content match a level descriptor? If so, which one?
- Does the content appear in one Key Stage only or does it appear at other levels? If so, which?

The statutory framework

As previously noted, the National Curriculum consists of 12 subjects. However, not all these subjects are required to be taught in each Key Stage and there are also significant variations between the curricula for England and Wales. The subjects presently included in the National Curriculum in each Key Stage are shown in Table 2.4. The statutory curriculum for KS4 contains fewer subjects than at other Key Stages. At KS4, secondary schools have the flexibility to offer a range of additional courses to meet students' needs (in line with the 1996 Education Act and the changes made for 2000) and these courses can lead to a range of qualifications including: GCSE, GCSE (short courses), specialist/applied GCSEs, key skills units in information technology and NVQs and NVQ units. Religious education, sex education and careers education are also statutory parts of the KS4 curriculum (QCA, 1998a) along with citizenship (QCA, 1999a).

The changes introduced in August 2000 and completed in 2002 created a 'new look' (QCA, 1999a, p2) National Curriculum incorporating revised PoS with a new structure and design, setting out the knowledge, skills, understanding and breadth of study required. PoS became less prescriptive in order to provide greater flexibility within the curriculum, requirements were reduced and a greater coherence within and between subjects was introduced.

A statutory inclusion statement replaces the previous statements on access. It sets out three principles for inclusion that teachers are required to take into account when planning or teaching:

1. setting suitable learning challenges;
2. responding to pupils' diverse learning needs;

Table 2.5 Subjects in each Key Stage for England and Wales

In England	
Key Stages 1 and 2	English, mathematics, science, design and technology, and information and communication technology, history, geography, art, music, and physical education
Key Stage 3	As Key Stages 1 and 2, plus a modern foreign language and citizenship
Key Stage 4	English, mathematics and science (single or double award), design and technology,• information and communication technology, a modern foreign language,• physical education and citizenship
In Wales	
Key Stages 1 and 2	English (except in Key Stage 1 in Welsh-speaking classes), Welsh, mathematics, science, technology (design and technology and information technology), history,* geography,* art,* music,* and physical education
Key Stage 3	As Key Stages 1 and 2, plus a modern foreign language
Key Stage 4	English, Welsh, mathematics, science (single or double) and physical education
Key:	• Section 363 regulations allow disapplication of design and technology and/or modern foreign languages. * Separate orders for England and Wales

3. overcoming potential barriers to learning and assessment for individuals and groups of pupils.

The principles support a more flexible delivery of the curriculum to provide increased access and challenge for all pupils to suit their abilities. This requires the teacher to develop appropriate strategies for differentiation across the ability range to include pupils with learning difficulties or disabilities and those with interrupted schooling, while providing challenges for those defined as gifted and talented.

Task 2.3: Planning for inclusion

Consider a topic or area that you intend to teach. How will you plan the activities in the classroom to ensure that all pupils are included and challenged?

General teaching requirements

The general teaching requirements include three new statutory statements. The use of language across the curriculum sets out what is expected in writing, speaking, listening and reading in Standard English as the predominant language in which knowledge and skills are learnt. Similarly a statutory statement on the use of ICT across the curriculum applies to all subjects (with the exception of physical education at Key Stages 1 and 2). Pupils should be taught to handle information, undertake research, develop ideas using ICT tools and develop evaluative skills. The ways in which teachers may accomplish ICT capability are suggested in the margins of all PoS. Finally, a statement on health and safety applies to science, design and technology, ICT, art and physical education practical sessions where pupils should be taught about hazards, risk assessment and control.

Task 2.4: Meeting the general teaching requirements

Refer to your subject booklet and find examples of opportunities to develop English, ICT or, if appropriate, health and safety. Consider how you would incorporate these into your lessons. Are there other opportunities that you can add for yourself?

Religious education

All schools must provide religious education for all pupils according to the Education Act 1996, unless parents choose to withdraw their children. Voluntary Aided Schools and those of a religious character are permitted to teach their own syllabus, but other maintained schools must teach religious education to a locally agreed syllabus. This syllabus should reflect the Christian traditions of the UK but may take into account 'teachings and practices of other principal religions represented in Great Britain' (DfEE and QCA, 1999c, p20).

Sex education

Schools must provide sex education but they may determine the detailed nature and content of the syllabus and once again parents are free to choose to withdraw their children from all or part of the programme. The lessons must include AIDS, HIV and other sexually transmitted diseases, and should support the values of family life and enable pupils to consider moral issues.

Careers education

During Years 9, 10 and 11 all schools are obliged to provide a programme of careers education and access to the Careers or Connexions Service at decision-making points in their pupils' education. There is also encouragement for schools to provide careers education prior to Year 9 and for Years 12 and 13. The statutory requirements are described in DfEE Circulars 5/97 and 5/98 and the QCA has published supporting material in 'Learning outcomes from careers education and guidance' (QCA/99/359).

Citizenship

From August 2002 schools have a statutory responsibility to teach citizenship at KS3 and 4 and PoS provide the content and foundation for planning schemes of work. In their planning, schools are asked to consider the general teaching requirements of inclusion, use of language and of ICT. Pupils should cover three areas in their study of citizenship:

1. knowledge and understanding about becoming informed citizens;
2. developing skills of enquiry and communication;
3. developing skills of participation and responsible action. (DfEE and QCA, 1999a, p14)

Links are also made to other subjects such as history, geography, science and English and these are cross-referenced in the margins of the subject booklets.

One end of Key Stage description for KS3 and another for KS4 summarize the type and range of performance that pupils should demonstrate at the end of each programme. At the end of KS3 the expectation is equivalent to levels 5/6 in other subjects. Pupils are expected to have a comprehensive knowledge and under-standing of, for example, topical events, their rights and responsibilities as citizens, forms of government and the legal and justice systems. Participation in school and community activities is supported by research skills, debating and the ability to express and develop an opinion on paper. Demonstration of personal and group responsibility in their attitudes and the development of evaluative skills are also expected outcomes at the end of the programme.

Learning across the National Curriculum

Cross-curricular themes have been replaced with Information on Learning across the National Curriculum, which is included in both primary and secondary handbooks and the individual subject booklets to promote spiritual, moral, social and cultural development for all pupils. Religious education, citizenship and the non-statutory personal, social and health education (PSHE) framework provide explicit opportunities to support this development.

The framework for PSHE aims to help 'pupils to lead confident, healthy and responsible lives as individuals and members of society' (DfEE and QCA, 1999c, p188). The programme is delivered in discrete lessons and incorporated in other subjects and in activities across the curriculum. At KS1 and 2, four areas are covered:

1. developing confidence and responsibility and making the most of their abilities;
2. preparing to play an active role as a citizen;
3. developing a healthy, safer lifestyle;
4. developing good relationships and respecting the differences between people.

In KS3 and 4 the second area is omitted as citizenship is now a foundation subject. Opportunities are highlighted for the development of PSHE in other subjects such as English, science, geography, physical education and design and technology. Breadth of opportunities is described for each stage, which include activities such as caring for the school environment or other people, organizing school events or participating in events in the local community.

Key Skills are also embedded in the National Curriculum and their development may now be followed though Years 12 and 13 at A-level and eventually to their inclusion in degree level study. The six key skills are:

1. Communication
2. Application of number
3. Information Technology
4. Working with others
5. Improving own learning and performance
6. Problem solving.

In addition, thinking skills are seen as complementary to key skills and as the key to 'learning how to learn' (DfEE and QCA, 1999c, p23); the following five are embedded in the National Curriculum:

1. Information processing skills
2. Reasoning skills
3. Enquiry skills
4. Creative thinking skills
5. Evaluation skills.

Financial capability, enterprise and entrepreneurial skills, work-related learning and education for sustainable development are also promoted as part of the revised National Curriculum. Their delivery is through PSHE or citizenship and in particular subjects such as mathematics, geography and science.

Flexibility in the National Curriculum

The 'one size fits all' approach has been modified to enable the school to make provision more appropriate to the individual needs of the learner. Although the content of the curriculum is prescribed, the allocation of time and the emphasis that may be put on subjects are not. Schools may place emphasis on literacy and numeracy or concentrate longer periods of time on specific subjects for particular year groups. Others, recognizing that the subjects do not have to be taught discretely, have adopted a modular approach 'for years 9, 10 and 11 integrating PSHE, work-related learning and community projects with ICT, history, geography, art and design and music' (QCA, 1999c, p2).

Blocks of time to follow community projects, arts projects or to complete practical coursework are allocated in some schools with time 'paid back' at other times during the year to the subjects the pupils missed for that period. If pupils complete PoS early during KS3 or 4 they may concentrate on other subjects or work towards additional qualifications. In some schools, mathematics GCSE is taken at the end of Year 10 and in Year 11 the pupils take statistics GCSE or study for an AS in mathematics.

In meeting the needs of individual pupils it is possible to modify or disapply some aspects of the National Curriculum. In September 1998 schools were able to disapply some aspects of the National Curriculum for work-related learning. Through local collaboration between schools, FE colleges and local employers, pupils have been provided with one or two days' work-related learning with appropriate work placements.

From September 2000, using section 363 regulations, schools could offer disapplication to a wider range of pupils. This change recognizes the needs of pupils who are making less progress than their peers and those who wish to build on particular strengths and talents. The former group, instead of struggling with another GCSE, may benefit from concentrating on literacy and numeracy. Other students may wish to emphasize sports-related subjects, humanities, arts and modern foreign languages and disapplication is the vehicle that permits them to do this.

Disapplication is also possible for pupils with a statement of special educational need as well as those for whom a temporary modification is thought to be appropriate. Such flexibility has also been explored as part of the curriculum developments and experiments in some Education Action Zones.

The desire to increase the flexibility of the National Curriculum and to increase the potential for schools to construct programmes for the individual student is at the core of *14–19: Opportunity and excellence* (DfES, 2002) and has led to the latest proposals for changes at KS4 (QCA and NFER, 2003). It is proposed that from September 2004 students will study a core curriculum comprising English, mathematics, science and ICT. Work-related learning will be included in the compulsory areas of learning described above – physical education, religious education, careers education and sex education.

Students will have an entitlement, however, to a modern foreign language, design and technology, the arts and the humanities. This means that schools *must* provide courses in all four areas if students wish to take them, and they may deliver them through partnerships with other schools or colleges. These proposals to modify the National Curriculum, so soon after the changes in 2000, are made so that schools may 'offer programmes that better meet young people's individual needs and strengths, whilst ensuring that they acquire the core of general learning and experience essential to later learning' (QCA and NFER, 2003).

The National Curriculum in action

As a trainee teacher you are likely to meet the National Curriculum at three levels:

1. *Whole-school policies* – that define, for example, the school timetable.
2. *Schemes of work* – that define, for example, the progression of subject content.
3. *Group and individual pupil activities* – these include, for example, the content of teachers' (and your) lesson plans.

Schools will have *policies* that embrace all aspects of the curriculum, including the non-statutory curriculum, and any individual priorities of the school. A principal aim of these policies will be to secure equality of opportunity and access to the 'whole curriculum' for each pupil. The effective management of the curriculum depends on establishing policies on, for example, attendance, homework, record keeping, pastoral code, codes of behaviour and discipline as well as the drawing up of the school timetable. The Education Reform Act indicates the statutory parts of the curriculum; however, it does not prescribe the amount of time that should be spent on any part of the curriculum. How subjects are timetabled is at the discretion of the school and there are considerable variations between schools.

In secondary schools, the curriculum is usually divided into subjects that have a number of timetable slots in a school week. There is considerable flexibility in the curriculum at KS4 and this flexibility has to be built into the school timetable. In primary schools, the curriculum is less frequently organized by subject, although the recent introduction of the literacy and numeracy hour is likely to result in schools introducing a regular time for these subjects each day.

Task 2.5: The curriculum timetable

Find out, for a particular year group, how the curriculum is organized in your school. Does your school have any curriculum priorities and how are these reflected in the school timetable?

A whole-school approach to planning the curriculum is essential and the school's schemes of work will contain details of the aims and objectives, learning activities, progression and assessment of the curriculum. It is likely that teachers in primary schools will start to plan the curriculum with a cross subject/whole-school approach (often referred to as a 'topic approach') although the literacy and numeracy hour is likely to have a self-contained structure. Recently, the DfEE has published non-statutory schemes of work for science and technology (DfEE, 1998b, 1998c). These should be available to you as a trainee.

In secondary schools, planning usually takes place within a subject department and it is common for members of staff to have responsibility for the curriculum at KS3 and KS4. It will be the responsibility of these staff to liaise with colleagues and construct a scheme of work matched with National Curriculum KS3 requirements and chosen KS4 examination syllabuses.

The PoS provide the basis for what should be taught in each Key Stage as a minimum statutory entitlement. As previously noted, they define the content agenda for the school curriculum. It is up to the school to decide how to teach the PoS and to what depth. The National Curriculum claims to have no implied teaching methodology; however, with the publication of non-statutory lesson plans, particular styles of teaching are increasingly emerging. How the curriculum is structured in terms of pupils and group activities is left up to teachers' professional judgement. Furthermore, teachers can decide whether to augment the specified content with additional materials.

The National Curriculum details the curriculum assessment. Assessment is an integral part of teaching and the National Curriculum provides a framework for day-to-day and end of Key Stage assessment (see Chapter 7). When developing a scheme of work or a lesson plan, attention must be given to the expectations of pupils' progress as represented by the ATs, level descriptors and end of Key Stage descriptors as previously indicated. The subject ATs define the level of experience and how the content should be sequenced. The National Curriculum contains no detail about the mechanisms of day-to-day teacher assessment.

A useful lesson planning sequence, incorporating the statutory requirements, is illustrated in Figure 2.1. Planning and assessing are explored in more detail in Chapters 5 and 7, respectively.

The National Curriculum and continuity and progression

Pupils moving from one school to another have always presented problems to teachers – what has the pupil achieved in the previous school and how to build on this in the new situation? This problem is, of course, potentially much greater when a change of phase is involved, for example from primary to secondary, or middle to secondary school. The resulting secondary teaching group may contain pupils from many different 'feeder' schools.

Prior to the introduction of the National Curriculum, the problem of transferring and interpreting the information was such that it was not uncommon for secondary subject teachers to state that it was more practical to assume that nothing had been done! The potential for reducing motivation because of repetitive or unchallenging work was very real. Research in the 1980s (Galton, 1988) suggested that pupils often regressed in attainment in the first years of secondary school. The National Curriculum is designed to alleviate this problem by providing a clear definition of content in the PoS, common standards in the ATs against which pupils can be assessed, national statutory end of Key Stage tests in the core subjects, and a common vocabulary to help plan for continuity in the curriculum and for describing a pupil's progress.

However, the 1993 Dearing Review suggested that there were still many concerns in this area. Consequently, after the National Curriculum was revised in

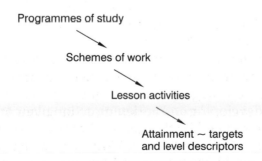

Figure 2.1 A National Curriculum planning sequence

1995, SCAA, now QCA (Qualifications and Curriculum Authority), produced booklets giving advice on how to promote continuity between Key Stages and make effective use of assessments (see 'Further reading', below). They have also promoted the development of software designed to reduce the administrative burden of transferring and analysing information.

Task 2.6: Primary-secondary transfer

Find out how your school makes use of information from pupils' previous schools on transfer.

The KS3 strategy

The increasing concentration by schools on their position in the league tables produced at KS4 has exacerbated the issue identified by Dearing and has led to a national KS3 strategy. This is a programme designed to raise standards for 11 to 14-year-olds and comprises five main strands. English (literacy) and mathematics (numeracy) were both introduced in 2001, science and ICT in 2002, followed by teaching and learning in foundation subjects, including religious studies. There are four key principles underpinning the strategy:

1. Expectations – to set high expectations and challenging targets.
2. Progression – to improve the transition from KS2 to 3 and from primary to secondary school.
3. Engagement – to provide approaches to teaching and learning that engage pupils and in which they actively participate.
4. Transformation – to improve teaching and learning through professional development and practical support.

The frameworks for teaching and the materials provided in the two initial strands of literacy and numeracy created an opportunity for teachers to reflect on their classroom practice and to develop it, particularly through planning for active learning and differentiation. The practice of auditing the standards and quality of teaching in the area, developing and achieving action plans and working alongside teachers to identify and meet their professional development needs have moved the spotlight from KS4 GCSE results to the early years in the secondary school. The long-term effects of the KS3 strategy are yet to be assessed but in its early stages it has moved the 'what' should be taught of the National Curriculum to 'how' it might be taught successfully. Whatever the results of the evaluation there is no doubt that over the last 15 years we have witnessed a dramatic development in both the design of the curriculum and its pedagogy.

The hidden curriculum

'The hidden curriculum' is a commonly used term to refer to the politics, attitudes and values promoted by school experiences. Much is learned in school that has nothing directly to do with the curriculum content of lessons but is implied by school structures, procedures and organization. For example, the subjects and structure of the school timetable and the mechanisms of school discipline all carry hidden messages. There is much written on the hidden curriculum. Illich (1973), for instance, argues that schools tend to inculcate a 'passive assumption' – an acceptance of the current social order. He goes on to argue that we should do away with schools in their current form and focus instead on providing information to people who want to learn as part of an endeavour to promote lifelong learning. Recently, these ideas have been linked with advances in communication technology and the Internet, which will potentially enable information to be available to larger audiences.

Task 2.7: The hidden curriculum
- What are the hidden messages in your teaching?
- What aspects of the hidden curriculum do you promote?
- Do you agree with Illich's argument that schooling tends to promote an acceptance of the current social order?

Further reading

Useful addresses and Web sites

The National Curriculum was last revised in 2000. The following Web sites contain up-to-date details about this revision and a list of recent policy publications. Many of these publications will be free to trainee teachers.

The Department for Education and Skills (DfES): http://www.dfes.gov.uk
The Qualifications and Curriculum Authority (QCA): http://www.qca.org.uk
The Office for Standards in Education (Ofsted): http://www.ofsted.gov.uk/ofsted.
   html
The Teacher Training Agency (TTA): http://www.canteach.gov.uk

Useful general publications

A good overview of the National Curriculum is provided by *A Guide to the National Curriculum*, School Curriculum and Assessment Authority, the Curriculum and Assessment Authority for Wales and the Teacher Training Agency (1996), HMSO, London.

Individual subject booklets are also available from HMSO publications, for example, *English in the National Curriculum*, DfEE (1995), HMSO, London.

Recent policy documents

At KS1 and KS2

Department for Education and Employment (1998) *The National Literacy Strategy*, DfEE, London
DfEE (1998) *The National Numeracy Strategy*, DfEE, London
DfEE and the Qualifications and Curriculum Authority (1998) *Information Technology – A teacher's guide: Scheme of work for Key Stages 1 and 2*, QCA, London
DfEE and QCA (1998) *Science – A teacher's guide: Scheme of work for Key Stages 1 and 2*, QCA, London
QCA (1998) *Maintaining Breadth and Balance at Key Stages 1 and 2*, QCA, London

At KS3 and KS4

Qualification and Curriculum Authority (1998) *Key Stage 4 Curriculum in Action*, QCA, London

References

Centre for Contemporary Cultural Studies (1981) *Unpopular Education: Schooling and social democracy in England since 1944*, Hutchinson, London

Department for Education (DfE) (1994a) *Religious Education and Collective Worship*, Circular 1/94, DfE, London

DfE (1994b) *Code of Practice of the Identification and Assessment of Special Educational Needs*, Circular 10/94, DfE, London

Department for Education and Employment (DfEE) (1998a) *Connecting the Learning Society*, HMSO, London

DfEE (1998b) *Excellence in Schools*, HMSO, London

DfEE (1998c) *The National Literacy Strategy*, DfEE, London

DfEE (1998d) *The National Numeracy Strategy*, DfEE, London

DFEE and QCA (1999a) *Citizenship*, TSO, Norwich

DFEE and QCA (1999b) *The National Curriculum. Handbook for primary teachers in England*, TSO, Norwich

DFEE and QCA (1999c) *The National Curriculum. Handbook for secondary teachers in England*, TSO, Norwich

DfES (2002) *14–19: Opportunity and excellence*, DfES, London

Department for Education and Science (DES) (1969) Black Papers, HMSO, London

DES (1977) *Education in Schools: A consultative document*, HMSO, London

Galton, M (1988) The implementation of innovation in primary education at the local level, *Western European Education*, **20** (3), pp 323–44

Illich, I (1973) *Deschooling Society*, Penguin, Harmondsworth

NCC (1990) *Curriculum Guidance 3: The whole curriculum*, NCC, York

Qualification and Curriculum Authority (QCA) (1998a) *Key Stage 4: Curriculum in action*, QCA, London

QCA (1998b) *Developing the School Curriculum: Advice to the Secretary of State on the broad nature and scope of the review of the National Curriculum*, QCA, London

QCA (1998c) *Maintaining Breadth and Balance at Key Stages 1 and 2*, QCA, London

QCA (1999a) *The National Curriculum for 2000. What has changed?*, QCA, London

QCA (1999b) *Learning Outcomes from Careers Education and Guidance*, QCA/99/359, London

QCA (1999c) *Flexibility in the Secondary Curriculum*, QCA, London

QCA and NFER (2003) *Consultation on Proposed Changes to the Key Stage 4 Curriculum*, QCA, London

SCAA (1994a) *Religious Education Model Syllabuses – Model 1: Living faiths today*, SCCA, London

SCAA (1994b) *Religious Education Model Syllabuses – Model 2: Questions and teachings*, SCCA, London

SCAA (1996) *A Guide to the National Curriculum*, SCAA, London

Simon, B (1988) *Bending the Rules: The Baker 'reform' of education*, Lawrence and Wishart, London

3   Children's Learning

Margaret Cox

The aim of this chapter is to introduce the trainee to the nature of pupils' learning and development. It considers a variety of learning theories and a range of views on how these theories can be implemented in the classroom and inform teachers on how pupils may learn more effectively. Consideration is given to pupils' learning and the context in which pupils may learn. These contexts are then discussed with a view to making teaching and learning more effective.

> ## Objectives
>
> By the end of this chapter, the trainee should have an understanding of:
>
> - a variety of learning and developmental theories;
> - how these theories can be used to enhance pupils' learning;
> - how these theories can inform teaching strategies;
> - how pupils can be motivated;
> - how pupils learn.

Introduction

There have been many theories developed and studies carried out about the nature of learning with both children and adults, and there continues to be a range of views about which theories are closest to the reality. From years of research and teachers' experiences in schools we now know that children's learning is affected by their everyday experiences in the world, giving them ideas some of which seem to conflict with those we are trying to teach. We also know that children don't learn in isolation but that their learning is influenced by collaborating with other children, interacting with the teacher and with their environment. How they feel about themselves, their abilities and position amongst their peers also has an effect on how well they learn. Teaching children is not, as is sometimes assumed, pouring knowledge into an empty vessel; it is about helping them to build ideas about the world and to understand how they learn. All of these factors and many more need to be considered when devising effective strategies for teaching.

In this chapter I start by briefly explaining some of the most widely known theories of children's learning and many other issues such as the learning context, pupils' attitudes and social position, which also affect the ways in which children learn. This is followed by a discussion of where teaching and learning activities have been influenced by these theories, leading to ideas for tasks that will help you make use of this knowledge.

How do children learn?

We begin by considering the learning theories that have influenced the world of education and which often form the basis for teaching strategies and curriculum materials. It would be impossible here to include all the theories that have been proposed over the years so I am only presenting briefly the theories most commonly used and discussed in education.

Skinner

One of the earliest theories of learning that is still used today by many educators but has been widely criticized by many others was proposed by Skinner (1974), an American behaviourist psychologist, who did extensive research mainly with animals. For example, his early research involved rewarding animals with food if they 'learnt' how to open doors. Behaviourism, which is a theory based on empiricism, assumes that knowledge is primarily acquired by the evidence of the senses (Nussbaum, 1989). Knowledge is what is confirmed through careful obser-vations and logic. From his research results, Skinner concluded that the award principle governed all behaviour, including that of human beings.

When Skinner applied his results to the teaching of children in the earlier part of this century, he believed that teachers were not making use of effective 'schedules of reinforcement' in the classroom. He argued that formal education was usually based on negative reinforcement. For example, when children behaved inappro-priately in lessons the result was sometimes punishment by the teacher with language or behaviour that was intended to humiliate, instead of the teacher showing interest in the formation and reinforcement of responses to be learnt. He saw lessons and examinations as a means of showing what pupils do not know and cannot do, rather than revealing and helping them to construct the material they know. In this way, he argued, children's behaviour was not formed effectively by negative reinforcement, the learning was not appropriate and often the learnt material was quickly forgotten. Concerned with the application of his theory to education, Skinner designed the first 'learning programmes' for use on teaching machines, the forerunner of drill and practice programmes and integrated learning systems using ICT, which are discussed in the next chapter.

In today's teaching, this theory of behaviourism is reflected in the rote learning of verbs or multiplication tables for example, where it is expected that if the pupils work through an exercise enough times they will memorize and learn the facts that are being taught. Behaviourists believe that the way to achieve pupils' 'correct' learning is through the procedure of careful and systematic teaching where each stage is monitored and where children are given regular feedback to confirm what they have learnt. As we know, there are still many examples of such teaching strategies today, but this theory did not take account of the stages in the intellectual development of all children nor the effects on learning of such factors as the learning context and the social milieu.

Piaget

Jean Piaget, a Swiss psychologist, studied the development of children for more than 40 years (Piaget and Inhelder, 1969). His theory presents, in detail, specific universal stages in human development and provides a possible explanation connected with when and how a child is ready to learn or develop specific forms of knowledge and understanding. In his theory, action and self-directed problem solving are basic factors in learning and development. While learners are interacting with their environment, they discover how to control it. He proposed that in human beings, the basic principle of thinking is formed when they learn how to act in the world and discover the consequences of their actions.

According to Piaget, in the development of intelligence, certain processes are happening behind all learning, whether it happens in simple organisms or in human beings. The two essential processes are adaptation to the environment, and organization of experience (in terms of action, memory, perceptions, or other kinds of mental activities). As children become older, they adapt to a sequence of environments and at the same time they organize their experiences in a more complex way. According to Piaget (1926), 'Attempts to teach the products of a "later" stage before previous stages have been passed through cannot facilitate development nor can it foster understanding.' This means that what children can learn will depend upon what mental stage of development they have reached, which can vary a lot at any age from one child to another.

Piaget and Inhelder (1969) distinguished three main periods in which cognitive development is quantitatively different. The first of these is the period of sensorimotor intelligence, which extends from birth until the appearance of language, approximately during the first 18 months of life. The second period, that of concrete operations, extends from this time until about 11 or 12 years. Here, children can think in a logically coherent way about objects that exist and which have real properties, and about actions or relations that are possible. The third period, that of formal operations, begins at about 12 years and is fully developed roughly three years later, when children are able to think in a more abstract and complex way. It involves the development of higher cognitive skills, such as classification, analysis, synthesis, deduction and drawing of inferences. According to Piaget, children develop through the same sequence of stages before they achieve mature, logical thought.

At each stage there are four main aspects of development during school years, which Piaget has defined as:

1. the directive function of language;
2. the formation of concepts;
3. translation of concrete experiences into verbal and symbolic terms; and
4. the evolution of logical thinking.

Piaget uses the terms 'schemas' or 'schemata' for well-defined sequences of actions. Although they may have a different nature or complexity, their main characteristic is that they are organized wholes that are frequently repeated and which can be recognized easily among other various and different behaviours. When new objects or experiences are incorporated into existing schemas, it is called 'assimilation'. Children assimilate experiences into a sequence of cognitive schemas or, put more simply, when children are taught something new this is added to their existing knowledge, which is reorganized to include the new knowledge.

The term 'accommodation' describes the process of modifying schemas in order to solve problems arising from new experiences within the environment. During the interaction of the two intellectual processes, children assimilate new experiences into their existing schemas and accommodate their schemas by extending or combining them (when meeting new situations). For example, a child pushing a toy brick along a slippery table may form a mental model of the rate of movement relating to their pushing effort. When she tries to repeat the process but this time pushing the brick on a carpet, she will find that the effort required is considerably greater. To assimilate this new experience will require modifying the previous mental model to include the effect of friction representing the influence of the nature of the surface across which the brick was being moved. To accommodate new knowledge children's schemas are very flexible and although they are

ed or modified, they keep their property of being organized wholes.
gh these procedures individuals develop an adequate number of schemas to
vith the events they meet and, in doing so, they become adapted to their envi-
ent; but it is a temporary adaptation only and is modified as the environment
changes or as the individuals act in a variety of ways.

Most of children's thinking in any one stage or period is characterized by a structure. This structure is distinct: the same for all children at this stage and different from other children or adults at other stages. As children grow older, the structure built at a younger age develops gradually and becomes an integral part of the structure of the following stage. For example, the idea that an object is a permanent thing, which is learnt gradually in the first period, is necessary to the notion of conservation of quantity, which is learnt in the period of concrete operations. Similarly, concrete operations form a basis for the system of formal operations that follows them; for example, to understand proportionality in adolescence, children must first learn to compare any two quantities or to equalize them, as they do in the period of concrete operations. The more complex and abstract hypo-thetico-deductive thinking is therefore generally developed in adolescence.

The periods of development appear to follow a constant series; there is a sequence as one structure appears to follow another. Though all children pass through these distinct sequential stages, they pass with different speed. Thus, the age at which a stage is distinguished cannot be fixed, because it is always relative to the individual characteristics of the child and the environment that may encourage, restrict or prevent its appearance. A stage may appear fairly early or late according to the relevant situation for each individual child. Thus, children who have not entered the stage of concrete operations may not be able to understand certain basic mathematical concepts, for example. Or, in the stage of concrete operations, they may not be able to understand certain kinds of scientific thinking.

As the nature of young children's thought affects what they can learn, it often limits their learning. It may result in a restriction of the knowledge they can hold, even if the range of the educational experiences offered is quite broad. This means that in a class of 11-year olds some pupils may be reaching the formal operations stage and be able to grasp quite difficult topics, where others in the same class may not, despite careful and well organized lessons. One of the hardest lessons to learn about teaching is that you cannot conduct your lessons at the pace of the least able because the progress of the whole group may then be too slow, but there are strategies that you can adopt which will help all pupils progress to an improved understanding. Figure 3.1 shows a diagrammatic representation of the stages in Piaget's theory of learning.

Piaget also observed that children learn faster when they cooperate with others; this cooperation develops and improves their formal thinking. For example, adolescents who show more socialization can exchange their ideas and discuss their different viewpoints, and this verbal communication is seen as a way of enriching their thinking. According to Beard (1969), collaboration:

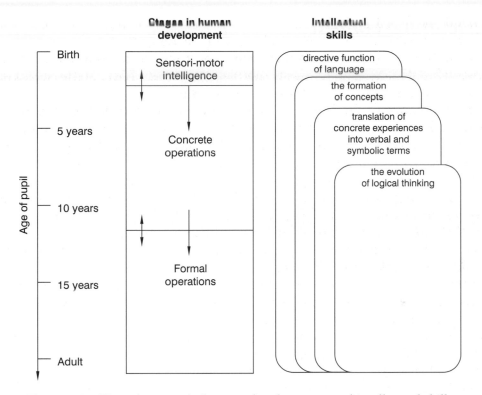

Figure 3.1 Piaget's stages in human development and intellectual skills

has the effect of leading children to a greater mutual understanding and gives them the habit of constantly placing themselves at points of view that they did not previously hold. Consequently they progress to making use of assumptions. In addition, discussion gives rise to an internalized conversation in the form of deliberation or reflection.

The role of language in Piaget's theory is similar to that of visual perception. Language is a system of symbols used by the individual to represent the world, and is distinct from actions and operations that lead to thinking. Yet, as will be shown later, pupils' linguistic abilities will strongly affect their reasoning and other mental activities.

Although Piaget wrote very little about the educational implications of his theories, many psychologists and educators explored the educational directions of Piaget's theory and transformed it into curricula, approaches to teaching and a whole philosophy of education (Wood, 1988). A very important part of these developments has been the studies on the effects of context on children's learning.

The learning context

Many researchers have developed Piaget's work further to include the effects of the environment in which pupils are learning. One particularly well-known Russian researcher was Vygotsky, who claimed that pupils' learning is affected by the culture of the learner and participation in society. He regarded these develop-mental interactions as a relationship between nature and culture. He maintained that learning can be enhanced through collaboration with others including through an adult tutor. He defined this influence as:

> the distance between the actual developmental level as determined by inde-pendent problem solving and the level of potential development as deter-mined through problem solving under adult guidance or in collaboration with more capable peers. (Vygotsky, 1978, p86)

This he called the 'zone of proximal development' and it has widely influenced teaching strategies at all levels of education. However, his theories mainly focused on the effects of the social environment on cognitive development, excluding the effects of pupils' understanding of the social world itself, their perceptions of themselves, how colleagues perceive them and their role and position within the class, the school and their own communities (Durkin, 1997, p381), all of which will play a part in the way they respond in lessons and their general behaviour.

From theory into practice

The theories discussed above provide useful foundations supported by an enormous amount of educational research about how children learn. Using these theories, educators have considered the implications for teaching and learning for a range of aspects of education. The following are important to consider if we are to achieve effective learning of our pupils:

1. stages in cognitive development;
2. ages and education levels of pupils;
3. existing preconceptions;
4. prior knowledge;
5. influence of the learning environment;
6. social influence and cognition;
7. children's attitudes towards learning, fellow pupils and themselves;
8. influence of literacy and numeracy skills.

Whether you are involved in primary or secondary teaching, to take account of all the aspects listed above you need to know your pupils. This is easier at primary than at secondary level. The following sections provide more information about these aspects, with ideas on how to include them in the planning and delivery of your teaching.

1. Stages in cognitive development

Piaget's theoretical arguments about the nature of thinking, cognitive development and of the relationships between what is seen, heard and understood have direct consequences for teaching and its effectiveness:

> Attempts to question, show or explain things to children before they are mentally 'ready' cannot foster development, though the child may learn some 'empty' procedures. Indeed, premature teaching and questioning may demoralize or frustrate a child who can't begin to understand what is being 'taught'. A teacher can provide appropriate materials and contexts for development, and organize time and space so that children are free to act upon the world with objects and tasks that serve to foster the emergence of operations and an understanding of invariance. (Wood, 1988)

Although the educational applications of Piaget's theory and the pedagogical implications of children's cognitive development continue to be discussed, there are some general teaching recommendations on which all the experts seem to agree. These particular recommendations may be grouped into three broad categories (Brainerd, 1978): the sequencing of curriculum material; the content of curriculum material; and the methodology of teaching. These recommendations are described briefly here but more detailed information about planning lessons is given in Chapter 4.

Sequencing of curriculum material

This category is concerned with when to introduce certain topics into your teaching programme. Piaget's theory emphasizes the readiness of pupils to be able to learn and understand the materials. First, the material taught to children should be in accordance with their present stage of cognitive development. Secondly, you should not try to force your pupils' progress through the material on a given subject. The third mentions that you should try, where possible, to teach children new concepts in the same order that these concepts appear during spontaneous cognitive development. In a Piagetian curriculum, teaching is always a two-stage process of diagnosis followed by instruction in the concepts for which the child is ready. It is therefore important to identify each of your pupils' present cognitive stage when planning the curriculum.

The content of curriculum material

This category is concerned with which specific topics should be part of the curriculum and the detailed content. For example, for primary pupils more of the curriculum should involve practical activities that depend upon concrete operations rather than more formal abstract reasoning. The content of your curriculum materials can also include activities with pupils working in groups to facilitate learning through peer interaction. Not only should the stage of cognitive development of each pupil with regard to the subject being taught be considered, but also the developmental stage of the language used by the pupils, which is discussed later in this chapter. For example, there are many curriculum materials designed for use by pupils of a particular age group but at a language level way beyond the abilities of those same pupils.

The methodology of teaching

This category is concerned with the strategies that you should adopt when dealing with children. There are three main aspects relating to the theories discussed earlier. First, consider the central role that children play in their own learning and try to make learning experiences as active as possible. Secondly, try to follow pedagogical strategies that make children aware of conflicts and inconsistencies in their ideas. Finally, you could make use of the child's peers for the facilitation of learning, building on the work of Vygotsky discussed earlier. Task 3.1 is to examine how well existing class and/or homework activities reflect these stages of development and how you can improve on these activities.

Task 3.1: Relating the learning tasks to cognitive development

This activity is based on the topic 'energy', which can be included in science, applied mathematics and technology. A similar approach can be used for other subject areas with an appropriate topic. Depending upon the complexity of the lessons this activity can be carried out at either primary or secondary level.

- Collect different homework and lesson activities already existing in your school on a particular topic for the year group that you plan to teach or are already teaching.

- In three columns, write out a list of all the concepts and skills you can find which are involved in these activities.
- In column 1 put all the concepts relating to the subject topic. For example, if the topic is conservation of energy, the concepts would include: temperature, heat, warmth, heat sources, heat gains, heat losses, etc.
- In column 2, note the concepts that you think could be taught corresponding to the concrete operational stage (by providing simple experiments pupils can do in the classroom to learn those energy concepts).
- In column 3, list the concepts that you think require more advanced abstract reasoning skills.
- Revise the activities into new assessment tasks which start with the easiest ones relating to the concrete operational activities followed by more advanced activities for pupils who may have reached the formal operational stage.

In most cases, planning assessment tasks for a group of pupils will vary with the age and the level of the pupils as given in the National Curriculum as well as their actual cognitive development. It is often the National Curriculum requirements that are uppermost in teachers' minds rather than the specific stages in cognitive development, and there are clear differences amongst the different National Curriculum subjects relating to the pupils' ability to reach a particular level according to their level of cognitive development.

2. Ages and education levels of pupils

The current requirements of the National Curriculum allow for pupils to be at different levels of attainment for a particular subject within the same class. Teachers are expected to progress their pupils through these levels to reach higher levels of achievement. When the National Curriculum was first launched in the late 1980s, primary school teachers were, in theory, expected to assess each of their pupils' achievements for over 260 attainment targets. In 1995 and again in 1999 the National Curriculum (DfEE, 1999; HMSO, 1995) was deliberately slimmed down to reduce this number to a much more manageable level, but it is still difficult to know how to measure what pupils have learnt which corresponds to these levels. Assessing pupils' achievements is discussed more fully in later chapters. Here it is important to recognize that being clearly aware of the ages and levels of achievement of pupils through assessment will give you insights into their relative cognitive and social development and how this will influence what they learn.

3. *Existing preconceptions*

Pupils frequently come to lessons with preconceived ideas about how the world works, particularly in science and applied mathematics. Extensive research by educators and psychologists has shown that, before children are taught many topics in school, they have acquired some knowledge about these through informal experiences. This knowledge is characterized by ideas sometimes different from the formally accepted ones, and moreover these ideas can be held strongly and be resistant to change. For example, in science education, researchers have found that pupils' prior ideas are an important factor in their understanding of school science and pupils whose observations and inferences about phenomena differ from the scientifically accepted ones, have different interpretative schemes.

The fact that children have their own scientific ideas that often differ significantly from the generally accepted scientific ones and that children often use their own words in everyday language about scientific phenomena, may reflect their current stage of cognitive development. Having a certain cognitive ability, pupils may not yet be able to understand and use the specialized language of some curriculum subjects and so they express themselves in their own words. It is therefore important, particularly if you are teaching science, mathematics or technology, to know what are the common informal ideas children have.

Researchers have identified an extensive background of children's conceptions about the natural world, and at the same time teaching strategies have been proposed to help them develop more scientist-like ideas. The proposals for teaching science, which apply to many other school subjects as well, take into account the way in which an improvement of pupils' knowledge can be achieved. To teach effectively it is safest to assume that your pupils have an existing conceptual scheme that is used in interpreting and making sense of new situations and phenomena. As a teacher, it is then important to acknowledge and build on these conceptual schemes. According to Piagetian theories, the learner relates the newly met concept to the pre-existing cognitive structure. Knowledge and skills acquired during one stage of cognitive development form the basis for the knowledge at the next stage. In this way, pupils' prior conceptions become an important factor in their understanding and therefore their prior ideas and assumptions and their willingness to use them have to be considered as a starting point for effective teaching.

When children are dissatisfied with their present viewpoints, it does not necessarily mean that this is an adequate reason for making them change their view. If children need to change their view, they must have access to a new and better idea that will replace the old one. According to Posner *et al* (1982) this new idea needs to be intelligible, plausible and fruitful:

intelligible, in that it appears coherent and internally consistent; plausible, in that it is reconcilable with other views the pupil already has; and fruitful in that it is preferable to the old ideas on the grounds of elegance, parsimony or usefulness in daily life and school situations.

By asking pupils questions and getting them to volunteer their ideas about a topic you can get some insights into their present viewpoints.

4. Prior knowledge

It should be clear from the discussion in the previous section that pupils' prior knowledge has a very important part to play in their learning. This prior knowledge is not restricted to preconceptions about the topic being taught, but extends to knowledge acquired from lessons already given on the same topic, or on related topics previously studied, or knowledge related to the subject but from another domain, such as mathematics for reading maps in geography.

One of the fundamental problems pupils have in learning is that of transfer: that is the transfer of knowledge between domain and/or contexts. Two well-known teaching approaches to help with transfer are discussed here. The first is to teach children very specific strategies for solving specific types of tasks. Brown (1981) found that this sort of teaching produced little transfer. However, more recently Cristafi and Brown (1986) found that when there was some variety in the original teaching materials, and the teaching included a specific generalization element that emphasized the underlying target (the reasons that make the strategy useful), then pupils showed a reasonable degree of transfer, within the specific type of problem.

The second approach has been to teach general learning strategies, relevant to those that are usually applied across a wide variety of types of problems (Feurstein, 1980). More recent studies have shown that pupils can learn more complex skills and processes in a context with which they are very familiar than when they are learning a formal academic subject in the school curriculum. When devising schemes of work it is then helpful to select activities that help pupils build on knowledge derived from other contexts. Identify what knowledge you expect the pupils to have already in the subject being taught and related subjects, including numeracy and literacy skills, and what particular conceptual weaknesses you might expect. A good scheme of work will also have lists of objectives and outcomes so that progression can be based on prior knowledge from each previous lesson and the learning outcomes achieved.

5. *Influence of the learning environment*

As was mentioned earlier, pupils' learning is influenced by the environment in which the learning takes place, which includes how the class is organized, what resources are available and whether the lesson is being taught in a relevant physical context. For example, in the case of using ICT, pupils are often taken to a room full of computers for a geography, history or science lesson, away from their normal classroom, which according to some studies produces an unreal context for the topic being studied (Watson, 1990).

In the previous sections most of the discussion is about pupils as individual learners, yet in the classroom situation there are often opportunities for pupils to work in pairs or groups where they benefit from sharing their expertise, challenging each other's knowledge and assumptions and contributing different views about topics and practical activities. Getting pupils to work in groups is also a way of finding out more about what they know through the conversations that occur and through the collaborative work they do. The main factor in cooperative learning is 'positive interdependence', pupils working together toward mutual goals in a way where the work is shared and members of the group must depend upon each other. Skills such as leadership, conflict resolution and decision-making are taught and practised in a cooperative learning situation. When working with ICT, which is explained more fully in the next chapter, students frequently form groups of various sizes. Straker (1989) observed that work with computers can contribute to the development of some group skills, such as communication skills, study and observation skills, problem solving skills, and personal and social skills.

Building on the research of Eraut and Hoyles into group work with computers (1988), task 3.2 can help you decide whether or not to put pupils into groups for the teaching of any topic, with or without ICT.

Task 3.2: Relating the learning tasks to group work

Select a set of learning objectives relating to a particular topic and National Curriculum level of the pupils. In the lesson plan, write out answers to the following:

- For what types of learning goal is group work most appropriate?
- What is its potential contribution to the learning activity?
- What kinds of tasks can be designed that facilitate group work?
- Is it possible to identify criteria for task design, group management and their interrelationships for effective group work to be established?
- What kind of grouping is best for achieving particular learning goals?
- How will the group work be prepared, implemented and evaluated?

Task 3.2 also needs to take account of the composition of the pupils in the class, the range of abilities, their ethnic mix and the opportunities available to them outside formal lessons. Issues of race, gender and class may also affect the way in which pupils can respond to the learning environment and to the influence of their fellow students (Cole *et al*, 1998; Hill and Cole, 1999). When planning the organization of your lessons you need to consider the learning objectives not only in terms of the topic being taught but also in terms of the broader objectives of fostering an enthusiasm for learning and for pupils to develop into socially responsible adults. Some of these issues are discussed in the next section.

6. Social influence and cognition

Most of the issues discussed above have focused on the cognitive development of pupils' learning, how well they come to understand a topic and what issues affect this growth in understanding. Yet there is now a large field of research into pupils' social cognition: the development of their understanding about the human world in which they live, themselves, their position amongst their peer groups, their standing in the community, and their future prospects as an adult (Durkin, 1997). Pupils' preconceived ideas about their peers can have a positive or negative effect on their attitudes and performance. For example, a study of boys working in pairs showed that:

the boys who had been forewarned that their partner was a bit of a trouble maker were less friendly towards them, talked less and put less effort into the joint task. For their part the alleged problem kids found the task less enjoyable, judged their dyad as not doing so well, and took less credit even for good performances. (Durkin, 1997, p343)

This study shows that if you can foster mutual respect amongst your pupils they are more likely to maintain good social relationships leading to fruitful collaborations in the classroom.

Being aware of the social and psychological influences on pupils should help you to understand the difficulties that pupils face and how these may affect their learning progression. This also applies to pupils coming from different social backgrounds and different cultures. For example, when planning a learning task for a class of pupils of mixed ethnic backgrounds, try and include resources that relate to the different pupils' culture and family experiences. If pupils show signs of lack of interest in a topic, this may be because they feel left out of the peer group or alienated from the culture in which the topic context is based. There are many activities described by other authors (see Cole *et al*, 1998 and Durkin, 1997, for example) that show teachers how to help pupils develop socially as well as academically through their educational experiences. Pupils' social awareness and cognition will also influence their attitudes to education, their fellow pupils and themselves. These social aspects clearly have an important influence on the pupil's ability to learn topics within the National Curriculum and to maintain an interest in education.

7. Children's attitudes towards learning, fellow pupils and themselves

The attitudes that children have towards themselves, their fellow pupils and their own abilities can have a strong influence on their motivation to study and learn. When designing lessons or other learning tasks it is important to recognize the distinction between pupils' positive motivation encouraged by success in achieving specific tasks and greater self-esteem, and negative motivation caused by a fear of failure. In the latter case this might lead to avoidance of engaging in particular learning tasks, for example using ICT, for fear of failing.

Motivating activities were mainly considered to influence emotions such as pride, shame, guilt and a general self-concept of the ability to achieve specific goals. Through the influence of Vygotsky and others, it has been recognized in recent years that the degree of motivation of individual learners is also influenced by social values and the context in which the learning takes place – hence the desire of the learner to do better than his or her colleagues, rather than improve his or her previous level of personal achievements. This aspect of motivation has implications for cooperation versus competition, and internal versus external rewards.

Ames (1992) analysed the work of many researchers into motivation to develop a framework for motivation relating to a belief in oneself and the ability of pupils to do better through long-term goals. She defined two types of motivation goals: mastery goals and performance goals, which involve different ways of thinking about oneself. Mastery goals relate to the belief that effort and outcome are interdependent. With such goals there is a motivation to learn by developing new skills, trying to understand the tasks, improving the level of competence and achieving a sense of mastery based on self-referenced standards. Achievement of mastery goals is therefore likely to lead to a longer-term high quality involvement in learning compared with achieving performance goals of particular tasks.

Performance goals on the other hand focus on one's ability and sense of self worth. 'Especially important to a performance orientation is public recognition that one has done better than others or performed in a superior manner' in achieving specific goals (Ames, 1992). These goals are directed towards achieving success in relation to the achievements of one's colleagues.

Research by Ames has also shown that:

> tasks that involve variety and diversity are more likely to facilitate an inte...
> in learning and mastery orientation. Students are more likely to approach and
> engage in learning in a manner consistent with a mastery goal when they
> perceive a meaningful reason for engaging in the activity.

This supports the earlier discussion about the importance of making the purpose of the teaching clear to the pupils and fostering positive self-esteem amongst your pupils.

Fostering positive self-esteem can be achieved by a careful balance between performance and mastery goals. The ideal teaching objective is to help pupils achieve mastery goals by developing their knowledge and skills across a wide range of subjects that provide them with the ability to progress. Performance goals can be introduced through assessment tasks, specific lesson activities and particular learning objectives, although care needs to be taken that pupils who regularly perform less well than their peers do not lose motivation and interest in their education. Devise a range of lesson and homework activities that help the least able to perform well in at least some aspects of the task.

8. Influence of literacy and numeracy skills

The effective learning of pupils across a range of subjects and ages requires a sound basis of good literacy and numeracy skills. These have very recently been emphasized through the government's introduction of a range of new requirements including both a literacy and a numeracy hour for all primary pupils, and the mathematics and English core within the ITT compulsory curriculum (DFEE, 1998). Competency in English and mathematics affects the pupils' abilities to learn other subjects well. For example, pupils are sometimes assumed to be poor at mathematics until the teacher realizes that it is because they can't understand the language of the worksheets or exercise books they are using. On the other hand, pupils with weaknesses in numeracy and mathematics more generally will also be handicapped in other subjects such as science, geography, technology and ICT.

Gilbert *et al* (1982) have observed patterns of pupils' understanding connected to their conceptions in mechanics that have implications for all curriculum areas and relates to pupils' literacy skills. The types of understanding the researchers have observed represent:

- The use of everyday language: when a term/word is connected to its everyday interpretation it is easier to understand. For example, children may use the words 'push' and 'pull' that appear commonly in their everyday vocabulary and experience instead of the term 'force'.

- A self-centred and human centred viewpoint. Phrases and situations are considered in terms of human experiences and values. For example, in the system bicycle-cyclist, children may indicate forces applied to the bicycle indirectly, through the cyclist's actions (such as pedalling).
- The endowment of objects with the characteristics of humans or animals. Objects may have the characteristics of feeling, will or purpose, and these words are often used without metaphorical meaning. For example, an object/box sliding on a slope may 'want to stand up and resist its motion'.

As children use words from everyday situations, it is necessary for you to know the correspondence of children's views to the formal ones – what formal term children mean when they use particular words. In addition, examples from everyday situations (in which reference to children's 'terms' is made) seem to facilitate pupils' understanding of many topics. The situation is even more complicated if the pupils' first language is not English. For example, for pupils originating from some African countries, there is no equivalent word for 'velocity' to distinguish it from 'speed', whereas for pupils coming from Inuit regions there are more than 10 different words for 'snow'.

The importance of pupils' numeracy and literacy skills for their learning of all subjects throughout their formal education and beyond cannot be overemphasized. Both Piaget's and Vygotsky's theories of learning, discussed earlier, stress the importance of language in the development of thinking skills; when a pupil has to study in a second language or has other language difficulties it can inhibit satisfactory progression in many National Curriculum subjects. By using a range of different teaching methods, including ICT, it is possible to overcome some of these difficulties through pictures, icons, graphs and models.

Pupils learning about learning

Research in recent years has shown that pupils' learning can be improved if they are helped to think about the way they learn and to develop methods of making their learning explicit (Adey and Shayer, 1994). There are several techniques that can be used to help learners organize their knowledge, such as Knowledge Ven diagrams, advance organizers, lesson outlines and concept maps, but the work of Adey and Shayer has been widely recognized as causing a learning revolution across the UK in the last 10 years. The application of the CASE (cognitive acceleration in science education) teaching methods has resulted in pupils consistently gaining higher GCSE results, not only in science but in other subjects as well. As a result of this the CASE team has developed an extensive in-service teacher training programme to train teachers how to teach cognitive acceleration in science and mathematics (CAME).

Another technique to help you develop teaching plans that present pupils' 'misunderstandings' involves constructing and using concept/proposition maps to make clear what is to be taught and to identify possible areas of 'misunderstanding' by pupils. The maps should be constructed according to concept hierarchies and cover the content of a microschema or unit. These maps are diagrammed facts, concepts, propositions, attitudes, processes and physical skills that need to be taught during the presentation of a taught unit. The information is arranged diagrammatically to show the interrelationships among the content. After the content of the unit has been mapped, the information can then be reviewed in each area of knowledge to locate potential 'misunderstandings' that pupils held before or during the teaching-learning process.

To help pupils think about the way they learn, encourage them to describe their own views, verbally and pictorially, and help them express these ideas clearly, in order to recognize what they can and cannot explain. If such activities result in pupils' dissatisfaction with their existing ideas and the teacher provides additional experiences that will lead to further dissatisfaction, this will probably cause conceptual conflict. Nussbaum and Novick (1982) suggest that this conflict must be sufficient to persuade pupils to recognize that their existing views require modification. Accommodation develops when pupils search for a solution to their conflicting ideas. Using this approach, concept learning is achieved by *exposing alternative frameworks*, *creating conceptual conflict*, and *encouraging cognitive accommodation*.

Task 3.3 helps you to develop strategies for helping pupils to think about the ways they are thinking and learning. If you choose to question the pupils orally it is important to ensure that over a period of time all pupils volunteer answers. Written questions can help overcome this problem.

Task 3.3: Helping pupils question their ideas

This task presents ways of helping pupils think about what they know when you are teaching a lesson.

- Plan a lesson that includes questions relating to the learning objectives.
- At the beginning of the lesson, question the pupils orally or hand out a prepared sheet of paper containing questions to find out the ideas children bring to the problem situation.

- Write the pupils' responses on the board so they can all see them.
- Ask the children to hold their ideas in their heads, and then present other possibilities they will evaluate later.
- Explain the 'new' idea by linking it to the pupils' existing ideas.
- Refer to the old ideas for comparison, with each other and with the new idea.
- Ask the pupils to explain which ideas they think are the right ones.
- If they have changed them, find out how their thinking led to this new knowledge.

Summarizing the above, the types of teaching strategies that have been suggested by various researchers as facilitating conceptual change and helping pupils think about their learning include:

- providing opportunities for pupils to express clearly their own conceptions about the topic so that they can be examined in detail;
- presenting examples that challenge children's prior ideas;
- using strategies that enable pupils to consider and evaluate alternative conceptions of presented phenomena;
- providing opportunities to use new conceptions. Long-term accommodation of a person's conceptions is not likely to happen if new schemas are not seen as useful;
- giving pupils opportunities to become aware of their own conceptions and how they change.

Influence of ICT skills

There is substantial research evidence of the effects of ICT on pupils' learning and its impact on the curriculum itself. In the last few years the government has announced two major programmes for the development of the use of ICT in education that have been widely claimed as the biggest investment in education, amounting to over £1.3 billion, since World War II. It is therefore crucial that all teachers should know about what will be expected of them as well as the ways in which ICT can actually contribute to pupils' learning. The uses of ICT in different curriculum areas and teaching ICT as a subject are discussed in more detail in the next chapter.

Conclusions

This chapter has discussed some of the theories about children's learning and presented ideas for accommodating these in your teaching. Table 3.1 shows a summary of the most important issues associated with these theories.

Table 3.1 Issues relating to how children learn and acquire knowledge

Issues	*Explanations*
Stages in cognitive development	Sensori-motor – concrete operational – formal operational. Pupils may be at different stages within the same class. Until they have passed one stage they will struggle with tasks that require higher-level cognitive development. Teaching and learning tasks should relate to the pupils' stage of intellectual development.
Ages and education levels of pupils	Key National Curriculum stages, intellectual levels of achievement. The nature of any learning task needs to match the intellectual level of the individual pupil. Achievement goals within one subject level descriptor of a National Curriculum level may include goals that are at different intellectual levels so that pupils may not be able to achieve all aspects of any level. National Curriculum programmes and levels should be examined and chosen to fit the intellectual levels of the pupils concerned.
Existing preconceptions	Pupils' everyday informal experiences outside the classroom will influence how they can assimilate new knowledge within the lesson. Regular informal experiences can lead to entrenched misconceptions, particularly in science and mathematics. Efforts should be consistently made to find out pupils' informal knowledge and misconceptions.
Prior knowledge	The robustness of the prior knowledge that the pupils have about a topic will influence how well they can understand the new topic being taught. Prior knowledge in a different but relevant area will also determine how readily pupils are able to acquire knew knowledge. Some pupils will remember and retain topics and concepts covered in previous lessons better than others. Knowing and taking account of pupils' prior knowledge will help all pupils progress to their maximum potential.
Influence of the learning environment	Whole class, group-work or individual work will all affect the ways in which the pupils learn. Group work can sometimes produce better learning outcomes than individual pupils working on their own.
Social influence and cognition	The social background, different cultures and/or ethnic origins of the pupils will influence their ability to learn in different groups and particular lessons. It is important to know about the backgrounds of all your pupils and to vary the lessons and curriculum materials to help pupils benefit and enjoy their learning.

Table 3.1 *continued*

Issues	Explanations
Children's attitudes towards learning, fellow pupils and themselves	Pupils already have well-established attitudes and personality traits before they come to school. Within a class there will be pupils who are confident and cooperative and those who are negative about themselves, their school and their teacher, resulting in lack of cooperation and aggressive behaviour. Organize tasks and lessons that help foster the achievement of mastery and performance goals.
Influence of literacy and numeracy skills	Pupils who have literacy problems may underachieve in science, for example Pupils whose first language is not English may need additional help in lessons that involve substantial text or oral presentations. Pupils with numeracy problems may need additional help with other subjects such as science, technology and geography, as well as with mathematics.
Influence of ICT skills	Pupils' ICT skills and experience will affect their ability to grasp subject concepts and may enhance or inhibit learning (see the next chapter).

Although the issues discussed in this chapter may be daunting for the student teacher, remember that in spite of all the differences between individual pupils and the additional difficulties this presents when planning and preparing lessons, pupils usually start school wanting to learn and have an amazing resilience to difficulties and problems that they meet through their formal schooling. At the end of the day, although you cannot assume that each and every pupil learns in the same way, at the same pace, or even consistently over time, given an interesting, committed and enthusiastic teacher, who tries to take account of the issues discussed here, most pupils will respond with cooperation, dedication and determination to do well in their education.

References

Adey, P and Shayer, M (1994) *Really Raising Standards*, Routledge, London

Adey, P, Shayer, M and Yates, C (1990) *Better Learning. A report from the Cognitive Acceleration through Science Education (CASE) project*, Centre for Educational Studies, King's College, London

Ames, C (1992) Classroom; goals, structures and student motivation, *Journal of Educational Psychology*, **84** (3) pp261–71

Beard, R (1969) *An Outline of Piaget's Developmental Psychology*, Routledge & Kegan Paul, London

Brainerd, C (1970) *Piaget's Theory of Intelligence*, Prentice-Hall, New Jersey

Brown, C (1981) The implementation of curriculum change by schools, in ed G Elliott, *The School Curriculum in the 1980s,* Aspects of Education, 26, The University of Hull

Cole, M, Hill, D and Shan, S (1998) *Promoting Equality in Primary Schools,* Cassell, London

Cristafi, M and Brown, A (1986) Analogical transfer in very young children: combining two separately learned solutions to reach a goal, *Child Development,* **57,** pp953–68

Department for Education and Employment (1998) *Teachers Meeting the Challenge of Change,* TSO, Norwich

Department for Education and Employment (1999) *The National Curriculum,* DfEE, London

Durkin, K (1997) *Developmental Social Psychology: From infancy to old age,* Blackwell, Oxford

Eraut, M and Hoyles, C (1988) Groupwork with computers, ESRC Occasional Paper, InTER/3/88, University of Lancaster, and *Journal of Computer Assisted Learning,* **5** (1) pp12–24

Feurstein, R (1980) *Instrumental Enrichment: An intervention program for cognitive modifiability,* University Park Press, New York

Gilbert J, Watts, D and Osborne, R (1982) Students' conceptions of ideas in mechanics, *Physics Education,* **17** (2) pp62–6

Hill, M and Cole, D (1999) (eds) *Promoting Equality in Secondary Schools,* Cassell, London

HMSO (1995) *The National Curriculum,* TSO, Norwich

Nussbaum, J (1989) Classroom conceptual change: philosophical perspectives, *International Journal of Science Education,* **11,** special issue, pp530–40

Nussbaum, J and Novick, S (1982) Alternative frameworks, conceptual conflict and accommodation: toward a principled teaching strategy, *Instructional Science,* **11,** pp183–200

Piaget, J (1926) *The Language and Thought of the Child,* Routledge & Kegan Paul, London

Piaget, J and Inhelder, B (1969) *The Psychology of the Child,* Routledge & Kegan Paul, London

Posner, G, Strike, K, Hewson, P and Gertzog, W (1982) Accommodation of a scientific conception: toward a theory of conceptual change, *Science Education,* **66** (2) pp211–27

Skinner, B (1974) *About Behaviourism,* Vintage Books, New York

Straker, A (1989) *Children Using Computers,* Basil Blackwell, Oxford

Vygotsky, L S (1978) *Mind in Society: The development of higher psychological processes,* Harvard University Press, Cambridge, MA

Watson, D (1990) The classroom or computer room, *Computers and Education,* **15** (1–3) pp33–7

Wood, D (1988) *How Children Think and Learn,* Blackwell, Oxford

Using Information and Communication Technologies (ICT) for pupils' learning

4

Margaret Cox

> If we didn't have computers life would be very difficult because they help a lot with all difficult subjects and make you understand the 'problem' better. (13-year old boy, cited in Cox, 1997)

This chapter introduces the trainee to the requirements and standards set for information, communication and technology (ICT) following Circular 4/98 (DFEE, 1998) and the National Grid for Learning (NGfL). The trainee is taken through what ICT means, its nature and provision in school, and how this affects the trainee's own learning. ICT is a key issue in the classroom, with a clear expectation that teachers will play the leading role in promoting it. This is part of the trainee's role.

Objectives

By the end of this chapter the trainee will have an understanding of:

- up-to-date policies for ICT in education;
- the implications of ICT for their teaching;
- the need for pupils to participate in ICT;
- the need to continually develop their own ICT skills and pedagogy.

Introduction

What is the difference between Information Technology (IT) and Information and Communication Technologies (ICT)? There has been considerable confusion amongst many educators about IT and ICT, especially in schools where, for example, many have now replaced the IT coordinator by the ICT coordinator. It is therefore important to be clear about the distinction especially as both are so important in teaching and learning.

Information technology (IT) is the design, study and use of processes for representing physical, hypothetical or human relationships employing the collection, creation, storing, retrieving, manipulation, presentation, sending and receiving of information. IT was one of the National Curriculum subjects to be taught at all school levels, but the most recent National Curriculum orders (DFEE, 1999) now call the subject ICT. ICT is taught as a separate subject in the majority of schools, although some of them try and teach the subject through other subjects instead. IT is still the name used for the majority of university courses and in commerce and industry.

Information and communication technologies (ICT) are electronic and/or computerized devices and associated human interactive materials that enable the user to employ them for a wide range of teaching and learning processes in addition to personal use. ICT is being included in many new government initiatives that will be discussed later on. The term ICT is increasingly being used, for both IT and ICT, by the UK and other European governments, particularly when talking about schools. For simplicity the term ICT will be used for the rest of the chapter.

ICT includes computers, videos, televisions, connections with other computers, sensors, switches, interface boxes, the Internet which links computers globally together, telecommunications, satellite connections, and all the software and materials that enable us as teachers to use them to teach our pupils. Just as a television would be useless without visual and audio material reaching it through an aerial, video or cable, which we can then watch, so a computer needs software to make it communicate with us, the user. These devices have an important place in education in all school subjects.

The development of ICT in education

It is only in recent years that the phrase Information and Communication Technologies has come to be used in society and in education. Before that the most common terms ICT in education were 'Computers in Education' and 'Microelectronics in Education'. The use of computers in schools goes back many years, long before the requirements of the National Curriculum, and there have been a series of government programmes since as early as 1974, with an investment of over £250 million to support the use of computers and more recently ICT in education. More recent programmes and centres include the Education

Support Grants (ESG, during the 1980s and early 1990s) for the appointment of advisory teachers and the provision of hardware, more widely known as the Grants for Education Support and Training (GEST); and the British Educational and Communications Technology Agency (BECTa) (1997 to the present) formed from a restructuring of the National Council for Educational Technology (NCET) but with a greater focus on communications ICT, and with special responsibility for the NGfL.

Evidence from research studies has shown that these and many other initiatives have had an impact on teaching and learning in schools, through extending learning opportunities (Abbott, 2002; Mellar *et al*, 1994), improvements to children's learning (Harrison *et al*, 2002; Watson, 1993), and enhanced motivation (Cox, 1997). Amongst these and many other research studies there is substantial evidence about the value of ICT to teaching and learning, with improvements that cannot be achieved through other means.

In May 1998 the government announced new programmes that would amount to new funding of over £1.2 billion towards the NGfL, ICT for all initial teacher trainees and an ICT training allocation of £460 for every practising teacher. However, in spite of these initiatives, government surveys show that ICT is not yet used substantially in most National Curriculum subjects.

With all the changes that have taken place in the school curriculum over the last 15 years since the introduction of the National Curriculum, it is understandable that many teachers, if not the majority, are still unwilling or unable to use ICT in their subject teaching. In fact, according to the last government survey of ICT in schools (DfES, 2002a), less than 35 per cent of teachers, apart from ICT and business studies teachers, reported making substantial use of ICT in their subject teaching.

The new national curriculum for ITT (DfEE, 1999) contains 14 pages of ICT requirements for all teachers of all subjects aimed at 'equipping every newly qualified teacher with the knowledge, skills and understanding to use ICT effectively in teaching subjects'. These include a wide range of skills from being able to 'successfully connect up ICT equipment, including input devices, eg touch screens, overlay keyboards, ... to the use of CD-ROMS, the Internet, information from weather stations... computer based modelling'. Although these requirements may seem overwhelming to most teachers it is not expected that pupils will spend their entire time in front of a computer screen but only that ICT should be used where it will enhance pupils' learning. There are five main aspects of ICT use in schools:

1. teaching ICT as a subject that involves studying the concepts, skills and applications of IT;
2. using ICT to enhance learning of all subjects;
3. pupils using ICT to support their private study and assessment tasks;
4. using ICT to manage pupils' learning programmes and progression; and
5. using ICT for teachers' personal use and administration.

The focus in this chapter will be on the second aspect, involving contributions of ICT to pupils' learning, although the other aspects are also important for the improvement of education.

The ICT curriculum

The purpose of teaching ICT, which takes some of its topics from computer science, is to teach pupils how to handle information, generate and communicate ideas in different forms, give direct signals and commands that produce a variety of outcomes, and create and use ICT-based models or simulations to explore processes and real situations, etc. In the most recent version of the National Curriculum (DFEE, 1999), the main themes have been radically changed even though the content and skills are mostly still the same. The current theme titles are given under two main areas as with all other National Curriculum subjects: knowledge, skills and understanding, and breadth of study. The main themes are:

Knowledge, skills and understanding:

- finding things out;
- developing ideas and making things happen;
- exchanging and sharing information;
- reviewing, modifying and evaluating work as it progresses.

Breadth of study for KS3 (this range differs for each of the Key Stages):

- working with a range of information to consider its characteristics, structure, organization and purposes;
- working with others to explore a variety of information sources and ICT tools in a variety of contexts;
- designing information systems and evaluating and suggesting improvements to existing systems;
- comparing their use of ICT with its use in the wider world.

These curriculum themes provide opportunities for pupils to learn new skills and concepts that will influence their learning in other curriculum areas. Many aspects of the ICT curriculum embrace the ICT skills and processes that are expected to be included in all subjects. Although you may not be expecting ever to teach ICT as a subject, there are many schools that are still trying to teach ICT through other subjects even though this approach has so far proved to be very difficult and unsuccessful (Goldstein, 1997). In most primary schools ICT is 'taught' across the curriculum, so for any new teacher it is important to know what is involved in the

ICT curriculum and which ICT skills and processes help pupils to use ICT in other curriculum areas. In secondary schools ICT is either taught as a separate subject or through other subjects.

In 2002 the Department for Education and Skills produced a scheme of work for teachers (DfES, 2002b) on how to teach and use ICT in the curriculum at KS3. This was followed by a scheme of work for primary schools for KS1 and 2. These schemes of work are available in packs and also downloadable off the DfES Web site at http://www.standards.dfee.gov.uk. They include a large number of units that provide many examples of the content of the ICT curriculum and the teaching approaches that might be used.

The primary level units include topics such as:

Unit 1B. Using a word bank
Unit 1C. The information around us
Unit 1D. Labelling and classifying
Unit 1E. Representing information graphically: pictograms
Unit 1F. Understanding instructions and making things happen
Unit 2A. Writing stories: communicating information using text
Unit 2B. Creating pictures for primary schools

At KS3 units include:

Unit 8. Public information systems
Unit 9. Publishing on the web
Unit 10. Information – reliability, validity and bias
Unit 11. Data – use and misuse
Unit 12. Systems – integrating applications to find solutions
Unit 13. Control systems
Unit 14. Global communication – negotiating and transferring data
Unit 15. Systems: managing a project

Each unit includes information about how it relates to the National Curriculum targets, recommendations about how many lessons the unit covers, details of the teaching and learning tasks, a list of resources needed, pupils' prior learning, the subject knowledge needed by the teachers, and outlines of each lesson. This is followed by a detailed account of how to conduct the lesson and then assess the pupils' learning. Other useful reference materials and sources are listed in the *ICT in Education Directory 2003/2004* (British Computer Society, 2003) and at the end of this chapter.

There is a widely held misconception among teachers, pupils and parents alike that teaching ICT is simply about pupils learning how to word-process, create spreadsheets and use the Internet, yet it is interesting to note that apart from generic packages such as databases or spreadsheets, not one specific application package nor

Item of hardware is mentioned in the ICT National Curriculum orders (DfEE, 1999). It is not possible to provide details of all the elements of the ICT curriculum in this chapter, but two examples are discussed briefly below to show the kinds of ICT knowledge and skills that should be part of the ICT National Curriculum.

In primary schools, pupils should be taught at KS1, for example:

> to gather information from a variety of sources [for example, people, books, databases, CD-ROMs, videos and TV] [and] to use text, tables, images and sound to develop their ideas.

At KS2, pupils should be taught:

> how to prepare information for development using ICT, including selecting suitable sources, finding information, classifying it and checking it for accuracy [for example, finding information from books or newspapers, creating a class database, classifying by characteristics and purposes, checking the spelling of names is consistent] (DfEE, 1999).

Often the ICT experience that pupils are given in primary schools is limited to irregular use of word-processors. However, ICT equipment can include sensors, switches and graphics tablets (more commonly called concept keyboards), which enable young children to interact with the technology in a very simple way. The important education objective is that the pupils should understand the purpose for using ICT, so the first stage would be to identify a problem such as, 'How can we find out how cold the classroom gets during the night when the heating is turned off?' The task for the pupils is to think of a temperature gauge that could be connected to a computer that would record the temperature every hour, for example. This simple activity would involve the pupils in planning the investigation, hypothesizing, estimating, collecting and analysing information, measuring, controlling equipment and so on.

Research into pupils learning science has shown that, if pupils engage in conducting experiments that enable them to confront their own misconceptions, they come to a better understanding of the processes and concepts involved (Brna, 1990). There are many different activities involving this process that can be undertaken in the ICT curriculum.

Learning about the function and uses of ICT equipment can be introduced at all stages in the curriculum and in many different curriculum areas. Task 4.1 will help you think of ideas for teaching the systems aspect of ICT and 'finding things out'. For more advanced A-level ICT/IT activities see, for example, Mott and Leeming (1998) and Heathcote (1998). Use Task 4.1 to identify a range of ICT equipment and/or software that can help pupils understand the impact of ICT on society.

Task 4.1: Using ICT equipment

Many aspects of our lives depend upon access to ICT.

1. List three pieces of equipment found in the home that contain micro-processors/computers, eg a washing machine.
2. Write down the task you think each one performs, eg operating the washing machine.
3. List all the things it will have to measure, eg water level, temperature, stage in the washing cycle.
4. List how these could be done without a washing machine, eg filling up a bowl with hot and cold water, using your eyes or hands to tell when you have enough water and whether the temperature is right for the clothes.
5. Prepare a table for the whole class to list the different machines they or you have thought of, their tasks and the manual equivalent, and discuss how they supplement or replace human activities.

This task will encourage pupils to think of the relationships between the many different machines we use, and the manual processes that ICT can now control or replace. Extending these kinds of tasks to include pupils thinking about cause and effect and how such mechanistic processes work, can help them develop causal reasoning skills. Studies of the use of problem-solving activities involving causal relationships (Mellar *et al*, 1994) have shown that pupils develop higher order thinking skills and autonomy of learning. The ICT curriculum also involves many of these skills, which are required in other subjects when using ICT.

When teaching ICT or even using it within another subject teachers often discard their best teaching practice and 'throw the baby out with bath water'. It is not the case that pupils using ICT within a subject should be put in front of computers for the whole of a lesson. At least half of the timetabled series of ICT lessons should involve pupils discussing ideas, drawing up plans, sequences and models on paper, collecting data and so on away from the computer.

It would be an amazing breakthrough if the ICT curriculum could be successfully taught within other subjects instead of as a separate subject. Many schools have adopted this approach to save money and to avoid the sensitive issues of staffing and timetabling. However, recent OFSTED (Office for Standards in Education) reports have shown that in the majority of schools where ICT is taught across the curriculum, the coverage is superficial with most pupils only reaching levels 4 to 5 in Year 11 and many schools not having any ICT at all at KS4 (OFSTED, 2002). The reality is that pupils are losing out on an important part of their learning because of the difficulties many schools face in delivering the ICT curriculum. However, since the government initiative in April 1999, which provided the equivalent of £450 for every state school teacher to obtain additional training in the use of ICT in their teaching, more teachers are starting to make productive uses of ICT to promote pupils' learning. Ideas for how ICT can promote pupils learning are discussed in the next section.

ICT to promote pupils' learning

A useful framework for considering the contribution of ICT to pupils' learning is the one based on the work of Kemmis *et al* (1977), which proposed four paradigms for computer assisted learning that are still relevant to today's technology. These paradigms are: instructional; revelatory; conjectural and emancipatory.

1. The instructional paradigm

The instructional paradigm applies to a learning task that can be broken down into a series of sub-tasks, each one involving its own prerequisites and objectives. These separate tasks are then structured and sequenced to form a coherent whole. ICT software, which fits this paradigm, is usually given names like 'skill and drill', 'drill and practice' and 'instructional dialogue' and is mostly based on Skinnerian theories of learning. Within this paradigm are included integrated learning systems (ILS), first devised by Skinner himself in the late 1960s, but which are now extensive programmed learning systems involving graphics, colour, sound and moving images. A few years ago these systems were promoted vigorously by some hardware companies and increasingly adopted by schools that had often obtained poor academic results. However, most of the evidence from research into this kind of software is that it is of limited value to pupils' learning and relates mainly to short-term performance goals rather than substantial understanding. Since then the uptake of ILS has been tailing off.

2. The revelatory paradigm

The revelatory paradigm relates to ICT environments that involve guiding a pupil through a process of learning by discovery. The subject matter, and its underlying model of the associated theory, is gradually revealed to the pupils as they use the program. This would include simulations of processes and situations, but not modelling. The use of simulations provides the pupil with the opportunity to investigate a scientific experiment that, for example, may be too expensive in materials and equipment, or take too long to be practicable, or cannot be undertaken in the laboratory because it is dangerous. The computer may facilitate the building or imagining of models or systems that are too complex to be understandable in any other way. When the pupils carry out simulated experiments that would be impossible to undertake under other conditions, allowing them to alter and experiment with variable factors, they take a greater part in controlling the direction of their investigations. When the calculation process is entirely managed by the computer, users can concentrate more easily on thinking (eg, making hypotheses about why things are happening), and this has been found to be a very effective stimulus to discussion when the activity happens in small groups. The skills promoted by the use of simulations are both practical and intellectual, involving reasoning, experimenting and interpreting.

The educational philosophy of most simulations is based on Piagetian theories of learning, where the pupils can challenge their existing schemas by exploration and build on this through practical observation of the results of their hypotheses and actions. An early example of a simulation is 'Indian Farmer', from the Computers in the Curriculum (CIC) project 1988, which simulates the life story of a Hindu family living in a hypothetical agricultural village on the Ganges Plain. The software displays pictures of each family member, their names and ages, the numbers of fields of rice and millet planted, and the amount of grain available for planting at the beginning of each year in a simple bar chart. An example of one screen display is shown in Figure 4.1

Figure 4.1 A family after the harvest and their grain store

The program allows the pupils to make decisions as though they were part of the family, about how many fields of rice and millet they should grow and whether to buy a bullock or not. The family story then varies according to those decisions, revealing the long-term social and economic aspects of life in a poor agricultural community. Although this simulation was designed for secondary pupils of all ages, it can be used with KS2 pupils to stimulate an appreciation of the problems faced by other societies and cultures and the impact of the weather.

During the period from 1973 to 1995 hundreds of useful simulations were produced in the UK, many of which are still available today, updated to run on current machines. Some of these are also available through the DfES' E-learning credits scheme[1] (see http://www.curriculumonline.gov.uk), which provides teachers with credits to buy educational software. However, while the educational design of many of them is relevant to the current curriculum, further resources are needed to make more of these programs compatible with today's technology. Simulations include history, geography, economics, role-playing and educational games, as well as many in science and technology. Research by the first Impact project (Watson, 1993) and many other projects provides convincing evidence of the positive contribution of simulations to pupils' learning.

3. The conjectural paradigm

The conjectural paradigm relates to increasing the control by the pupil over the computer by allowing the pupil to manipulate and test his or her own ideas and hypotheses. The range of programs that relate to this paradigm include modelling, where pupils can propose and construct relationships and then test them against real processes. Modelling programs include programming languages such as LOGO, for which there have been widespread claims for many years about the contributions to pupils' learning. Papert (1980), who invented LOGO, found in his research studies during the 1980s that pupils using LOGO developed higher order thinking skills, including problem solving, hypothesizing and logical reasoning, which could be applied across a range of subjects.

Although there is conflicting evidence from research studies about the value of modelling in learning particular concepts, one common agreed finding is the importance and value of modelling in education because it facilitates and extends investigations, exploration and confrontation of one's own conceptions in an interactive and immediate environment.

There are two types of modelling activities generally referred to in education: quantitative and qualitative modelling. Quantitative modelling involves pupils constructing mathematical relationships of real-life processes, while qualitative modelling involves rule-based logical relationships using, for example, Boolean Logic.

Although you can build your own models with general purpose software such as the spreadsheet package EXCEL, or the data-handling package ACCESS, there are very comprehensive modelling packages that have been developed specifically for education. A Windows based modelling system, Model Builder (Booth and Cox, 1997) has been designed to be used with pupils aged from 9 years up to adulthood and includes a simple modelling language (incorporating natural language). Using this environment, the learner can explore the models provided with the resource pack or build models themselves. Models can include pictures, diagrams, graphs and tables, and can vary between very simple models with only two or three parameters to very complex models, involving sub-models and different modes of operation. Various ideas for using this kind of modelling software are described below.

At the primary level, pupils can explore models such as HOUSE.MDL, shown in Figure 4.2, which performs a simple set of calculations of the energy gains and losses in a home. Alternatively, they can build their own models of their home showing how it gains and loses heat and how to save energy, by starting with HEATING.MDL, shown in Figure 4.3.

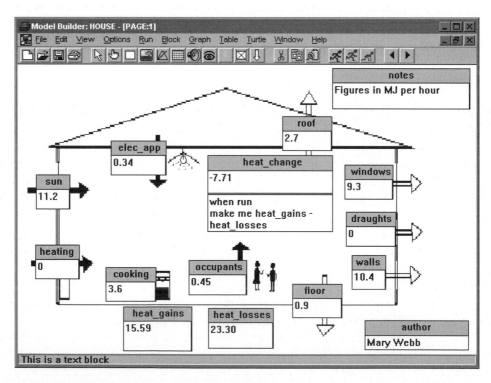

Figure 4.2   Example of a simple model, HOUSE.MDL, to investigate energy gains and losses (Model Builder, 1997)

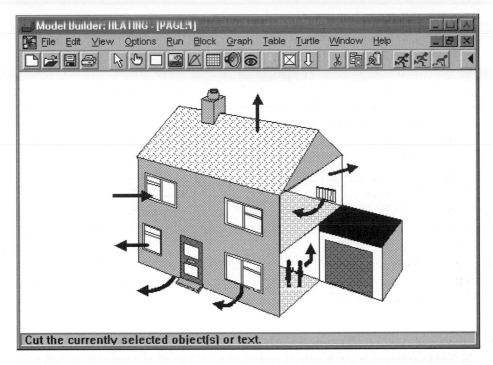

Figure 4.3   Example of a simple model, HEATING.MDL, for pupils to create their own model (Model Builder, 1997)

Similar kinds of investigations can be carried out using the spreadsheet package EXCEL as shown in the Energy Expert curriculum pack (Cox, 1993). Each modelling application, eg Model Builder, EXCEL, has its own set of metaphors for the way the information is displayed on the screen. It is important that when choosing which one to use, you consider the level of ICT skills of the pupils and their ability to use different types of commands and interpret the information. For example, for KS1 pupils, EXCEL is not easily usable since pupils are not yet capable of understanding a tabular format that allows text, numbers and relationships inserted into any cell.

Model Builder or EXCEL can both be used to help pupils build simple mathematical models, such as the relationship between the volume of a cube and its dimension, or simple everyday models such as MONEY2. MDL, in Model Builder. Figure 4.4 shows a model that can be constructed by KS2 pupils to investigate the relationships between their income, expenditure and savings.

At KS3 and 4, there is a whole range of models provided with Model Builder suitable for the ICT curriculum and for many other subjects. These models enable pupils to study, for example, the processes of the carbon cycle in order to investigate the amount of carbon dioxide produced in the atmosphere by the industrial combustion of fossil fuels, and to take into consideration the rate of absorption by

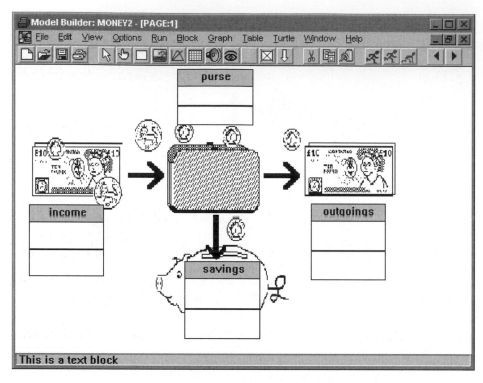

Figure 4.4   Example of a simple money-saving model, MONEY2.MDL
(Model Builder, 1997)

plants and the oceans. Figure 4.5 shows the model CCYCLE.MDL, which can be investigated or extended to enable pupils to understand the uses, advantages and disadvantages of this particular modelling technique for studying the way human behaviour affects our global environment. Pupils at KS3 and 4 can build similar models either working in small groups to create sub-models or using sections from the sample models provided in the pack.

For GCSE and GNVQ projects there are many ideas within Model Builder and the curriculum pack, Energy Expert (Cox, 1993), suitable for longer activities that involve the pupils gathering data and building a model of a topic relevant to a range of subjects. For example, pupils can follow Activity 10, Designing a Home, described in the Energy Expert curriculum pack. This Students' Guide provides a series of staged tasks involving initial ideas, research, evaluating your own ideas, the detailed design, evaluating the design and presenting your design.

Similar kinds of modelling activities can also be achieved with software such as EXCEL, but using a more formal mathematical language for building the models. Figure 4.6 shows the sample model FORECST2.XLS, built by pupils using EXCEL (Energy Expert, 1993) which enables pupils to forecast energy demand by consumers,

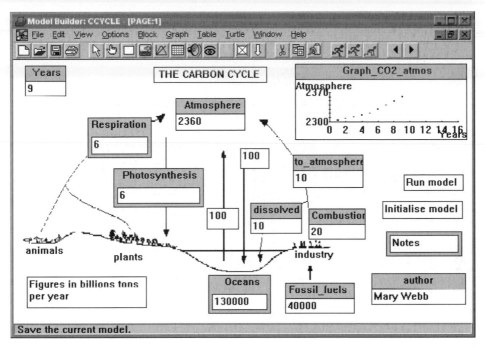

Figure 4.5   Example of an environmental science/geography model of factors contributing to the world's carbon cycle (Model Builder, 1997)

depending on the outside temperature, the inside temperature, hourly energy use and weighting factors. This model can be built and evaluated by pupils to compare their own home energy use with that forecast by their model. This model can then be extended to suit different weather patterns, different types of communities and longer periods of time.

Activities such as those described above using modelling software, enable teachers to include computer-based modelling in many different areas of the National Curriculum, from KS1 to above KS4, not only in ICT, but also in design and technology, science, mathematics, geography, physical education, economics and business studies. With the tools now available, modelling can be applied to almost any curriculum area.

The modelling packages referred to above are principally designed for quanti- tative model building through algebraic relationships. Qualitative tools, such as the expert system shell, Expert Builder[2] (Booth *et al*, 1994) have been developed to allow the learner to construct models in the form of conditional relationships. This is done by constructing a logical network of phrases comprising questions, facts, rules and advice, displayed on the screen as boxes linked together through logical connectors. While the model is being constructed, it can be interrogated by the pupils to test their logic and reasoning behind the model. This kind of system is

Microsoft Excel - Forecst2.xls

File   Edit   View   Insert   Format   Tools   Data   Accounting   Window   Help

	A	B	C	D	E	F	G	H
1								
2				Gas Consumption Forecasting				
3								
4	Base Temperature		20.0 °C			Energy Factor	0.8	
5								
6	Date	Outside Temp.		Degree Day	Smoothed De	Hourly Energy Use		Weights
7	1	7.0 °C		13.0 °C				1
8	2	10.0 °C		10.0 °C				2
9	3	11.5 °C		8.5 °C				3
10	4	12.0 °C		8.0 °C				4
11	5	13.0 °C		7.0 °C	9.1 °C	7.2 KwH		
12	6	12.5 °C		7.5 °C	7.9 °C	6.3 KwH		
13	7	10.0 °C		10.0 °C	7.6 °C	6.0 KwH		
14	8	12.5 °C		7.5 °C	8.5 °C	6.8 KwH		
15	9	12.0 °C		8.0 °C	8.2 °C	6.6 KwH		
16	10	11.0 °C		9.0 °C	8.2 °C	6.6 KwH		
17	11	13.5 °C		6.5 °C	8.5 °C	6.8 KwH		
18	12	14.0 °C		6.0 °C	7.7 °C	6.1 KwH		

FORECST2

Figure 4.6   Sample model FORECST.2, using EXCEL on forecasting energy demand (Energy Expert, 1993)

based on formal logic and inference rules. Figure 4.7 shows an example of a model, CREEPY.EBD built by secondary, KS4 school pupils for the classification of insects and other animals. This model is constructed by typing in the characteristics of a creature in each box, then linking them together in logical sequences.

A simpler version of this could be built by younger pupils at KS2 or 3, with pupils bringing in small insects and other animals, or visiting the local museum or zoo to collect data to help construct their animal classification system. Expert Builder can also be used to create or explore fault-finding procedures for devices in technology, conditions for the development of a town in history, dietary factors and healthy eating in food technology and biology, human behaviour leading to desertification in geography, and conditions for illnesses in biology.

Using modelling software and simulations enables pupils to investigate their own ideas about different subject processes and concepts, at the same time as learning ICT skills about model building, graphical representations, and using computers for simulating complex physical, economical, or geographical processes. There is no in-built teacher control except for the constraints imposed by the modelling framework. The topic and level of complexity are determined by the learner and not the software developer.

Computer models can also be built using any programming language such as BASIC, LOGO, PASCAL, Prolog or Smalltalk, although the use of some of these in

(a)

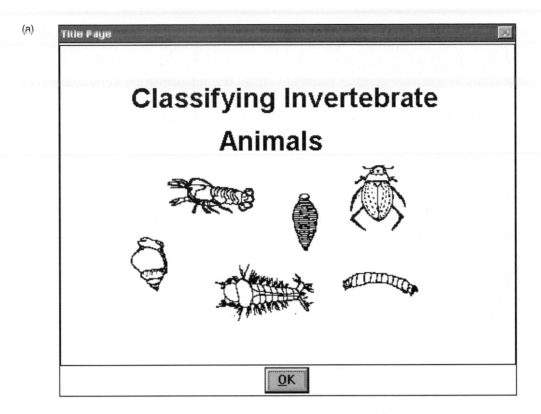

(b)

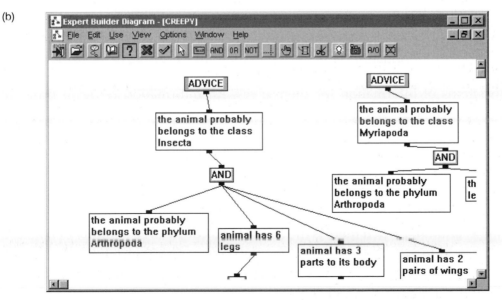

Figure 4.7 Example of an animal classification model, CREEPY.EBD
(Expert Builder, 1994)[2]

the classroom is still very rare. An additional difficulty in using most programming languages is that the routines for the input and graphical displays have to be created as well as for the model itself.

Data analysis software enables pupils to study the relationships between sets of experimental data and perform statistical analyses, thereby engaging in many of the processes of modelling. The types of software that can be used for simulating and modelling are almost limitless and include many activities now available over the Internet. Examples of these are discussed in relation to the emancipatory paradigm.

Chapter 3 explains that a major contribution to pupils' progression in learning is made by helping pupils think about how they learn. The interactive nature of modelling using ICT enables them to do this through, for example, the creation of a model of a process where the pupils can see an immediate result of their model in relation to the outcomes of a real process.

4. The emancipatory paradigm

The fourth and final paradigm suggested by Kemmis and MacDonald means being emancipated: the learners have more control over the computer, and use it as and when they want as an aid in the learning process. It involves the use of ICT as a 'labour-saving device', to perform calculations, to plot graphs, to retrieve information, to manipulate text and, in general, to deal with some given task. In this type of ICT use, the information handling abilities of the computer are exploited so as to improve the quality of the learning experience by taking the monotony out of some kinds of tasks.

By using an 'information retrieval' program, pupils can store their own information on a computer, they can display this information, and they can access specific items of information for themselves. An information retrieval program allows the person using it to form a database. This can be defined as 'an organized collection of related data, where the structure of the data is independent of any particular application'. Data handling and analysis are a major part of the ICT curriculum and also a major ICT activity relevant to science, history, geography and many other curriculum areas at both primary and secondary levels.

Data analysis packages have some strong advantages in particular curriculum applications. They enable pupils to recognize patterns or tendencies in the data they are examining. When there is the need to consider a large quantity of data or a wide range of observations, the use of a database package facilitates the organization or management of information. Data processing is one way for the pupils to develop a more systematic approach to problem solving, especially in cases where, for instance, planning, categorization and formal reasoning are demanded. When the computer generates results of simulated experiments, pupils may analyse the results to discover the underlying operating relationships. Moreover, they have more time to interpret patterns of data and results from investigations, and to gain confidence when they summarize information.

Data handling skills are perhaps one of the most important ranges of skills that pupils need to be taught today because of the expanding growth of information and methods of access through the Internet and other telecommunication systems. Cox and Nikolopoulou (1997) investigated the strategies and skills of pupils aged 13–15 who were using a computer-based data analysis package, compared with similar classes of pupils who used sets of data on paper cards, and found that the pupils using ICT outperformed the control group and developed important data handling skills, previously only found among older pupils.

This study and previous ones have shown that the following skills and understanding are promoted by the use of database software:

- formulating queries;
- using Boolean logical operators (and, or, greater than, less than, equal to);
- conducting single and multiple condition searches;
- performing two parallel logical reasoning tasks;
- classifying and interpreting data;
- specifying ranges of numbers;
- recognizing patterns in unfamiliar data.

Although data handling is a cross-curricular activity it usually takes place in a subject-specific context. The skills mentioned above can be promoted in many different curriculum applications. For example, in history, census schedules are commonly used to encourage enquiry learning through pupils formulating and testing their own hypotheses. In biology pupils are required to develop the skills of classifying insects and other animal forms, and in chemistry pupils use and construct chemical databases to speculate about conceptual links, about correlations and trends in chemical behaviour, and about causal relationships.

An early study by Underwood (1988) evaluated the investigations undertaken by teachers and pupils using computer-based information handling packages in 18 primary and secondary classrooms, across a range of subjects, and compared the expressed objectives/intentions of teachers using databases against recorded classroom outcomes. Types of teachers' intents included:

- skills and knowledge (cognitive, communication, computer) acquired from the exercise;
- teaching and learning strategies employed (eg emancipation, motivation);
- social and psychological climate of the classroom; and
- societal issues (eg life skills).

Although not all the recorded transactions and outcomes matched the teachers' intentions, the results of these 18 case studies showed that computer-based information handling packages can be beneficial to pupils' learning. Teachers were aware of the wide range of skills and knowledge that could be stimulated by database use, and the emphasis in the transactions and outcomes was very much towards the cognitive skills (in particular formulating hypotheses and questions), communication skills, and the organization and management of the classroom. The data handling skills and National Curriculum attainment levels are shown in Table 4.1.

Table 4.1   Data handling skills and National Curriculum attainment levels

Elementary skills Levels 2, 3, 4 (ages: 7–11)	Intermediate skills Levels 5, 6, 7 (ages: 11–14)	Advanced skills Levels 8, 9, 10 (ages: 14–16)
• collect data • select data • retrieve data • sort and classify discrete data • compare and contrast (observe similarities and differences) • ask questions	• select relevant information • formulate and test hypotheses • classify (against one or two criteria) • interpret (graphics, relationships) • predict relationships • make decisions • organize and analyse data • analyse patterns • draw conclusions	• analyse results to test a hypothesis • compare and contrast • identify patterns • interpret evidence • make predictions • evaluate information • analyse complex information

Task 4.2: Relating data handling tasks to the National Curriculum

1. List the number of fields for the data; eg height, weight, name.
2. Write down the number of records; ie a record is all the information for one item,
3. Write a set of procedures to enable the pupils to follow through the data handling activity.
4. Identify the skills in Table 4.1 involved in the task you have devised.

The second example of an ICT activity that relates to the conjectural as well as the emancipatory paradigm is communicating information.

This involves understanding what information is, the different forms of information and how it can therefore be communicated. For example, in the primary classroom pupils might be asked to bring in and study different kinds of information sources, such as leaflets, labels, bus tickets, posters, letters, postcards, etc. They can then be asked to examine them for their content, the audience, the purpose of the information, its design, the time it might be accessed and so on. The next stage would be to consider what kinds of information might be enhanced with the use of a word-processor for example, or desktop publishing program, planning the design to take account of the purpose, the message and the audience.

Schools that have access to the Internet could include an activity involving downloading and printing out a few Web pages to examine the different ways in which information is presented. Figures 4.8 a, b and c present three very different types of Web pages, showing the different emphases the Web designer has placed on the information provided. Lessons can be planned around an evaluation of these Web pages, why they were produced, what kind of information they hold and how this differs from paper-based information.

The teaching of general information handling skills without computer use seems to be organized according to pupils' experience and development. Piaget and Inhelder (1969) assert that the mastery of basic operations like seriating and classifying is important to cognition and a prerequisite for success at later cognitive tasks. To these skills can be added instruction in comparing, contrasting and observing, and these come before teaching more complex skills such as analysing, synthesizing and evaluating.

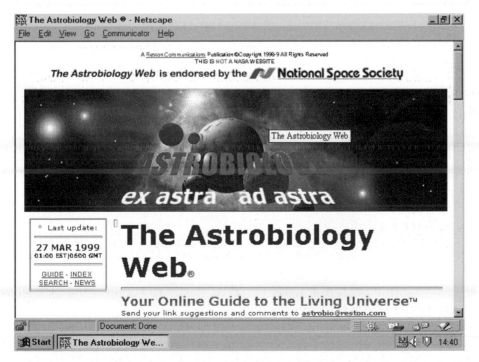

Figure 4.8a   The Astrobiology Web at http://www.astrobiology.com

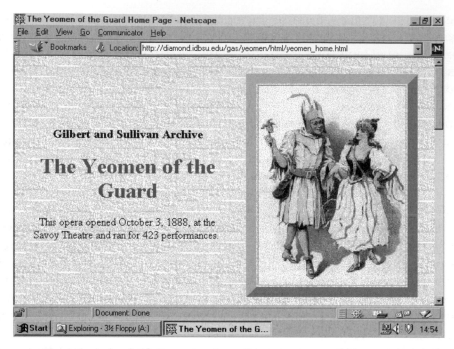

Figure 4.8b   Yeoman of the Guard at http://www.geocities.com/queens_yeomen/

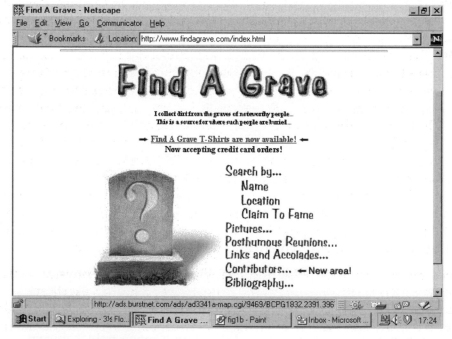

Figure 4.8c   Finding a grave at http://www.findagrave.com/index.html

When using a computer for information handling, tasks also need to be structured and sequenced. Hunter (1987) suggested that pupils should start with activities that develop prerequisite skills, such as locating, classifying and interpreting information, before they take on tasks requiring more complex skills (like analysing, formulating hypotheses and evaluating). Parker (1986) states that the lower order thinking skills with database work might include entering data, retrieving factual information, and using databases to organize lists. On the other hand, the higher order thinking skills might include determining the information needed to test a hypothesis, reorganizing and synthesizing data to test ideas and find non-obvious relationships, selecting between relevant and irrelevant information, and drawing inferences.

In the examples above, the ICT uses have involved stand-alone or networked computers without any peripheral equipment except printers. However, one of the most important aspects of ICT is the use of sensors, switches and other alternative devices that enable pupils to collect a wide range of scientific and other data both directly or remotely. According to Joseph Deken, technology curator at the California Museum of Science and Industry (Deken, 1990), measurement and control devices form the main components of robotics, which 'is a new and universal medium, which will certainly make obsolete all the primitive machines and computers of the 20th century'.

There are many experiments that are difficult or impossible to carry out in the classroom without the use of measurement and control devices. This is because the time scales required are either very short, such as the speed of a falling object, or very long, such as the rate of change of humidity in the air. Alternatively, the changes may be minute, and impossible to measure without accurate gauges connected to a computer. Frost (1994) has provided many examples of how sensors and switches can be used by pupils to collect simple scientific data. For instance, pupils can measure the speed of a moving object by the computer recording the exact time it passes through two light gates. Using sensors, pupils can collect accurate information and then compare their results with their own theories of the process. It also enables them to see the results immediately and avoid the sometimes laborious process of recording the data by hand then carrying out calculations. Barton and Rogers (1994), who researched into pupils using motion sensors and light gates to measure the movement of objects, found that in both cases 'the immediate presentation of data connects the investigation and the results. This has the effect of freeing pupils to spending most of their time analysing, interpreting and predicting skills which are at the heart of scientific investigation'.

Practical examples of measurement and control activities include:

- pupils measuring their pulse and changing their rate of physical activity to investigate the relationship between pulse rate and human exertion;
- measuring the variation in temperature levels over a period of several days in various locations in the school, using remote sensors to determine the highest sources of heat loss;

- measuring the levels of infrared radiation as a detector of human presence to trigger an alarm.

Task 4.3 provides ideas for introducing measurement and control concepts to pupils. A visit to a local canning factory or car manufacturing plant provides very stimulating insights into how important measurement and control devices are in our lives.

Task 4.3: Measurement and control devices

This task can be used for either primary or secondary pupils; the detail will depend upon the intellectual stage of the pupils.

1. Organize a visit with the pupils to the local supermarket.
2. At the supermarket get the pupils to record all the devices they can see which measure things or might be controlled (eg automatic doors; bar code readers at the checkout; lighting, car park gates, fridges, burglar alarms).
3. Get the pupils to make a second list of the different types of food and produce in the supermarket (eg fresh, canned, non-foods).
4. In the following lesson, with the pupils in small groups, ask them to identify the kinds of sensors these devices might have (eg light, sound, position). For younger pupils, this might need ideas from the teacher.
5. List their results on the board and discuss the reasoning of their results.
6. For more advanced work, provide a list of questions for the pupils for homework for them to propose what kinds of sensors and switches might be needed in providing the food in the different types of containers. (For example, what sensors and switches might a machine need that fills coke cans and then seals them?)

The examples in this chapter of ICT uses are just the tip of the iceberg in terms of resources and different curriculum applications. New ideas and resources are arriving on the Web every day and a few useful Web sites are given at the end of the chapter. The overwhelming ICT resources available on the Internet make it even more difficult to decide what to include when using ICT in one's teaching.

ICT whole-class resources

All the activities described above can be used in a variety of ways in the classroom with different ICT resources. It is not possible to describe all the ICT hardware devices that could be used in teaching, but there are two major ICT developments that need to be explained in more detail here because they are being adopted by innovative teachers and have been shown to be very beneficial to pupils. These are the electronic whiteboard and video-conferencing.

Electronic whiteboard

The electronic whiteboard is a white screen that has a matrix of cells embedded within it that pass signals to and from a computer. This enables the teacher to display computer software, Power Point slides, Web sites, etc to the whole class. The other important feature is that the user (teacher or pupil) can draw on the whiteboard, and the pictures, diagrams or text can be stored on the computer for further use. This is very useful for recalling previous screens and for keeping materials for later lessons. Schools are now using them widely for whole-class demonstrations, to promote class discussion and to build up a body of resources that can be shared by other teachers.

One of the problems with networks of individual work stations has been that teachers tend to encourage pupils to work in isolation. As I explained earlier, this does not always lead to useful pupil activity. Using whiteboards, on the other hand, can enable the teacher to use a simulation with a whole class, or build a computer model when every pupil is volunteering ideas for the activity. There are clearly many other whiteboard uses that extend the ICT opportunities within most subjects.

Video-conferencing

Although not many schools are yet using video-conferencing there are teachers who have connected their pupils to a class in another school so they can share ideas about their work. There are international projects that are linking classes of pupils in different countries, eg Japan and England, and there are examples of pupils speaking through a video-conference link to an expert in a relevant field. Video-conferencing is also becoming an important component of some distance learning courses and some schools are running distance learning courses for A-level subjects where the pupil numbers are small.

These and other ICT resources make it difficult for teachers to decide when and where to use ICT in a very busy curriculum. The final section explains some of the issues, which might help with these decisions.

Organizing ICT in one's teaching

Since the publication of Kemmis *et al*'s paradigms in 1977 the ICT environment has changed almost beyond all recognition, although the Internet was around then and computers look the same from a distance! Most software on sale today is very versatile and dynamic with pictures, icons, sound and moving images. The use of the Internet and the material available through it is profoundly changing society and education. The teacher of today has the difficult task of trying to organize a powerful resource into subject lessons and into a crowded timetable. For example, one CD-ROM designed for use in teaching geography, Distant Places (Advisory Unit, 1998) has enough material for pupils to spend hours longer on it than on other geography topics. Therefore the teacher has to decide how to plan a series of useful lessons without having to leave out many other geographical skills and concepts also included in the National Curriculum.

The main issues that have to be considered when planning how to include ICT in one's teaching are to relate the ICT activity to the learning aims and objectives of the curriculum. Ten golden rules to follow when planning and using ICT in the curriculum will help you in ensuring that it is used to enhance pupils' learning:

1. Identify the learning aims and objectives for the pupils that can be enhanced by the use of ICT.
2. Select appropriate ICT resources to meet the learning aims.
3. Ensure that the pupils have enough ICT skills to be able to carry out the activity.
4. Plan the timing of the activity to include non-ICT tasks such as question and answers, group work and pupils' discussions.
5. Plan enough lessons to enable the activity to be completed.
6. Decide on the groupings of the pupils – they do not always have to work alone.
7. Introduce the lesson to all the pupils first before working on any ICT resource.
8. Intersperse the ICT activity with whole-class guidance and direction.
9. Allow enough time for the pupils to reflect on and evaluate their achievements at the end of the lesson.
10. Allocate homework or other assessed work in which the pupils extend their thinking about the activity, and through which you can find out what they have learnt.

It would be impossible to address all the Teacher Training Agency's new requirements for teachers using ICT in schools (TTA, 1999) in this chapter, although it is important to bear in mind that OFSTED will be including assessing the uses of ICT in its school inspections more extensively in the future. Although the New Opportunities Fund training scheme for all teachers is more or less completed, training programmes continue to be offered by LEAs, colleges and universities as well as many companies that provide online training. There are also many subject and government Web sites that provide curriculum resources and ideas for using ICT in one's teaching. Considering the vast array of ICT resources that are now available to schools, it is essential to plan for lifelong professional development in the field of ICT in education.

Conclusions

ICT is becoming one of the most important aspects of education today. Some people have claimed that this is a bigger revolution than the industrial one. New government programmes require all teachers to use ICT widely in their teaching and it will no longer be an optional activity. The range of ICT skills required of teachers makes the numeracy and literacy skills pale into insignificance, yet the time needed to acquire all these new teaching skills is rarely available to the over-worked teacher. The important point to remember is that it is not necessary to change or discard all the pedagogical practices used with more traditional resources since most of these are relevant to teaching with ICT.

The first reason for being a teacher is to help pupils learn. The most compelling reason for using ICT is that there is convincing evidence that children can learn some things more effectively with the use of ICT and that its uses can motivate pupils who have been disillusioned with education. Denying pupils the opportunities to use ICT in their learning will impoverish their education and make their education less relevant to today's world of new technologies. Using ICT in lessons makes it fun to teach as well as to learn!

Further reading

A Glossary of Computing Terms, 9th edn, 1998, British Computer Society, Swindon

The ICT in Education Directory 2003/2004, British Computer Society, Swindon (contains an extensive list of useful education Web sites)

The ImpacT Report – An evaluation of the impact of Information technology on children's achievements in primary and secondary schools, 1993, King's College, London

Information Technology. Exemplification of Standards, School Curriculum and Assessment Authority, 1996, TSO, Norwich

Information Technology for Advanced Level, Julian Mott and Anne Leeming, 1998, Hodder and Stoughton, London

Useful Web sites

The Association of Science Education – http://www.ase.org.uk
BECTa – http://www.becta.org.uk
Department for Education and Skills – http://www.dfes.gov.uk
The National Association for ICT in Education – http://www.acitt.org.uk
National Curriculum On-line – http://www.nc.uk.net/home.html
The National Grid for Learning – http://www.ngfl.gov.uk
The Qualifications and Curriculum Authority – http://www.qca.org.uk
The Virtual Teachers Centre – http://vtc.ngfl.gov.uk
The Education Market Place – http://www.education-net.co.uk/
The Guardian – http://www.guardian.co.uk/
Journal of Computer Assisted Learning – http://www.blackwellpublishing.com/journals/jca/

References

Abbott, C (2002) (ed) *Special Educational Needs and the Internet: Issues in inclusive education,* London, Routledge Falmer

ACITT (1999) *Informatics at Key Stage 3,* National Association of Co-ordinators and Teachers of IT, Barking and Dagenham LEA, The Westbury Centre, Barking

Advisory Unit (1998) *Distant Places. Geography Pack,* The Advisory Unit, Hatfield

Barton, R and Rogers, L (1991) The computer as an aid to practical science – studying motion with a computer, *Journal of Computer Assisted Learning,* **7** (2), pp 104–13

Barton, R and Rogers, L (1994) The computer as an aid to practical science: studying motion with a computer, *Journal of Computer Assisted Learning,* **7**, pp 104–13

Booth, B et al (1994) *Expert Builder (qualitative modelling software environment),* The Modus Project, Harpenden

Booth, B and Cox, M J (1997) *Model Builder,* The Modus Project, Harpenden

British Computer Society (2003) *The ICT in Education Directory 2003/2004,* BCS, Swindon

Brna, P (1990) A methodology for confronting science misconceptions, *Journal of Educational Computing Research,* **6** (2), pp 157–82

Cox, M J et al (1993) *Energy Expert,* The Modus Project, Harpenden

Cox, M J (1997) *The Effects of Information Technology on Students' Motivation: Final report,* NCET/King's College, London

Cox, M J and Nikolopoulou, K (1997) What information handling skills are promoted by the use of data handling software?, *Education and Information Technologies,* **2**, 105–20

Deken, J (1990) Robotics, computers the next step, Inside Science No.30, *New Scientist*, 29 September

Department for Education (1995) *Information Technology in the National Curriculum*, TSO, London

Department for Education and Employment (DfEE) (1998a) *Requirements for Courses of Initial Teacher Training*, Circular 4/98, DfEE, London

DfEE (1998b) Survey of information and communications technology in schools, *1998 Statistical Bulletin*, 11/98

DfEE (1998c) *Teachers Meeting the Challenge of Change*, TSO, London

DfEE (1999) *The National Curriculum*, DfEE, London

DfES (2002a) *Survey of Information and Communications Technology in Schools 2002*, DfES, London

DfES (2002b) *Key Stage 3 National Strategy. Launch of the ICT Strand.* Resource pack for teachers, DfES, London; see also http://www.standards.dfee.gov.uk

Frost, R (1994) Computer software for science teaching, *School Science Review*, **76** (287), pp 19–24

Frost, R (1994) *The IT in Secondary Science Book: A compendium of ideas for using information technology in science*, The Association for Science Education, Hatfield

Goldstein, G (1997) *Information Technology in English Schools: A commentary on inspection findings 1995–1996*, Falmer Press, London

Harrison, C, Comber, C et al (2002) *ImpaCT2: The impact of information and communication technologies on pupil learning and attainment*, 48, British Educational Communications and Technology Agency, Coventry

Heathcote, P M (1998) *A-level Computing*, 3rd edn, Letts Educational, London

Hooper, R (1977) *National Development Programme in Computer Assisted Learning*, Final report of the director, Council for Educational Technology, London

Hunter, B (1987) Knowledge-creative learning with databases, *Social Education*, **51** (1), pp 38–43

Kemmis, S, Atkin, R and Wright, E (1977) How do pupils learn?, *Working Papers on CAL, Occasional Paper 5*, University of East Anglia: Centre for Applied Research in Education, Norwich

Mellar, H et al (1994) *Learning with Artificial Worlds: Computer-based modelling in the curriculum*, Falmer Press, London

Morrison, H, Gardner, J, Reilly, C and McNally, H (1993) The impact of portable computers on pupils' attitude to study, *Journal for Computer Assisted Learning*, **9** (3) pp130–41

Mott, J and Leeming, A (1998) *Information Technology for Advanced Level*, Hodder and Stoughton, London

Office for Standards in Education (2002) *ICT in Schools. Effect of government initiatives. Progress report*, April, HMI 423, London

Papert, S (1980) *Mindstorms: Children, computers and powerful ideas*, Harvester Press, Brighton

Parker, J (1986) Tools for thought, *The Computing Teacher*, **14** (2), pp 21–23

Piaget, J and Inhelder, B (1969) *The Psychology of the Child*, Routledge & Kegan Paul, London

Qualifications and Curriculum Authority (1997) *Teaching Information Technology in Primary Schools*, QCA, London

TTA (1998) The use of ICT in subject teaching (Annex B of DfEE Circular 4/98), DfEE, London

TTA (1999) *The Use of Information and Communications Technology in Subject Teaching: Identification of training needs. Secondary Information Technology*, Teacher Training Agency, London

Underwood, J (1988) An investigation of teacher intents and classroom outcomes in the use of information-handling packages, *Computers in Education*, **12**, pp 91–100

Underwood, J (1988) An investigation of teacher intents and classroom outcomes in the use of information-handling packages, *Computers and Education*, 12 (1) pp91–100

Watson, D M (ed) (1993) *The ImpacT Report – An evaluation of the impact of information technology on children's achievements in primary and secondary schools*, King's College, London

Notes

1. E-learning Credits (eLCs) are a new form of funding made available to maintained primary and secondary schools, non-maintained special schools and pupil referral units in England. They are being distributed via the Standards Fund Grant 618, £50 million for the academic year 2002–2003. eLCs' credit are for buying Curriculum Online certified digital learning resources published on the Curriculum Online site. Local education authorities were asked in November 2002 to release the first tranche of £30 million to schools. Only Curriculum Online registered Retailers can accept eLCs.

2. Although Expert Builder was first published in 1994, it is continuously updated with more models and features, many of which have been contributed by teachers who have used it with their pupils.

Planning, Expectations and Targets for Effective Learning and Teaching

5

Mike Waring

Irrespective of the subject, phase or ability of the pupils being taught, regardless of the nature of government reforms in initial teacher training (ITT) and despite the erosion of time for all teachers, planning and the associated preparation remain fundamental in facilitating an effective and progressive learning experience for all pupils (and for that matter, trainees).

> Good lesson planning translates school policies and subject guidance into informed classroom practice; it identifies learning objectives, making provision for the different learning needs of pupils, and specifies the activities to be pursued in the lesson, the use of time, the resources, any assessment opportunity and any link to cross-curricular themes and spiritual, moral social and cultural development. (OFSTED, 1998, p78)

It should be no surprise, therefore, that some of the criteria used by the Office for Standards in Education (OFSTED) inspectors for judging teaching quality and effectiveness (OFSTED, 1999a; 1999b; 2000), and a significant portion (section 3.1)[1] of those standards for the award of qualified teacher status (QTS) as outlined in *Qualifying to Teach* (DfES/TTA, 2002) and which form the statutory assessment of trainee teachers in ITT, refer specifically to planning.

Objectives

By the end of this chapter you should be able to:

- explain the need for planning and preparation;
- recognize the mechanics of planning and preparation;
- identify standards and the planning process;
- review the relevance of pedagogic and subject knowledge to the planning process;
- recognize the need to specify clear and directly measurable educational objectives (intended learning outcomes);
- recognize the need to select and organize appropriate learning materials and activities;
- review the importance and nature of evaluation procedures to promote pupil (and trainee) learning;
- discuss successful preparation;
- describe joined up planning (and thinking) as part of the planning cycle.

So why plan?

Each trainee has to satisfy all of the standards for QTS as outlined in the statutory requirements as part of *Qualifying to Teach* (DfES/TTA, 2002). Some of these standards relate to teaching: planning, expectations and targets (Section 3.1). There are a number of other reasons, however, that a trainee needs to plan even though, as McIntyre (1997) notes, these may not initially appear to be those driving the trainee. Planning is an expression of intent by the teacher. Trainees need to give themselves an opportunity to check all aspects of their thinking about a lesson: what is to be learnt, how the environment is to be managed, the content delivered and the learning activities progressed. This is articulated in the first instance via a number of plans. These will ensure that the trainee remains focused not only on the immediate learning outcomes, but also the way in which these progressively contribute and relate to the medium and long-term learning objectives and outcomes. The whole process of writing things down allows trainees to be very clear about what they want the pupils to learn in lessons. It also allows them to explore and experiment with the organization and management of the environment and class so that most mistakes are made outside of the lesson and that best facilitates the desired learning outcomes. Not only does this aid organization, but it also allows the trainee to get a feel for the amount of time to devote to particular portions of the lesson. It also highlights and makes sure that the trainee is clear about how the learning activities relate to the lesson's overall learning outcome. In other words – it allows trainees to check what they are asking the pupils to do, and whether when and how it will be assessed are appropriate to achieve and measure the lesson's stated learning outcome.

It is essential that trainees allow themselves (and their mentor) as much of a chance as possible to try and anticipate pupil reactions and outcomes, consequently giving themselves a chance to plan for contingencies to achieve the same learning outcome(s). Planning enables the trainee teacher to do this and take into account pupil differences and the necessary teaching and learning activities that might be appropriate to combat any problems linked to variation in ability. Griffey and Housner (1999) acknowledge a difference between trainees and experienced teachers in terms of the overt detail of their planning. This difference is important in that trainees must never think that because their mentor does not produce the same detailed planning documents, yet achieves high quality progressive learning outcomes, they have not gone through the same planning process. They have: it is merely a more internalized process due to their previous experiences (both positive and negative).

> While student teachers on teaching practice are usually required to make explicit lesson plans, experienced teachers more often rely on their extensive experience to form a mental framework of how they want the lesson to proceed. This does not necessarily mean that the lesson plans of established teachers are any less detailed than those of beginning teachers, simply that the lesson plans have become internalized through repetition. (Kyriacou, 1991, p17)

Significantly, there always remains a degree of flexibility with any detail of planning. No plan is 'set in stone'. It is a guiding framework that can and should be interpreted by trainees in the context of their lesson and the pupils' reactions. Having worked through a plan, the majority of issues/problems can be resolved. However, for a variety of reasons unexpected circumstances can make redundant or less effective certain portions of a lesson plan. This is not a fault or criticism of trainees or their planning, it is a natural consequence of teaching. Things will happen unexpectedly, but thorough planning will provide trainees with an invaluable tangible framework that can be used to support them as they manoeuvre around the problem/issues at the same time as maintaining a focus on the learning outcome for that lesson.

The link between planning, monitoring and assessment is an extremely important one. Even though the standards for QTS separate these under Section 3 'Teaching', they are very much interrelated and should be considered and developed together. Whatever learning a trainee teacher plans for, it should be directly measurable and the learning activity used to achieve it should be appropriate. If it is not measurable, how can the trainee know if the pupils achieved it? A trainee should be able to justify any learning activity given to the pupils in terms of its progressive contribution to the lesson's learning outcome(s). Detailed planning facilitates these.

Planning also allows trainees the opportunity to focus on and develop finer points of their delivery in that it allows them to concentrate on a more manageable amount of variables during the lesson. For example, being secure in the knowledge that the necessary resources have been selected, prepared and organized prior to the lesson, along with being confident that there is appropriate progression in the content, means that the trainee can extend and explore teaching styles and strategies, or concentrate more on the nature of the assessment of learning activities.

Evaluating the learning of the pupils and the trainee in each lesson is an essential element in what should be a holistic process of teaching, if the learning of both is to be progressive. As part of the constant self-reflection trainee teachers are involved in (and teachers generally), they should address issues that impact not only on their own learning, but how that and their practice impact on pupils' learning. To do this trainees should be asking questions that look at their teaching skills and the planning of pupil learning experiences. On the basis of the evaluation, the nature, structure and content of future lessons can be amended and enhanced appropriately. Planning exists as a prerequisite around which this developmental teaching and learning process consistently evolves.

The critical association between planning and preparation needs to be dealt with here. Simply put, planning leads on to preparation of the materials, resources and props that will be needed in the lesson. If these materials are prepared prior to the lesson, the teacher is in a much better position to differentiate the activities successfully, as well as to cope with maintaining the smooth and effective progress in learning throughout the lesson for all pupils.

The reduction in stress and anxiety for the teacher that comes from identifying and minimizing potential problems before entering the teaching context is one outcome of effective planning that should not be underestimated. Such room for manoeuvre and associated increase in teacher confidence allows the teacher to organize alternative resources, tasks and styles if others in the lesson do not appear to facilitate the learning outcomes the teacher may have intended in the first instance. This is supported by Clark and Yinger (1987, p88) when they give three main purposes of planning:

- planning to meet immediate personal needs (eg reduce uncertainty and anxiety, to find a sense of direction, confidence and security);
- planning as a means to an end of instruction (eg to learn the material, to collect and organize materials, to organize time and activity flow);

- direct uses of plans during instruction (eg to organize students, to get an activity started, to aid memory, to provide a framework for instruction and evaluation).

Planning and preparation can be seen as essential components of effective teaching for a myriad of interrelated reasons. Not least of these is that they minimize ambiguity for the teacher and pupils, thus forming the foundation on which realistic and effective assessment, recording and reporting can be based.

Numerous authors have attempted to articulate the progression of elements to be addressed in effective planning. Table 5.1 provides a simple summary of a selection of these. Highlighted to the left is Tyler's (1950) linear, rational objectives-based planning model. Such a model has been advocated as an appropriate approach for teachers to use when planning their teaching (Mawer, 1995). Others, such as Taylor (1970), have

Table 5.1 The suggested elements of effective planning and their progression

	Tyler (1950)	Kyriacou (1986)	Kyriacou (1991)	Leask and Davison (1995)	Kelly and Mayes (1995)	Williams (1996)	Taylor (1970)
1	Specify objectives	General aims and specific educational outcomes	Decision about objectives	How do pupils learn?	Who am I teaching?	What are pupils going to learn?	Content being taught and teaching context
2	Selection of learning material	Take account of the context	Selection and scripting of lesson	Requirements of the curriculum	What am I teaching?	What tasks are going to be set during lesson and in what order?	Pupil interests
3	Organization of learning activities		Preparation of all props to be used	Most appropriate methods of teaching the topic and resources available	How can I teach it?	How will teacher help pupil answer the task? What organization issues are there?	Aims and objectives of course: course philosophy
4	Specification of evaluation procedures	Monitor and evaluate	How to monitor and assess	Evaluations of previous lessons		How will teacher assess pupil learning?	Criteria for evaluation

proposed an alternative model, which acknowledges the content being taught and the teaching context, rather than objectives, as the primary consideration. This variation in planning is considered to be a consequence of the relative experience of the teacher. Table 5.1 identifies other models that are variations on this theme.

Do as I say not as I do...

Critically, bound up in the relationship between trainee teachers and their mentors is the potential tension of any novice-expert exchange. This has already been highlighted in relation to the development of planning for the trainee teacher; however, it is essential to remember that the notion of an objectives model of planning (eg Tyler, 1950) is only one of a number of variations, as illustrated in Table 5.1. As with the increasing range of teaching styles that teachers are able to adopt and practise with, and more 'effectively' adopt through their increasing exposure and experiences, similarly they are able to *internalize* elements of the planning process.

On a superficial basis it might appear to the external observer that such internalization constitutes neglect by the experienced mentor/teacher[2] of certain aspects in the planning process, such as the pre-specification of learning objectives and evaluation procedures. This would be an unfortunate misreading of the situation. The fact is that they have rehearsed their planning so many times that they can afford to redirect the bulk of their overt attention to other aspects in the teaching and learning process. This is certainly not to state that they are no longer important – they are. They remain fundamental even to the experienced teachers although not as overtly evident. As Borko and Niles (1987) argue, supported by the research literature on teacher planning (Mawer, 1995), pre-service and inexperienced teachers should still approach planning through the pre-specification of objectives and evaluation procedures, because they do not have the breadth and depth of experience of experienced teachers.

Consequently, in order to appreciate and begin to 'internalize' the planning process it is important, especially for trainee and novice teachers, that they adopt an objectives model of planning. Inevitably this will mean that mentors should expect trainees to adopt different models of planning to themselves. Both parties need to be aware of the reasons for this. Within the context of this chapter the objectives model of planning will be explored to highlight the most significant aspects of effective planning.

Bearing this in mind and considering the predominantly school-based model of ITT in the UK, it is essential that trainees, mentors and tutors are able to share in a common translation of an objectives model of planning as it relates to *Qualifying to Teach* (DfES/TTA, 2002) section 3.1, planning, expectations and targets, as this is part of the basis on which all trainees' work is assessed regarding their QTS.

Standards and the planning process

Table 5.2 identifies on its left-hand side an example of an objectives model of planning with each stage numbered, as in Table 5.1. Listed and labelled to the right side are each of the statements on 'planning, expectations and targets' from *Qualifying to Teach*. The numbers written centrally suggest those elements of the objectives model that might correspond to that particular statement from *Qualifying to Teach*.

Table 5.2 The potential relationship between elements of an objectives model of planning and the planning portion of the standards for the award of QTS in *Qualifying to Teach*

An objectives model of planning		*Planning, expectations and targets (Qualifying to Teach, DfES/TTA 2002)*	
1 Specify objectives	1, 2, 4	They set challenging teaching and learning objectives which are relevant to all pupils in their classes. They base these on their knowledge of the pupils; evidence of past and current achievement; the expected standards for pupils of the relevant age range; the range and content of work relevant to pupils in that age range	3.1.1
2 Selection of learning material	1, 3, 4	They use these teaching and learning objectives to plan lessons and sequences of lessons, showing how they will assess pupils' learning. They take account of and support pupils' varying needs so that girls and boys, from all ethnic groups, can make good progress	3.1.2
3 Organization of learning activities	1, 2, 3, 5	They select and prepare resources and plan for their safe and effective organization, taking account of pupils' interests and their language and cultural backgrounds, with the help of support staff where appropriate	3.1.3
4 Specification of evaluation procedures	3, 5	They take part in, and contribute to, teaching teams, as appropriate to the school. Where applicable, they plan for the deployment of additional adults who support pupils' learning	3.1.4
5 Preparation of materials, resources and props	1, 2, 3, 4, 5	As relevant to the age range they are trained to teach, they are able to plan opportunities for pupils to learn in out-of-school contexts, such as school visits, museums, theatres, field-work and employment-based settings, with the help of other staff where appropriate	3.1.5

Pedagogical content knowledge

Before exploring an objectives model of planning in more detail, it is necessary to consider the foundation on which it is to be built. If trainee or novice teachers are to plan effectively over any kind of time frame, where do they start? Yes, they need to look at the objectives; however, it is important to understand and appreciate the context in which these will apply. Shulman (1986) coined the term 'pedagogical content knowledge' as a way of conceptualizing the essential knowledge required to be able to teach subject content knowledge. Cochran *et al* (1993, p263) have extended this by stating that:

> Pedagogical content knowledge (PCK) differentiates expert teachers in a subject area from subject area experts. PCK concerns the manner in which teachers relate their subject matter knowledge (what they know about what they teach) to their pedagogical knowledge (what they know about teaching) and how subject matter knowledge is a part of the process of pedagogical reasoning.

Consequently, a great deal of background knowledge needs to be generated by the teacher regarding the learners, the curriculum and the context of teaching the activity, prior to specification of learning objectives. This requires familiarization with the National Curriculum for the particular subject area (as well as others regarding cross-curricular dimensions); the activity areas to be taught; the particular school and departmental context; the pupils; and resources. Once this foundation on which to construct the more overt planning process has been achieved, the teacher can then consider the nature of the learning experience he or she wants the pupils to have.

Kyriacou (1986, p115) states that when planning one must ensure that the learning experience fulfils three psychological conditions necessary for pupils' learning to occur:

1. *attentiveness*: the learning experience must elicit and sustain pupils' attention;
2. *receptiveness*: the learning experience must elicit and sustain pupils' motivation and mental effort;
3. *appropriateness*: the learning experience must be appropriate for the educational outcomes desired.

Cohen's (1987) concept of 'instructional alignment' is one that supports Kyriacou's in relation to the need for certain elements to be complementary. Instructional alignment basically means that there is a close affiliation between those intended learning outcomes for the pupils and the tasks that facilitate them, and that the assessment of the learning or achievement supports both of them. The conclusion to all this is that if this cohesion is to be achieved, trainees must have a sound knowledge of the activity they are about to teach. However, limited depth and breadth of knowledge across the subject area is a concern consistently reported by those involved in the ITT process (Hardy, 1996; McIntyre, 1997). This is a significant factor in the planning process, a) for the trainee due to the amount of time and energy it can involve; and b) allowing the mentor and tutor to facilitate this process. The consolidation and enhancement of the trainees' subject knowledge base, in conjunction with all the other knowledge they have to gather in order to prepare to plan (eg concerning the context of the department and school, knowledge of the pupils and resources), is extremely time and energy consuming. For many trainees this can also be a demoralizing portion of the planning process, as they realize they only have the material with which to build, and not the building. However, if a trainee does realize this, it is certainly a significant movement along the road to internalization of the planning process. The challenging and exciting part of the planning process ie, the manipulation of the subject and pedagogical content knowledge to achieve instructional alignment, still has to be addressed.

Having outlined some of the necessary background information and knowledge required to develop the objectives model of planning, each of the elements involved in planning the model will now be discussed.

Specifying educational objectives

The identification of clear educational objectives has consistently been seen as an essential feature in planning (DES, 1985, 1988; OFSTED, 1993, 1998). It allows teachers to facilitate a structure and purpose to their planning. However, in order to do so it is essential that each objective describes an aspect of pupil learning. Hence, the term 'objective' is often used interchangeably with the term 'learning outcome'. The potential for confusion, especially for the trainee, is generated by a belief that planning is merely the organization of activities, something that is reinforced by imprecise thinking about the educational objectives (and lack of structure in the whole planning process).

The wording of the learning outcome or objective is vital in that they have to be directly measurable. The verb used could be one like state, describe, identify or demonstrate. Verbs such as understand, appreciate and know should be avoided because the pupils' understanding (other than inference by their behaviour) cannot be directly measured. Therefore, the selection of the outcome verb is crucial. The way in which the trainee assesses whether or not the outcome is achieved will be determined by the verb. For example, if it says describe – the pupils will need to be given the opportunity to do this (eg describe it to a partner); or to plan – the pupils need to be given the opportunity to plan (eg plan a sequence/activity, devise a checklist to ensure everything that should be, is in the sequence). Table 5.3 identifies a number of suitable outcome verbs for use in planning.

As demonstrated at the end of this chapter, the structure of the National Curriculum (NC) highlights the varying degree in specificity of educational objectives within planning. This emphasizes the essential concept of continuity in pupil learning over time through different phases of planning: long, medium and short term. In other words, this refers to a scheme of work, a unit of work and a lesson plan respectively. A scheme of work is drawn from the NC subject programmes of study and contains what is planned for the pupils over a Key Stage or a year, regarding the knowledge, skills and understanding required for each activity area. A unit of work represents a teacher's medium-term planning covering a shorter block of time (eg a few weeks or a term). A unit of work is derived from a scheme of work. The number of units may vary between areas and the number of lessons in each unit may vary from school to school. A unit should introduce pupils to a new aspect of learning, build on previous learning, identify the most appropriate teaching styles to be used, and identify available resources/facilities and how they might be used. Sometimes the terms 'schemes of work' and 'units of work' are used interchangeably – this is not really a problem as long as the concept of continuity and progression in pupil learning is acknowledged and maintained through increasingly more specific planning.

Importantly, the trainee must appreciate that what 'is' to be learnt has to be linked with what 'has' been learnt, if planning is to be effective. This means that the process of planning is not really linear in its organization, even though initially the trainee may deem it to be so. It should be considered more of a spiral so that

Table 5.3 Measurable outcome verbs to use in the writing of learning outcomes for lessons (adapted from National Coaching Foundation, 1995)

| | Outcome Verbs | |
Rote Learn	Reorganize	Apply and Analyse
Define	Translate	Interpret
Repeat	Restate	Apply
Recognize	Discuss	Employ
Recall	Describe	Use
List	Categorize	Solve
Name	Review	Calculate
Identify	Summarize	Analyse
State	Explain	Compare

elements can be practised and consolidated to support effective learning for pupils. The formulation of learning objectives for a future lesson will be dependent on the trainee's interpretation of the pupils' background and the evaluation of the achievement of learning outcomes in the previous lesson.

Selection of learning material

Kyriacou (1986) makes an important distinction between 'content' and 'lesson organization' when referring to the selection of learning activities. The selection of learning material can come under the banner of content. Even with the NC framework and the need to work to the programmes of study for the area, there is still a great deal of autonomy for teachers when selecting learning material. Fundamentally, teachers must know what the pupils already know, so that they can extend their knowledge and understanding from 'where they are'. As with the establishment of the learning objectives, when selecting appropriate learning materials the teacher must ascertain the pupils' present knowledge, understanding and skills related to the area of study, but must also ensure that these, or a development in them, can satisfy the learning outcomes established for the lesson.

It is the whole planning process that allows the teacher to consider the best breakdown of conceptually appropriate steps in order to achieve the desired educational objectives for the particular pupils in the given context. However, this is also one of the most challenging and daunting aspects of planning for trainees. Not only does it require them to select content, but to separate the topic into sections that are progressive, meeting the needs of all the learners in achieving the learning outcomes. This is a complicated and interrelated process for any teacher, but especially the trainee. Therefore, what is the repertoire of demands placed on the trainee to achieve this? Once again good content knowledge is important, along with an awareness of how to sequence elements of the topic relative to the needs of the pupils.

Organization of learning activities

Lessons can be structured in a wide variety of ways depending on the nature of the subject, as well as the particular learning focus within it. If one considers what is probably the most basic organization for a lesson, it would be one that has three reinforcing components. The first is the introduction to the lesson, in which the topic would be outlined. The second component comprises the main learning activities. Finally, there is a review of the learning that has occurred in the lesson.

It is essential when deciding on the structure of the lesson that it is considered in a holistic manner. In other words, what is the total learning experience that the pupils will receive and will it achieve the intended learning outcomes of the lesson? Whatever the organization of the lesson and the learning activities, they must sustain the interest, attention and motivation of the pupils. In order to do this there has to be variety in the activities. This equates to the use of a variety of teaching styles that help to facilitate different ways of learning in conjunction with opportunity for pupils to practise, give and receive feedback, read and listen to theory about how to do it. The selection of elements and the amount of time that teachers spend on the activity and the way in which they organize it in the given context will be significant in influencing the tone and atmosphere of the learning environment.

Everyone can have difficulty in planning for differentiation, not only the trainee. However, if all pupils are to learn effectively, then differentiation is important. Table 5.4 identifies a variety of ways in which one could differentiate an activity that can and should be incorporated in planning to assist pupils to achieve personal learning targets, including those pupils with special needs. One must remember that special needs equates not only to the less able but also to the very able.

Specification of evaluation procedures

In order to determine whether the lesson is effective in terms of being able to achieve the learning outcomes, a teacher needs to monitor and assess pupils' progress and attainment. Concurrently, the teacher will be receiving feedback on what aspects of the original plan are satisfactory or may require modification in order to achieve learning outcomes. As Kyriacou (1991) identifies, 'this requires more than just being responsive and reactive to feedback'; it requires the teacher 'to be active, and to probe, question, check whether the progress and attainment intended is occurring'. Therefore, there is a great deal of forethought required by the trainee. For example, the bridging organization or transitions within lessons are ideal times to involve the whole class, small groups or individuals in questions and evaluation of learning outcomes so far. This is an ongoing approach in lessons. There are also the more formal homework and tests that can assess certain learning outcomes.

Table 5.1 Various forms of differentiation (Adapted from Williams, 1996 and Mawer, 1995)

Differentiation through:	
Outcome	In which the teacher may set tasks that are appropriate for the pupil's starting level, or pupils might answer the task as set according to their level of ability.
Content	Appropriate tasks – differentiation may be achieved offering a range of more difficult tasks in which pupils may choose to enter the learning situation, or in which different individuals or groups may have different roles or responsibilities. Pupils should have the opportunity to experience all of these roles
Pace	The pace at which pupils perform may well be a function of physical fitness and capacity as well as cognition or concentration (eg PE)
Level	This may be related to differentiation through pace. Where taskcards are progressive, perhaps through setting increasingly demanding and complex tasks, pupils may be working at different levels as well as at a pace appropriate to their abilities
Teaching Style	Use of a range of teaching styles and approaches can elicit different responses from pupils. Some of these responses will match individual's preferred learning styles better than others
Grouping	Appropriate pupil groupings (eg by friendship, ability, group or individual activities). The majority of groupings are selected by the teacher to maintain safety and differentiate; however, some contexts allow pupils to choose whether they work alone, in pairs or in larger groups and may also accommodate individual differences and preferences
Resources	Do all pupils have to have the same resources or potential for some variation dependent upon ability? Appropriate equipment for different levels of ability (eg different size/weight of ball, varying target size/height, varying distances from the target, increased size of work cards)

Integral to this process is the self-reflection of trainees regarding their planning and teaching performance. As a consequence of the pupil responses the teacher needs to alter and modify schemes, units and lessons:

> Without a well thought out and structured self-reflection strategy, it is easy to drift aimlessly into a limited form of reflection based purely on aspects of teaching that cross your mind at a particular moment in time. A well-structured self-reflection strategy worked out in advance ensures that all aspects of your teaching performance are reflected upon during the unit of work. (Mawer, 1995, p89)

There are a myriad of questions that could be asked about numerous elements of the lesson when a trainee comes to evaluate it. Therefore, it is important to maintain some kind of progressive focus. But on what? If one considers three categories regarding the pupils, the material and the teacher, certain questions can be asked of the trainee such as:

Pupils: How many pupils had difficulty learning the tasks set? Which pupils and why?
            How many pupils found the tasks set too easy? Which pupils and why?
            Did the class always understand the explanations? If not why not and how could this be improved?

Materials: To what extent were lesson objectives achieved? How do you know?
            To what extent were the activities appropriate for the age and ability of pupils?
            How successful were attempts to differentiate activities during the lesson?

Teacher: How will you modify the learning activities and objectives in the light of answers to the above questions?
            What aspects of the lesson caused most time to be wasted? Why?
            How effective were the teaching approaches used? Were they appropriate for the objective for the lesson, the pupils and the activities being taught? If not, how will you modify your teaching approaches in the light of answers to other questions? (adapted from Mawer, 1995)

So many questions could be asked after each lesson. However, the important aspects are, a) there is a clear focus to the evaluation and self-reflection by trainees and their mentor, and that it is relevant to the trainees' understanding and stage of development; and b) they demonstrate how the assessment of the learning outcomes in each lesson informs the planning of their next lesson. The focus of the lesson evaluation should be a follow-up from the previous lesson to see how the action points for learning (for pupils and the trainee) that were established have been addressed and developed. Of course new elements will be identified in terms of action points, but it is the notion of development and progression in the learning of the pupils and the trainee that needs to be highlighted, understood and facilitated at this point, collaboratively by the mentor and trainee.

Preparation of materials, resources and props

The preparation and organization of the teaching environment and the equipment that is required for the lesson are essential if it is to be successful and fulfil the learning outcomes planned for. Preparation also includes the need to prepare assessment materials. Such materials need to be built into the planning of lessons both generally and specifically, and a formal note made of pupils' learning. When doing this, the teacher needs to be clear about the realistic number of assessments to be made in a lesson, as well as the procedures that will be adopted. As a result of this, advanced planning about how records are to be made and kept will also be required. This task is further enhanced when one considers that a variety of assessment materials need to be used and types of responses given (eg based on direct observations of pupils' behaviour, questioning in verbal and written form, paper and pencil tests, and normal coursework, including homework) (Kyriacou, 1991).

It is essential that materials are of good quality and care has been taken to present them in the best manner possible. The time and effort taken to prepare them is likely to be reflected in a positive attitude towards them from the pupils. Why should pupils read a scrap of scruffy paper when it is clear it has just been thrown together at the last minute, they can't read it all, and it contains errors? Relevant CD-ROM footage and differentiated, colourful, laminated and word-processed task cards with bold inspiring images on, are much more stimulating items that are motivating and create a much more positive and successful working environment.

When using equipment or materials of any kind for a practical session or experiment, it is important that teachers undertake some form of rehearsal to familiarize themselves with the equipment and identify potential problems that may occur. It is important to note that the rehearsal should include an evaluation from the perspective of the pupil. One needs to ask, is it user-friendly for the pupils? Regardless of the length of time spent preparing, and the belief that nothing could go wrong, the trainee should always have an alternative available that will be able to satisfy the learning objectives of the activity as they contribute to the learning outcomes for the lesson.

Any materials that may be produced or purchased as part of the preparation for a lesson must always be appropriate to the intended learning outcomes for the lesson. Resources should not be selected merely because they are readily available.

Prepare to be successful

Every trainee (as with every pupil) comes with a different set of experiences that impact on their learning and practice. It is essential that everyone is included and extended relative to their ability in any learning activity that they embark on – the planning for which is one of the challenges and rewards of teaching. The remainder of this chapter presents a suggested outline 'planning process and framework' that allows each trainee to plan effectively as they strive to demonstrate some of the characteristics of a very good trainee: their planning is consistently of a very high standard; and objectives, activities, resources and outcomes are very well matched to the needs of the varying groups of pupils taught (OFSTED, 2002).

Why reinvent the wheel?

A lot of time and expertise has been used to develop all aspects of the NC. This includes extensive material on the Web, which is an important resource that can enhance the planning of all trainees. Not all of these resources connected with the NC site are 'good'. However, what the NC Web content (NC homepage: www.nc.uk.net/home.html; subject schemes of work, primary and secondary: www.standards.dfes.gov.uk/schemes) does offer trainees is an ideal opportunity of 'understanding' and internalizing a 'joined-up' planning process over the long to short term, rather than struggling to amass as much (and sometimes irrelevant) content as they can for the lessons they teach.

Initially the interrelated aspects that have to be considered as part of the process of planning can be overwhelming for the trainee. Therefore, the planning framework has to be systematic in nature. Trainees should be provided with an approach that ensures that they have documented and considered the essential relationship between the knowledge, skills and understanding, and breadth of study in the programmes of study, as well as the programmes' relationship with the attainment target. A trainee also has to consider, facilitate and evaluate a raft of other variables such as special needs, language for learning, and the many other cross-curricular dimensions and factors that impact on their planning. The NC handbooks for each subject assist in this by providing a 'referencing system' that links other subjects and elements of each subject curriculum. However, the use of a 'base' framework of pro formas (see the appendix to this chapter) for planning is still very important for trainees. They need to experience and work with a 'joined up' planning process not just to understand what planning is about, but so that they can manipulate it relative to their particular school context. To deviate from this 'base' in the first instance is not advisable. However, a trainee's justification to vary his or her planning and the pro forma is a very useful indication of his or her understanding for the mentor and/or tutor.

Joined-up planning (and thinking)

Figure 5.1 outlines the planning process using the pro formas 1–4, which ensures that 'joined up' planning takes place and that the best use is made of the extensive subject-specific information provided in the exemplar schemes of work available on the Web (www.standards.dfes.gov.uk/schemes). It also provides trainees, and anyone involved in their development, with evidence of how they use their assessment of learning to inform their planning, and vice versa. The digital format makes the exchange and debate of planning practice a very supportive, rewarding, immediate and developmental activity for trainees and mentors.

Figure 5.1 identifies some of the key things that trainees should be thinking about during the planning cycle. It also identifies what they should be 'cutting and pasting' from the exemplar schemes of work to help them maintain consistency in their planning over different terms. All of the information demanded by the pro formas is on the schemes of work Web site and to a great extent is self-explanatory. However, there is a certain aspect of pro forma 2 that requires some clarification. There is a column called 'assessment of learning objectives (LOs)' on this pro forma. Each learning objective that is identified by the trainee from the relevant unit in the exemplar scheme of work, knowledge skills and understanding and presented in the first column should be given a number. There should be at least one corresponding learning activity that assesses each learning objective. Of course there

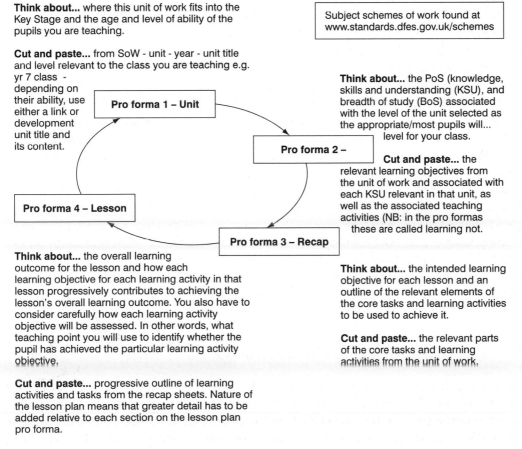

Figure 5.1 The baseline 'joined up planning' (and thinking) process

may be a number of objectives that can be assessed by one learning activity. Hence, in the 'assessment of LOs' column relative to each learning activity, the trainee should identify the learning objective that it assesses. This ensures that the learning objective is being assessed, as well as the trainee having to consider whether the learning activity will actually assess the learning objective it is supposed to.

It is worth noting again that the evaluation of the lesson by the trainee is an essential part of the planning process. OFSTED (2002, p43) identifies the following as some of the characteristics of a very good trainee: 'Evaluation of their teaching is rigorous, accurate and focuses specifically on what pupils have achieved in lessons. It is used effectively to improve their teaching.' Trainees must demonstrate that their assessment of the pupils' learning in a lesson has been used to inform the planning of the next. The lesson plan (pro forma 4) demands that trainees consider and record the action points from the previous lesson regarding the pupils' learning, as well as their own learning. As part of more general self-reflection, trainee teachers should address issues that impact not only on their own learning but how that and their practice impact on the pupils' learning. To do this trainees must ask questions that look at their teaching skills and the planning of pupils' learning experiences. As Mawer (1995) acknowledges, the important thing when doing this is to have a positive attitude towards putting their practice and expertise under scrutiny. Only then will their planning of pupil learning experiences be effective, and the trainees become truly reflective practitioners.

The planning process outlined here ensures that the trainee is immersed in the language of the NC and readily shares in the expertise that constructed the levelled, joined-up and progressive content on the NC Web site. With this process there is an automatic appropriate level-ness and consistency to their planning, and it clearly identifies the assessment of each learning objective so that the learning activities are appropriate and the means of assessment are relevant, clear and specific.

> Planning is therefore an essential feature of pedagogical thinking and reasoning. Planning appears to mediate between a teacher's basic knowledge of the subject being taught and his or her ability to teach the subject effectively, because it brings into play the teacher's general pedagogical content knowledge. This includes knowledge of theories and principles of teaching and learning, knowledge of the learner, and knowledge of the techniques and principles of teaching such as class management. The plan for a lesson, unit or course is the result of a considerable degree of thinking on the part of the teacher. (Mawer, 1995, p55)

This is a continual and evolutionary process towards internalization for every teacher, and the nature of the framework that guides it remains fundamentally the same. However, it is the emphasis placed on certain elements at certain times that focuses the attention of trainee teachers in their quest to facilitate the most effective pupil learning.

Appendix

Pro forma 1
UNIT OF WORK

About this Unit	Expectations After carrying out the activities and core tasks in this unit….	Prior Learning
Activity Area:		
Key Stage:	Most pupils will:	
Unit of Work No.:		
Number of lessons:		
Start Date:		
Finish Date:		
Where the Unit fits in:	Some pupils will not have made so much progress and will:	Language for Learning
	Some pupils will have progressed further and will:	

Pro forma 2

Name of Unit:				
Year				
Learning Objectives (LOs) (a description of what pupils should know, do and understand as a result of taking part in the lesson)	Learning Activities (an indication of what the pupils will do in lessons to realize the learning objectives) *Opportunities for pupils to:*	Assessment of LOs	Points to note: Inclusion Principles (A, B, C); teaching approaches; ICT Opportunity; . Spiritual, social and moral; Links with other subjects; Health and safety	Resources (the equipment required and for which activity during this teaching unit)
Knowledge, Skills and Understanding				

Pro forma 3

LESSON 1	
Learning Objective for the Lesson	
Content	

LESSON 2	Recapitulation:
Learning Objective for the Lesson	
Content	

LESSON 3	Recapitulation:
Learning Objective for the Lesson	
Content	

LESSON 4	Recapitulation:
Learning Objective for the Lesson	
Content	

LESSON 5	Recapitulation:
Learning Objective for the Lesson	
Content	

LESSON 6	Recapitulation:
Learning Objective for the Lesson	
Content	

LESSON 7	Recapitulation:
Learning Objective for the Lesson	
Content	

And so on....

Pro forma 4

Date:	Area of activity:		Class:	Duration in minutes:
Unit Lesson No.	No. of Pupils:		Age:	Facilities/Venue (working area):

For pupils' learning: ACTION POINTS FROM PREVIOUS LESSON: for your own learning:
QTS standards in focus:

Intended learning outcomes for pupils – *by the end of this lesson pupils should be able to know, do and understand the following:*

Identified pupils with SEN: Nature of SEN:

TIME	LEARNING ACTIVITY OBJECTIVE	ORG. OF LEARNING ACTIVITY and TEACHING STRATEGY	TEACHING/LEARNING POINTS (ASSESSMENT CRITERIA and DIFFERENTIATION)	RESOURCES

Notes

1. In its entirety Section 3 is headed: Teaching, and incorporates 3.1 Planning, Expectations and Targets; 3.2 Monitoring and Assessment; 3.3 Teaching and Class Management. The fact that planning has been highlighted in this chapter should not detract from the essential interrelationship that exists between each section in achieving learning objectives.

2. The term 'teacher' is used here as well as 'mentor', because within the mentoring process trainees will not only work with their assigned mentor within their particular subject department, but they must also experience the approach, work, etc of other members of the department so that they can appreciate the essential individuality they will ultimately generate in their teaching approach and style. The crucial thing here is the timing of this process relative to the experience and needs of the trainee.

References

Borko, H and Niles, T (1987) Description of teacher planning, in *Educators' Handbook: A research perspective*, ed V Richardson-Koehler, pp 167–87, Longman, White Plains, NY

Clark, C M and Yinger, R J (1987) Teacher planning, in *Exploring Teachers Thinking*, ed J Calderhead, pp 84–103, Cassell, London

Cochran, K F, De Tuiter, J A and King, R A (1993) Pedagogical content knowing: an integrated model for teacher preparation, *Journal of Teacher Education*, **44** (4)

Cohen, S (1987) Instructional alignment: searching for the magic bullet, *Educational Researcher*, November, pp 16–20

DES (1985) *Education Observed, 3: Good teachers*, DES, London

DES (1988) *The New Teacher in School: A survey by HMI in England and Wales 1987*, TSO, Norwich

DfEE (1997) *High Status, High Standards: Requirements for courses of initial teacher training*, Circular 10/97, DfEE, London

DfEE (1998) *Requirements for Courses of Initial Teacher Training*, Circular 4/98, DfEE, London

DfES/TTA (2002) *Qualifying to Teach*, TSO, Norwich

Fink, J and Siedentop, D (1989) The development of routines, rules and expectations at the start of the school year, *Journal of Teaching in Physical Education*, **8** (3), pp 198–212

Griffey, D and Housner, L D (1999) Teacher thinking and decision making in physical education: planning, perceiving, and implementing instruction, in eds

C A Hardy and M Mawer, *Learning and Teaching in Physical Education*, pp203–14, Falmer Press, London

Kyriacou, C (1986) *Effective Teaching in Schools*, Basil Blackwell, Oxford

Leask, M and Davison, J (1995) Schemes of work and lesson planning, in eds S Capel, M Leask, and T Turner, *Learning to Teach in the Secondary School: A companion to school experience*, Routledge, London

National Coaching Foundation (1995) *Tutor Trainer's Pack*, NCF, Leeds

Hardy, C (1996) Trainees' concerns, experiences and needs: implications for mentoring in physical education, in *Mentoring in Physical Education: Issues and insights*, ed M Mawer, Falmer Press, London

Kelly, T and Mayes, A (1995) *Issues in Mentoring*, Routledge, London

Kyriacou, C (1986) *Effective Teaching in Schools*, Blackwell, Oxford

Kyriacou, C (1991) *Essential Teaching Skills*, Stanley Thornes, Cheltenham

McIntyre, D (ed) (1997) *Teacher Education Research in a New Context: The Oxford Internship Scheme*, Paul Chapman Publishing, London

Mawer, M (1995) *The Effective Teaching of Physical Education*, Longman, Harlow

OFSTED (1993) *Handbook for the Inspection of Schools*, revised edn, TSO, Norwich

OFSTED (1998) *Secondary Education 1993–97: A Review of Secondary Schools in England*, TSO, Norwich

OFSTED (1999a) *Handbook for Inspecting Primary and Nursery Schools*, HMI No. 0–11–350109–9, TSO, Norwich

OFSTED (1999b) *Handbook for Inspecting Secondary Schools*, HMI No. 0–11–350110–2, TSO, Norwich

OFSTED (2000) *Framework 2000 – Inspecting Schools*, Ofsted.gov.uk/publications (web only)

OFSTED (2002) *Handbook for the Inspection of Initial Teacher Training (2002–2008)*, OFSTED, London

Shulman, L (1986) Those who understand: knowledge growth in teaching, *Educational Research*, **15** (2), pp 4–14

Taylor, P H (1970) *How Teachers Plan Their Courses*, National Foundation for Educational Research, Slough

Tyler, R W (1950) *Basic Principles of Curriculum and Instruction*, University of Chicago Press, Chicago, IL

Williams, A (1996) *Teaching Physical Education: A guide for mentors and students*, David Fulton, London

6 Teaching and Class Management

Mike Waring

Introduction

The intention in this chapter is to highlight some of the key aspects of teaching and class management that can be identified and manipulated by the trainee and mentor relative to their particular context. In so doing they can explore the meaning and underlying processes associated with each in an attempt to enhance their development as an effective teacher.

> ## Objectives
>
> By the end of this chapter you should be able to:
> - recognize potential phases in their own development as a teacher and their impact on their class management;
> - identify the need to establish effective learning environments;
> - explain the need to establish rules and routines with pupils;
> - discuss the importance of creating a positive learning climate in lessons, recognizing some of the factors that will influence it;
> - recognize the need to establish appropriate monitoring strategies for class behaviour;
> - identify the importance of reflection and evaluation in developing teaching and class management.

The standards and requirements in *Qualifying to Teach* (DfES/TTA, 2002) were written with the aim of giving providers of teacher training an increased flexibility in the way they designed their programmes, and to encourage increased use of professional judgement. Such relative autonomy is to be encouraged, but it is important to appreciate from the outset that the standards identified in Table 6.1, the teaching and class management (Section 3.3) of the standards for the award of QTS do not stand independently of each other. Nor should they be isolated from the other teaching standards that make up Section 3: 3.1 planning, expectations and targets, and 3.2 monitoring and assessment. They are very much interrelated in terms of the impact they will have on the development of a trainee's teaching and class management.

Table 6.1 Teaching and class management (Section 3.3 in Qualifying to Teach, DfES/TTA, 2002)

Those awarded Qualified Teacher Status must demonstrate all of the following:

They have high expectations of pupils and build successful relationships centred on teaching and learning. They establish a purposeful learning environment where diversity is valued and where pupils feel secure and confident.   3.3.1

They can teach the required or expected knowledge, understanding and skills relevant to the curriculum for pupils in the age range for which they are trained.   3.3.2

In relation to specific phases:

(a) Those qualifying to teach Foundation Stage children teach all six areas of learning outlined in the *QCA/DfES Curriculum Guidance for the Foundation Stage* and, for Reception children, the objectives in the National Literacy and Numeracy Strategy frameworks competently and independently.

(b) Those qualifying to teach pupils in Key Stage 1 and/or 2 teach the core subjects (English, including the National Literacy Strategy, mathematics through the National Numeracy Strategy, and science) competently and independently. They also teach, for either Key Stage 1 or Key Stage 2, a range of work across the following subjects:

history *or* geography
physical education
ICT
art and design *or* design and technology, and
performing arts

independently, with advice from an experienced colleague where appropriate.

(c) Those qualifying to teach Key Stage 3 pupils teach their specialist subject(s) competently and independently using the National Curriculum Programmes of Study for Key Stage 3 and the relevant national frameworks and schemes of work. Those qualifying to teach the core subjects or ICT at Key Stage 3 use the relevant frameworks, methods and expectations set out in the National Strategy for Key Stage 3. All those qualifying to teach a subject at Key Stage 3 must be able to use the cross-curricular elements, such as literacy and numeracy, set out in the National Strategy for Key Stage 3, in their teaching, as appropriate to their specialist subject.

(d) Those qualifying to teach Key Stage 4 and post-16 pupils teach their specialist subject(s) competently and independently using, as relevant to the subject and age-range, the National Curriculum Programmes of Study and related schemes of work, or programmes specified for national qualifications. (This could include work-related learning.) They also provide opportunities for pupils to develop the Key Skills specified by QCA.

They teach clearly structured lessons or sequences of work which interest and   3.3.3
motivate pupils and which:

make learning objectives clear to pupils
employ interactive teaching methods and collaborative group work
promote active and independent learning that enables pupils to think for themselves,
and to plan and manage their own learning.

They differentiate their teaching to meet the needs of pupils, including the more   3.3.4
able and those with special educational needs. They may have guidance from an
experienced teacher where appropriate.

They are able to support those who are learning English as an additional language,   3.3.5
with the help of an experienced teacher where appropriate.

They take account of the varying interests, experiences and achievements of boys   3.3.6
and girls, and pupils from different cultural and ethnic groups, to help pupils
make good progress.

They organise and manage teaching and learning time effectively.   3.3.7

They organise and manage the physical teaching space, tools, materials, texts and   3.3.8
other resources safely and effectively, with the help of support staff where appropriate.

They set high expectations for pupils' behaviour and establish a clear framework for   3.3.9
classroom discipline to anticipate and manage pupils' behaviour constructively, and
promote self-control and independence.

They use ICT effectively in their teaching.   3.3.10

They can take responsibility for teaching a class or classes for a sustained and   3.3.11
substantial period of time. They are able to teach across the age and ability range
for which they are trained.

They can provide homework and other out-of-class work which consolidates and   3.3.12
extends work carried out in the class and encourages pupils to learn independently.

They work collaboratively with specialist teachers and other colleagues and, with the   3.3.13
help of an experienced teacher as appropriate, manage the work of teaching assistants
or other adults to enhance pupils' learning.

They recognise and respond effectively to equal opportunities issues as they arise   3.3.14
in the classroom, including by challenging stereotyped views, and by challenging
bullying or harassment, following relevant policies and procedures.

Note: non-statutory guidance on the standards is also available from the TTA in the publication, *Qualifying to Teach Handbook of Guidance* (www.canteach.gov.uk/).

Good planning and preparation allow trainees to develop many areas of their teaching, not least their confidence. However, when trainees are attempting to create and maintain an 'effective learning environment' in their lessons, one of the biggest concerns that they have is related to class control, management and organization (Docking, 2002; Hardy, 1996). Furlong and Maynard (1995) provide interesting and important conclusions from their work on the 'stages of student development', which assist in understanding the development of a trainee's class management skills. They explain that rather than the stages (and associated concerns) being discrete and changing at each transition, they are continual concerns that evolve throughout the trainee's school experience. Guillaume and Rudney (1993, p79), from similar research findings, state that the trainees 'did not so much think about different things as they grew, they thought about things differently'. This becomes an important factor in relation to trainees' achievement and development of their class management skills, especially when one also considers the impact it has on the way in which they view the nature of the content they employ and the pupils they teach.

Of the five stages Furlong and Maynard (1995) identify, the second stage is called 'personal survival'. This involves 'classroom control' where the trainee's concern is very much about keeping control and the class quiet. They note that several student teachers maintained that, at this stage, all of their effort was put into keeping the class quiet, and when they did have the children's attention, it was a case of, 'quick tell them everything I know' (Furlong and Maynard, 1995, p80). They also note at this stage that any perceived lack of control also influences their perception and purpose of the content: their view of the content of activities changed over time. Initially it was viewed primarily as a medium of control, then as a chance to impress, before finally becoming a vehicle for learning (Furlong and Maynard, 1995, p97).

The changes in the trainees' view of pupils progressed from seeing them as 'children' and as allies, to viewing them as a whole class and even as enemies, before finally seeing them as individual learners. Knowing this predisposition is important for the trainee and mentor in that it provides them with an awareness of some of the influences on their class management and their likely interrelationships. The need for this awareness is reinforced when Wragg's (2001, p7) definition of class management is considered: class management is what teachers do to ensure that children engage in the task in hand, whatever that may be. There are many different ways of achieving this state.

Establishing an effective learning environment

Turner (1997) makes a simple but very important distinction in the nature of the application of the skills and understanding of the teacher when he asks: 'managing behaviour or managing learning'? One could then ask, can you have one without the other? It is important that the trainee has a sound grasp of the fundamental class management skills to facilitate and maintain appropriate behaviour because it is on such a foundation of management and good planning that effective learning will be based and developed. The establishment and sustainability of an effective learning environment follow from a number of predominantly proactive, rather than reactive decisions made by the trainee teacher.

Rules and routines within class management

Brophy's (1983) term 'proactive problem prevention' is one that highlights the need for advanced planning and detailed consideration by trainees of the kind of learning environment they wish to establish and maintain. This not only relates to each individual lesson, but over a period of time. A trainee's concerns will once again impact on this. However, another important factor influencing trainees' perception and implementation of rules and routines in a class is what and how they observe and copy from their mentor and other teachers. Significantly, the copying of the rules and routines adopted by a teacher in another lesson does not mean that the trainees necessarily understand them. If this understanding is lacking, trainees may well 'get by' in their lesson, but they are less likely to be able to develop the personal relationships and class management strategies and skills that will allow them to become more effective teachers. Therefore, this 'understanding' is something that has to be fostered by the trainee and mentor in their (collaborative) observations and discussions. There is a close link here between the nature of the rules and the nature of the relationships that the trainee is able to foster and build.

What are the rules and routines in the context of class management? Rules identify general expectations for behaviour that cover a variety of situations (Siedentop, 1991, p95). Mawer (1995, p93) develops this further by stating that a rule defines general expectations of acceptable and unacceptable behaviour that will cover different situations; for example, expecting pupils to be quiet and attentive when the teacher is talking. Rules must remain flexible in the light of the changing circumstances of the context – that is the interrelationship between the teacher, pupil, content and classroom. However, the teacher must endeavour to enforce rules on a continual basis. Teachers also need to consider the extent to which they intend to specify consequences for rule violations. Once again these decisions will have a bearing on the way in which the relationship between the teachers and the pupils will be framed and maintained and subsequently the nature of their planning.

To have no rules would lead to anarchy, chaos and endanger the pupils in the class. To have too rigid a set of rules would lead to paralysis in the class. Routines should be considered to be the compromise between those established by the school, the pupils' expectations from other classes, and the teacher's own values and ideas (Turner, 1997). More specifically, Siedentop (1991, p95) identifies routines as procedures for performing specific behaviours within a class, particularly those behaviours that recur regularly. Consequently, routines have to be established from the very beginning of those encounters between the teacher and the class and need to be reassessed and reapplied throughout the year. The effective use of routines can save a great deal of learning time and minimize disruption within the context of the lesson. However, if they are to be effective, they need to have the consent of the pupils. This consent is facilitated by teacher and pupils sharing a clear rationale. A learning environment that is governed by accurately planned, open and well understood routines is more likely to be an effective one.

The distinction between rules and routines has fundamental implications for the way in which a trainee and mentor work towards developing the teaching and class management standards of the trainee. For example, a rule is different from a routine in that it attempts to specify a generalized behaviour that can occur in a number of differing situations, whereas a routine is a constant procedural matter specific to the context. This means that the management of the situation will require different skills and techniques to initiate and maintain a positive and effective learning environment.

Rules tend to relate to the following areas (adapted from Siedentop, 1991 and Mawer, 1995):

- respect for others, pupils and teacher;
- respect for the learning environment;
- safety;
- support the learning of others/attitude to work rules.

As Turner (1997, p66) points out, 'classroom rules need to be positive, logical and relevant to the situation. Positive rules are those that stress what can be done rather than what cannot be done.' This is something that Cohen and Manion (1989) acknowledge, along with 'relevance' and 'meaningfulness', as part of their rationale for the recommendation that rules should be kept to a minimum. It is therefore possible to identify some simple guidelines that a trainee and mentor can consider in creating the most appropriate class rules:

- Keep the rules 'short and sweet', very much to the point and explicit.
- State the rules positively and make them realistic, providing mainly positive, but also negative examples. A community orientation to the wording is also recommended; for example, 'We will…'.
- Ensure that the terminology used for the rules can be understood by those they apply to.
- Ensure that the rules are supported by and consistent with departmental and school-wide rules.
- Negotiate (where possible) with the pupils.
- Identify and consistently apply consequences to rules, ensuring that you are willing to enforce them.
- Do not provide too many rules to any given context – a maximum of six.

Routines can relate to a number of things, but fundamentally they can exist in three guises. The first are those around managing relationships. These reflect a consistency in firmness, fairness and friendliness – qualities pupils acknowledge in an effective teacher. The second can be said to manage the work and movement of pupils. The third are those that refer to teachers and pupils gaining attention. Kelly *et al* (1997, p79) develop these further when they outline the organizational issues associated with the teacher (being organized and the presentation of self); the environment/working space (preparation before lesson, establishing authority and expectations); the pupils/equipment (planning and strategies for organizing); and the timing of the lesson (planning and progression). Teachers have to be consistent in their approach (Rogers and Freiberg, 1994), and remember they are a role model. Therefore, they should set a good example by being prepared and organized prior to each and every lesson. Once again the issue of planning is shown to be a significant foundation on which to be an effective teacher. Kelly *et al* (1997, p80) offer the checklist shown in Table 6.2 to organize the start of the lesson.

Table 6.2   Checklist for trainees to organize the start of the lesson

Prepared the lesson:	Learning outcome(s) clearly identified in advance for the lesson.
	Learning objective for each individual learning activity identified, and clear about how they contribute to the lesson's learning outcome(s).
Marked homework:	Meeting deadlines and positive, useful feedback; associated with motivation of pupil
Checked the working space:	Is it available and safe to use?
Checked and counted all equipment:	Is it readily available and in good order?
Established entry into the classroom:	Orderly and quiet
Established routines:	Attending to such tasks as coats and bags and handing out books
Taken the register:	This needs to be done without wasting too much time (during organization of books, etc)
Established routines:	Organizing the taking out, re-distribution and collection of equipment.

Have resources ready to use in the appropriate place (visual aids, work cards, additional materials, etc)

Such a checklist supports the identification of various routines offered by Mawer (1995) when he explores Fink and Siedentop's (1989) five different kinds of routines adopted throughout a lesson:

1. *Preliminary routines* – entering/leaving the classroom; introductory activity; pupils' method of gaining teacher's attention; teacher's method of gaining pupil attention and request for quiet.
2. *Transitional management routines* – pupil dispersal (eg to the work area); pupil gathering (eg for demonstrations); equipment movement (eg taking out and putting away); group work (movement into pairs, small and large groups).
3. *Instructional management routines* – starting activities; defining boundaries of work area (whole group, small group and individual).
4. *Housekeeping routines* – record keeping; accidents; collecting valuables.
5. *Closure routines* – finishing the activity; leaving the work space.

These are all routines trainees need to consider, experiment with and develop in order to organize their lessons, as well as to address not only the class management standards, but to appreciate and develop the essential association with the relevant aspects of the planning standards. Observing other teachers and discussing with their mentor the most appropriate rules and routines for them to use and develop in the context of one or a series of lessons, are important components in understanding and developing these standards. However, it is never straightforward: a trainee has to constantly consider the complex evolving interrelationship between the teacher and the pupils on a personal as well as a practical level.

A positive climate for learning

The climate in the classroom facilitated by the teacher will have a significant effect on the nature of the learning environment. Embroiled in the creation and maintenance of a positive learning environment are a number of interrelating factors. Kyriacou (1986, p101) makes the distinction between teaching *qualities* and *tasks*:

> In looking at effective teaching a useful distinction can be drawn between the general *qualities* of effective teaching and the component *tasks* involved. The qualities focus on broad aspects of teaching which appear to be important in determining its effectiveness, such as good rapport with pupils or pitching the work at the appropriate level of difficulty. The tasks refer to the activities and practices involved in teaching, such as planning a lesson or assessing pupils' progress.

As Kyriacou continues to point out, these are very much interrelated. However, the search for *qualities* is explicitly judgmental in character and may cut across a number of different *tasks* involved in teaching. With this in mind the next portion of this chapter will discuss issues related to the creation and maintenance of a good/positive learning environment.

What constitutes the best kind of classroom climate in order to facilitate pupil learning? It has been described as one that is purposeful, task-oriented, relaxed, warm, supportive and has a sense of order (Kyriacou, 1991). The creation of such an environment influences the motivation of the pupils, creating a positive attitude towards their learning. It can also be seen to marry with their feelings about what makes a 'good' teacher: 'those who are at once firm, friendly and fair, who take an interest in individuals and show humour whilst also "helping you to learn" and explaining things clearly' (Docking, 2002, p36).

In terms of teaching skills, creating a purposeful and business-like classroom climate means that the teacher should not only be well organized and well prepared, but start lessons on time, keep lessons running smoothly and monitor pupils' work and progress (Mawer, 1995). It is the acceptance by the pupils of the teacher's organization and management of tasks, as well as their willingness to produce a positive effort in relation to the task, that characterizes the purposeful and task-oriented environment. This positive orientation is facilitated by the teacher establishing challenging yet realistic opportunities for successful learning within the lessons. Such challenges have to be differentiated by the trainee to cater for the ability of all pupils – including the most able and well as the less able. This allows learners the opportunity to build their self-esteem through productive, constructive and supportive experiences. Once again it is teachers who are the catalyst for this in terms of their planning of interesting and meaningful learning activities and experiences, and the positive language they use to support them, as well as taking into account the individual differences that promote challenging and realistically attainable learning targets. If this is achieved the likelihood is that pupils' feeling of confidence and competence will be promoted, as will their motivation to work at the learning activity (Weiner, 1979).

Of course there is the other side of the coin in terms of a negative 'self-fulfilling prophecy' in which the teacher's prior knowledge and experience of a pupil may interfere with the kind of support he or she offers the pupil, which in turn influences the pupil's learning, creating a negative cycle. To prevent this and retain a positive learning environment, teachers should try to keep their expectations flexible and current, adopting a present perspective rather than an 'historical' one. They can also avoid direct comparison with other pupils and instead concentrate on the individual's current understanding. The trainee's differentiation of learning activities should allow all pupils to meet and understand on a personal level the realistic challenges they are presented with. Having set clear and realistic goals, which the pupil can achieve, it is important that these outcomes are acknowledged, valued and extended within the lesson using positive and constructive language and feedback.

Relationships

Day (1999) reminds us that the relationships between a teacher and pupil are certainly not uniform and they do not always follow a standard professional blue-print. It is very much a movement along a continuum from appropriate intimacy to distance in a variety of contexts. The type of relationship teachers establish with their pupils will influence the classroom climate. A positive climate is most likely to be achieved where there is mutual respect and rapport between the teacher and the pupils. It is important that the trainee is able to convey a sense of understanding and value of the pupil's perspective on an array of issues (academic, personal and social) in order to facilitate a caring and empathetic relationship. This has to be a two-way process where the pupils similarly reciprocate respect for the teacher's point of view. However, there are potential problems associated with a trainee attempting to create such a rapport, not least being over-friendly with the pupils so that the necessary divide between teacher and pupil is blurred or lost. It is a difficult skill to achieve, but as Kyriacou (1991) points out, 'as an adult, and given your role (*teacher*), it is up to you to have a major influence in establishing such a harmonious relationship in the classroom'.

A sense of humour is another element of the relationship with pupils that can create uncertainty for the trainee, in that it is something that has the potential to be misinterpreted or to get out of hand. A sense of humour is consistently cited as an important element in the teacher-pupil relationship (Docking, 1987, 2002; Kyriacou, 1991; Mawer, 1995; Wragg, 1993), but it must be used appropriately. That is, it should be used to complement strategies for behaviour management, for example to diffuse a situation or break the tension of a particular moment in the lesson. Humour must not be used too frequently or at the expense of pupils, as these have negative consequences with regard to over-familiarization and inhibiting pupil self-esteem respectively.

Monitoring the class

Regardless of the fact that a teacher may establish clear, challenging and realistic learning activities, there will be pupils who work to negotiate the boundaries of teacher expectations with a view to expanding their own terms. In an attempt to maintain the necessary 'dominance' in the relationship a teacher needs to monitor what the pupils are doing and assess their compliance with the task. This is not to negate appropriate notions of pupil self-discipline or negotiation. Trainees, as well as pupils, must understand why certain rules apply. In essence it is not what is up for negotiation or what should be negotiable, but how pupils can understand the need for rules.

Pupils should be accountable for their work and behaviour, adhering to clear expectations, but the teacher needs to monitor the learning environment through deliberate strategies. Effective monitoring is achieved through good movement around the class and positioning. It is essential that teachers circulate in such a way that they are able to see the entire class. This usually demands moving around the periphery of the class. By keeping the whole class in view a teacher is able to interact on a number of levels with individuals, pairs and small groups as well as the whole group, while at the same time being confident that if anything untoward were to happen in the learning environment (such as pupils being off task or safety issues) the teacher is able to pre-empt or quickly deal with them. The issue of safety is very important, especially if the nature of the activity is such that problems could occur (eg an experiment or gymnastics lesson). Trainees should also remember that it is not just the monitoring of negative aspects of behaviour that should be the focus of the teacher: they should identify and highlight the positive outcomes too. Reinforcement by the teacher of good work and application by the pupil(s) (having the potential to enhance their motivation) is also facilitated by good positioning and constant scanning of the class.

There are a variety of grouping strategies employed in schools (Hallam *et al*, 2002), the organization of which are significant in that they will influence trainees' selection and application of their class monitoring strategies and techniques. Whatever grouping criteria trainees adopt (ability, friendship, gender, developmental, random) for/in a class, they have to consider variables such as the nature of the learning activity, the time and space available, the resources required and their position in the learning environment, the position of the groups in relation to one another and the potential for each of these to change during the lesson. With these considerations in mind, the trainee will select and plan for the best strategy to facilitate the effective monitoring of the group. The monitoring of the class, along with the rules and routines that the teacher establishes and reinforces in lessons, is a significant class management skill.

Misbehaviour

The potential sources of disruption or misbehaviour and monitoring techniques that might be employed are shown in Table 6.3. It is worth noting at this point Wragg's (2001, p6) comment that 'the ability to control behaviour, in whatever manner, is a "threshold" measure – if you have enough of it, you are over the threshold and can display the rest of your repertoire of professional skills, but too little of it and these may never become apparent'.

The task for the trainee and mentor is to match the most appropriate monitoring techniques with aspects of misbehaviour and their origins so that they can attempt to incorporate the techniques more effectively in their preparation and delivery of the lesson.

Table 6.3 Matching the aspects of misbehaviour and their origins with potential monitoring techniques (adapted from Turner, 1997)

Aspects of misbehaviour and its origins		Monitoring techniques	
Cause	*Characteristics or origin*	*Technique*	*Characteristic*
Boredom	Lack of relevance to activity. Work too hard or too easy. Demands prolonged concentration.	Scanning	Frequently look around the room; site yourself where you can see most pupils while you talk to pupils.
Excessive intellectual demand	Work is too hard or takes too much time.	Circulating	Move around the work area, look at work, give praise or support, anticipate problems, ensure pupils are on task.
Frustration	Work is too difficult or language is too hard. Other pupils can do it easily. Unable to contribute to class or group activity.	Making eye contact	Address whole class and engage them; use eye contact for control; avoid interrupting flow of lesson.
Low self-esteem	History of past failures causes lack of confidence. Easier not to do the work than fail again. Often feels 'picked on'.	Asking questions	Target pupils; involve as many people as possible over the lesson period.
Emotional difficulties	Unable to adjust to working with others; not valued at home, or even abused. Is a bully or sustains bullying from peers. Employs attention-seeking behaviours.	Using space	Circulate among the pupils. When needed, use the whole room to separate pupils or groups from the main class.
Lack of perceived pastoral structure in school	Unclear code of conduct and/or sanctions. Teacher does not apply rules fairly or consistently. May be construed as lack of care.	Supporting	Give appropriate help, either motivational or academic; acknowledging the progress made inhibits off-task behaviour.
Teacher, school ethos	Pupil seen as a problem instead of the system failing the pupil. School unable to respond to pupil's needs.	Changing activity	Alter the pace of work; signal changes; acknowledge those pupils who have yet to finish earlier work and ensure they know what to do.
Peer pressure	Some pupils may be influenced by other pupils with apparent credibility in the wider world; or who bully or offer inducements.	Encouraging individuals	Ensure that all know that you are aware of their progress; encourage or praise good work for each pupil. Keep the individual in mind.

Dislike of teacher	Teachers are disliked who are unfair, have favourites, apply rules arbitrarily or pick on people, do not prepare their lessons, arrive late.	Acting	Insist on courtesies between pupils and between you and the pupil; confront disrespect. Address misbehaviour when it occurs or, if possible prevent it. See scanning and circulating, above. Remind pupils of rules and address violations.

So far the emphasis has been predominantly on teaching *qualities*. However, if we turn our attention to teaching *tasks* we can identify the underlying interrelated aspect of a teacher's decision making. In so doing it will help illustrate for trainees and their mentor the significant principles underpinning their teaching.

Moving towards a proactive style: reflection and evaluation

Forming a continuous cycle underlying the teacher's decision making, there are considered to be three main aspects: planning, presentation and monitoring, and reflection and evaluation (Kyriacou, 1991). Planning is a fundamental component of effective teaching and class management. Similarly the presentation and monitoring of lessons inform the teacher's decisions about the nature of the progression in learning and interpretation of the learning context. In other words, the teachers' teaching skills, used in carrying out tasks of teaching, will determine the extent to which pupils learn based on the three psychological conditions of attentiveness, receptiveness and appropriateness (Kyriacou, 1991). The notion of planning has been explored in detail in Chapter 5, so the focus of the remainder of this chapter will be on the reflective aspects trainees have to continue to develop if they are to enhance the quality of the learning experience for all pupils.

In an attempt to make the learning environment an effective one in the delivery of the lesson(s) trainees have to consider a myriad of different but interrelated aspects, both practical and theoretical. It is essential that the trainee evaluates and reflects upon each lesson in terms of class management, ie have the class management strategies worked to facilitate the desired learning outcomes? For many teachers and especially trainees, the primary consideration when evaluating and reflecting on their lessons on a day-to-day basis will be whether their class management style has been good enough to deliver what was intended. However, such a limited focus ignores pedagogic styles. A trainee should not consider class management style in complete isolation from pedagogic style. If trainees are considering factors that contribute to acceptable pupil behaviour, they are also considering in many instances factors that contribute to effective learning. Therefore, in order to become effective proactive managers of a class and each pupil's learning in that class, a trainee has to consider and develop strategies associated with behaviour and pedagogy (DES, 1989; DfE, 1994; Docking, 2002).

Reflection on their teaching allows trainees to reconsider what is effective and arrive at developmentally appropriate advances or alternative interpretations that will make their teaching and the environment more sensitive to the learning of the pupil. As part of this there is the need to reflect upon the assessment and recording of the educational progress of the pupils. The formal assessment of learning in school (marked work, examinations, etc) are a source of feedback on a pupil's academic attainment. They also form a vehicle whereby the teacher can diagnose difficulties and problems that can then be remedied by feedback accompanying the marking, and be addressed specifically in future lessons (Kyriacou, 1991, p128). When teachers have evaluated and reflected upon their teaching and its outcomes, those alterations and amendments that have been put in place also need evaluating and reflecting upon. It must be emphasized that teaching is intended to promote learning; however, if the priority of the lesson becomes class management, then learning will not be the focus of the evaluation of the lesson:

> Class management tasks overshadow learning management. In such circumstances, assessment is often confined to reporting attainment rather than to inform teaching. However, you need to assess if the lack of attention to learning strategies has caused the class management problems in the first place... The focus on class teaching because of class management priorities may reduce the opportunities to promote cognitive development. (Turner, 1997, p83)

This can be easily done. As Newell and Jeffrey (2002, pxvi) remind us, the orientation of a number of factors plays a vital role in managing behaviour in lessons, all of which can credibly form part of a trainee's evaluation and reflection. These are well planned, carefully organized, defined learning outcomes that are communicated to pupils; clear explanations and examples; effective questioning; a variety of activities that match the ability and maturity of the pupils; activities that are challenging and interesting; high expectations; pace; and colourful and interesting resources. However, trainees and mentors must not lose sight of the fact that it is the management of 'learning' that has to be the trainees' primary focus, rather than the management of behaviour when evaluating and reflecting upon their class management. Even though the latter helps to facilitate the former, it remains crucial that the trainee and the mentor constantly critique the 'learning' achieved by the pupils (and trainee) as a consequence of the trainee's management of the particular context.

Of course what has been discussed here takes place as part of the trainees' increasing 'awareness of self' (Furlong and Maynard, 1995). They are things that evolve, with the help of their mentor and tutor, to allow trainees to increasingly understand the meaning and interrelationships between their actions and those of others as part of their teaching. In so doing it enables them to become increasingly proactive in their management and pedagogic strategies to enhance pupils' learning, rather than merely 'coping'.

References

Brophy, J (1983) Classroom organization and management, *Elementary School Journal*, **83**, pp265–85

Cohen, L and Manion, L (1989) *A Guide to Teaching Practice*, 3rd edn, Holt, Rinehart and Winston, London

Day, C (1999) *Developing Teachers: The challenges of lifelong learning*, Falmer Press, London

DES (Department of Education and Science) (1989) *Discipline in Schools*, The Elton Report, TSO, Norwich

DfE (Department for Education) (1994) *Pupil Behaviour and Discipline*, Circular 8/94, TSO, Norwich

DfES/TTA (2002) *Qualifying to Teach*, TSO, Norwich

Docking, J W (1987) *Control and Discipline in Schools: Perspectives and approaches*, 2nd edn, Paul Chapman, London

Docking, J W (2002) *Managing Behaviour in the Primary School*, 3rd edn, David Fulton, London

Fink, J and Siedentop, D (1989) The development of routines, rules and expectations at the start of the school year, *Journal of Teaching in Physical Education*, **8** (3) pp198–212

Furlong, J and Maynard, T (1995) *Mentoring Student Teachers: The growth of professional knowledge*, Routledge, London

Guillame, A and Rudney, G (1993) Student teachers' growth towards independence: an analysis of their changing concerns, *Teaching and Teacher Education*, **9** (1) pp65–80

Hallam, S, Ireson, J, and Davies, J (2002) *Effective Pupil Grouping in Primary School: A practical guide*, David Fulton, London

Hardy, C (1996) Trainees' concerns, experiences and needs: implications for mentoring in physical education, in ed M Mawer, *Mentoring in Physical Education: Issues and insights*, Falmer Press, London

Kelly, L, Whitehead, M and Capel, S (1997) Lesson organization and management, in ed S Capel, *Learning to Teach Physical Education in the Secondary School: A companion to school experience*, Routledge, London

Kyriacou, C (1986) *Effective Teaching in Schools*, Blackwell, Oxford

Kyriacou, C (1991) *Essential Teaching Skills*, Stanley Thornes, Cheltenham

Mawer, M (1995) *The Effective Teaching of Physical Education*, Longman, London

Newell, S and Jeffery, D (2002) *Behaviour Management in the Classroom: A transactional analysis approach*, David Fulton, London

Rogers, C R and Freiberg, H J (1994) *Freedom to Learn*, Macmillan, New York

Siedentop, D (1991) *Developing Teaching Skills in Physical Education*, 3rd edn, Mayfield Press, CA

TTA (Teacher Training Agency) (2002) *Qualifying to Teach Handbook of Guidance*, TPU 0934/10–02, TTA, London

Turner, A (1997) *Learning to Teach Science in the Secondary School*, Routledge, London

Weiner, B (1979) A theory of motivation for some classroom experiences, *Journal of Educational Psychology*, **71**, pp3–25

Wragg, E (1993) *Primary Teaching Skills*, Routledge, London

Wragg, E (2001) *Class Management in the Primary School*, Routledge/Falmer, London

7 Assessment

Rita Headington

This chapter directs the trainee to aspects of monitoring and assessment that need to be developed in order to reach the standards laid down in *Qualifying to Teach* (TTA, 2002). The trainee is introduced to the concepts of monitoring and assessment, including the types of assessment they will be involved in. These include discussion on baseline assessment, National Curriculum assessment, GCSEs, GNVQs and A-levels, as well as the whole concept of formative and summative assessment processes. Key terms used in assessment are considered, as are their implications in recording and reporting the assessments made. Assessment is examined and explained, from the everyday classroom perspective, including marking and homework, to the wider perspective of statutory testing and examinations. The trainee is then introduced to the importance of recording and reporting assessments to a variety of audiences.

Objectives

By the end of this chapter the trainee should have a clear understanding of:

- the nature of monitoring and assessment;
- formative, summative, diagnostic and evaluative assessment;
- key terms in assessment;
- the nature of recording and reporting;
- the nature of marking and the need for effective marking and pupil feedback;
- key issues relating to recording;
- the need to report to a variety of audiences.

Introduction

Assessment is central to all areas of the National Curriculum and its Key Stages. Assessing pupils' work is not a new venture: it is a daily feature of classroom practice at all levels. But within recent years greater emphasis has been placed on the formal aspects of assessment, from baseline assessment and National Curriculum end of Key Stage assessments, through to GCSEs, GNVQs and A-levels.

Assessment is needed for a variety of purposes within teaching and learning. *Assessment for learning* provides teachers with detailed information on pupil progress so that teaching can be developed and enhanced to meet the needs of the pupil's learning. *Assessment of learning* provides the school, parents, LEA and DfES with information on the pupils' levels in relation to statutory assessment activities so that provision can be made to support teaching and learning.

This chapter is in two parts: monitoring and assessment, and recording and reporting. First, it will discuss monitoring and assessment: what they are, the purposes of assessment and its relevance to teaching and learning. There are tasks to help understand assessment within the context of the classroom.

Monitoring and assessment

Headington (2000) defines monitoring as 'the skill of being able to have a constant, clear and accurate overview of pupils within a learning situation'. She states that 'Assessment is more specific than monitoring. Where monitoring provides the teacher with an overview of the learning of many, assessment provides detailed information about the learning of one or more pupils...'.

The monitoring and assessment of pupils' learning and progress is central to effective teaching and learning. As far back as 1988 the Task Group on Assessment and Testing (DES, 1988) stated:

> Promoting children's learning is a principal aim of schools. Assessment lies at the heart of the process. It can provide a framework in which educational objectives may be set, and pupils' progress charted and expressed. It can yield a basis for planning the next educational steps in response to children's needs. By facilitating dialogue between teachers, it can enhance professional skills and help the school as a whole to strengthen learning across the curriculum and throughout its age range.

Reactions to assessment are rarely neutral; they are frequently influenced by prior experience and exposure to the assessment process, either as pupils in school or as students in higher education or professional activities.

In recent years the teachers' role in monitoring and assessment has become a central task and a major influence on their professional activities. This has increased their workloads and required even greater organizational skills to allow monitoring and assessment activities to be conducted systematically and effectively.

As aspiring teachers it is essential to understand the range of assessments that are used and to be able to distinguish between their formative, summative, diagnostic and evaluative purposes.

Purposes of assessment

Formative assessment informs future planning, teaching and learning. It is an ongoing process, relates directly to the learning that is taking place and is necessarily detailed. The aim of formative assessment is to promote effective further learning by pupils. This is achieved in a variety of ways including:

- identifying the pupils' current understanding;
- identifying pupils' future learning needs;
- giving pupils constructive oral and written feedback;
- providing the teacher with feedback on pupils' progress and teaching strategies.

The main focus of this form of assessment is to identify strengths and shortcomings, such as errors and difficulties, in the pupils' work. It also informs the teacher of the nature of advice and information needed to improve pupils' future learning outcomes.

Without formative assessment teachers would not be able to function effectively. Formative assessment also provides the basis of communication about individual pupils to teachers, other professionals and parents.

Summative assessment provides a summary of a pupil's attainment and progress at a given point. It is normally carried out at the end of a period of teaching or instruction and would include National Curriculum end of Key Stage assessments (Tests and Teacher Assessment), end of term examinations and end of course assessments. The outcomes of such assessments are typically the grades or percentages used on school reports of attainment, National Curriculum levels, or results from external examinations. Audiences for summative assessment include parents, teachers in other schools, providers of further education and training and potential employers.

Diagnostic assessment takes place when teachers diagnose a pupil's work to ascertain the cause of a difficulty. The assessment may take the form of a detailed analysis of a pupil's written work or a close observation of how the pupil tackles an activity. At another level it may be through the application of a commercially designed test for a particular learning difficulty and be undertaken by the teacher or a fellow professional (eg SENCO, educational psychologist).

Evaluative assessment draws upon the results of individual pupil assessments. At each summative assessment point the results of individual pupil assessments are collated and analysed by the school to provide information about the strengths and needs of the cohort as a whole, to evaluate and monitor the school's performance. At the end of KS2 and 3, and at GCSE and A-level, these collated results are published alongside those of other schools in LEA performance tables. They are also published in the school prospectus and annual governors' report, with comparisons with previous years, to demonstrate the performance of the school. The publication of results is a statutory requirement for the purpose of accountability. In addition to this, National Curriculum data, detailed in the PANDA report (Performance and Assessment), is used by schools and OFSTED for comparative purposes.

The range of assessment for formative, summative, diagnostic and evaluative purposes, and the variety of audiences who seek assessment information, has led teachers to become involved in a diversity of assessment practices. There are a number of key terms teachers should be aware of within the assessment framework.

Key terms in assessment

Referencing

In order for the result of an assessment to be understood it is measured 'in relation to a scale or compared to another assessment of the same or a different pupil… This is called referencing' (Headington, 2000). Three types of assessment referencing used by schools are norm-referencing, criteria-referencing and ipsative-referencing.

In *norm-referenced* assessment all the pupils' scores are put into rank order and a certain percentage are assigned to each grade (eg only 10 per cent will gain a Grade A, 20 per cent a Grade B and so on). Alternatively a cut-off point is chosen for passing, allowing a certain percentage to pass and the rest to fail. So, the grade pupils achieve and whether they pass or fail depends partly on the performance of other pupils.

In *criterion-referenced* assessment the pupil's performance is not measured in relation to other pupils but against set criteria. Work is marked or graded according to whether the criteria have been met. In this form of assessment there is no limit on how many pupils achieve a given level (see Gipps and Stobart, 1993).

The national criteria for assessment are encapsulated in the Attainment Targets as described in the Level Descriptions of the National Curriculum. The intention is that it should be a criterion-referenced system in which pupils' attainments are assessed in terms of national levels, which are determined with reference to statements of their attainment.

Ipsative-referenced assessment is 'judged against previous personal performance' (Headington, 2000), putting the individual pupil at the centre of the assessment process. Support for involving pupils in their own assessment has grown since the publication of an extensive review of effective assessment practice by Black and Wiliam (1995), which championed the cause of assessment for learning.

For ipsative-referenced assessment to be effective pupils must know what they have learnt, what they are to learn and how this learning will show itself. The teacher's role is to share and negotiate learning objectives with pupils and work with them to develop and meet personal targets. The motivation of the pupils should then increase as targets are met and they recognize the intrinsic value of learning.

Types of assessment

Internal assessments are teacher-oriented tasks. They are devised, implemented and marked by the class teacher. Teachers often use internal assessment as part of their own teaching programme. These can be tests, homework projects or practical tests. Internal assessment informs the teacher of continual individual progress.

External assessment activities and tasks are those devised by examiners outside the school and are usually marked outside the school. They include end of Key Stage National Curriculum tests, GCSEs, GNVQs and A-levels. Marking is then 'moderated' by external assessors to ensure accuracy.

Informal assessment takes place as part of normal classroom life and practice. It is usually observational, where the teacher observes performance and makes notes for future reference. *Formal assessment* is made following prior warning that assessment will occur. This gives pupils the opportunity to revise and prepare for the assessment process.

Continuous assessment is becoming a significant method. It requires teachers/ assessors to base the final assessment on the standard of attainment achieved on a variety of pieces of work over a long period of time. This technique is particularly relevant to GCSE and GNVQ qualifications. *Terminal assessment* is based on standards of achievement reached at the end of course, module or programme of work.

Each type of assessment has to be used in the context of teaching and learning. It is important for teachers to realize and understand the rationale of each type of assessment so that the approach used matches the purpose of the assessment.

Why do teachers assess pupils?

As discussed earlier, assessment has many faces and can be used for a variety of purposes. However, there are, for the teacher and learner, three fundamental reasons for assessment: feedback, progress and motivation.

The TGAT Report (DES, 1988) used the expression 'feedback and feed-forward'. Assessment gives the teacher feedback about pupils' progress, which allows the teacher to evaluate how effective the teaching is, by assessing how well learning objectives have been achieved. This then allows the teacher to feed-forward by correcting misunderstandings, giving further support if required, or extending the learning of pupils who found little challenge in the activity.

Assessment also enables direct feedback to be given to pupils. It shows them where their attainment is in relation to previous personal performance, to other pupils, to expected standards and to national standards. Constructive written and oral feedback can direct pupils in their own improvement and enable target setting.

Assessments that are recorded can, over the short or long term, enable the teacher to track pupil progress. Analysis of records of pupil progress should be key to teachers' long-term planning, helping to inform teachers of any decisions they need to make about the future learning needs of pupils. Records have been described as 'the essential interface between assessment and reporting' (Daugherty, 1995) and as such provide information for communication with parents and other professionals about each pupil's progress.

Motivation is a key factor in encouraging pupils to achieve and take interest in and responsibility for their own learning. Motivation can be intrinsic and extrinsic, and in many cases both. Positive feedback and success in assessment tasks are very effective mechanisms for future improvement and motivation. In summary, assessment enables teachers to:

- support pupils in their own learning;
- motivate pupils;
- provide feedback and feed-forward;
- measure what pupils know, understand and can do;
- undertake future planning;
- track pupil progress;
- diagnose learning difficulties;
- set targets;
- evaluate their own effectiveness;
- provide information to parents and other professionals;
- provide grades and levels of attainment.

Task 7.1

- Within your phase or Key Stage establish the types of assessment that take place within your school and evaluate the purposes for which they are used.
- Try to investigate and understand how the National Curriculum assessments affect teachers' assessment activities.

Assessment in the classroom

This can take many forms, but in the first instance a trainee will be involved in the following aspects:

- observation and questioning;
- marking;
- everyday classroom tasks;
- homework;
- externally set tests and examinations;
- teacher-based assessments.

Each form of assessment is important, but a clear view must be kept of the purpose or purposes of the chosen type of assessment. The road to success for the trainee is to set achievable targets for learning the skills and techniques of assessment, using clear collective goals derived from experience, practice and discussion with skilled practitioners. Trainees should always ensure they know about assessment practices within the school they are working in by reading the school's assessment policy. It is also essential that they keep up to date with developments in assessment practices and procedures by reading the work of key specialists in the field (eg, Black and Wiliam, 1995; Broadfoot, 1994; Gipps, 1994) and the latest documentation on external assessment matters (eg, from QCA, examination boards).

Task 7.2

Check the assessment policy for both the school and the department you are working in. Examine how your views and knowledge of marking fit with established policy.

Task 7.3

Discuss with your mentor the school/departmental assessment policy and examine how marking is used within the department. Establish which elements are essential for your training placement.

Observation and questioning

In the classroom, assessment of the processes pupils use is often as relevant as assessment of the work they produce. A key skill used in the classroom is observation and this is supported by questioning. It is the teacher's role to ask questions of pupils to ascertain their thinking about given tasks, including questions on strategies used or levels of motivation experienced.

Two types of questioning used by teachers in assessment are 'closed' and 'open'. A closed question provides one answer only and enables the teacher to find out whether pupils know a particular fact. An open question has many possible answers and encourages pupils to draw on their previous knowledge and experience to gain an understanding of the current situation.

Marking

Marking is a regular part of classroom practice taking place inside and outside lessons. It needs to be thorough, systematic and prompt. Feedback to pupils should be constructive, informative and based on the learning objectives in which they were engaged when the task was undertaken. Black and Wiliam (1995) found that grading could be detrimental to pupil's learning, emphasizing 'competition rather than personal improvement'. In contrast the teacher giving useful advice in relation to the learning objective was far more beneficial to the pupil's development. Good marking motivates the pupils to achieve more by commenting on the quality of the work completed and setting targets for future learning.

Marking has two distinct stakeholders: the pupil and the teacher. From the teacher's perspective marking should:

- check pupils' understanding of the learning objective;
- direct future lesson planning and teaching;
- track pupils' progress;
- enable work to be set at appropriate levels;
- enable formative feedback.

From the pupils' perspective marking should help them to:

- recognize progress;
- identify areas of strength and weakness;
- determine areas for future development;
- become more motivated and value their learning.

Marking involves a variety of skills. The teacher needs to check for accuracy of content and not focus solely on presentation. When marking, the teacher should focus on the purpose of the work and whether it was to establish a level of under-standing, to ensure the completion of a task, to judge progress in relation to a topic and concepts within the topic area, or to make an overall assessment of pupils' attainment over a long period of time.

To do this the teacher will need to:

- determine whether the learning objectives have been met;
- identify areas of strength;
- identify areas of weakness;
- consider the next steps to improve the pupil's learning;
- provide a written comment that gives accurate feedback and motivates the pupil;
- provide an achievable target for future learning.

Task 7.4

- With your mentor decide on a piece of work you are going to teach and mark.
- Identify how you will set, mark and report your assessments.
- Having completed the task, evaluate how effective you were in achieving your objective.

Marking is an activity that is public – all who have access to pupils' books can see what has been marked or ignored. It is open to scrutiny by parents, colleagues, mentors, senior teachers and OFSTED and can provide a quick judgement about the teacher's approach. It is always good practice to be consistent, systematic and constructive in the marking of pupils' work.

Using everyday classroom tasks for assessment

Assessment is both essential and integral to effective teaching and pupil learning. As discussed earlier there are many different ways to assess pupils' work. The everyday classroom task is an excellent way of collecting a variety of information about pupils. Conventional marking is just one form of assessment; observation, questioning and listening are also key components of the skills of assessment, all of which the trainee needs to practise and develop. Evidence of pupils' work can be collected from:

- oral work: reading, discussion, questions, role play;
- written work: drafts, notes, scripts, poems, investigations, experiment notes;
- design work: models, drawings, construction;
- physical skills: co-ordination and manipulative skills.

A broad range of examples of pupils' potential allows the teacher to gain evidence of progress from a wide variety of activities, and as a result report the extent of pupil achievement.

Task 7.5

With your mentor discuss and identify ways in which you can collect evidence from classroom activities you plan for your pupils.

Monitoring class work will produce evidence of learning. Both formal and informal classroom assessments are important as they allow teachers to make judgements about pupil progress and alter their style of teaching to facilitate learning. Feedback from pupils enables teachers to measure the effectiveness of lessons.

As a teacher there is a need to distinguish between monitoring informally through integrating assessment tasks into normal activities, and setting formalized tests. For example, is the teacher listening to a child read as a means of encouraging and estimating progress, or is it a means of predicting the pupil's reading level? Similarly in science investigations, is the teacher questioning to assess level or to help move pupils' thinking along in a positive way? In each case pupils need to know what the teacher is doing and why. The purpose of the assessment and monitoring has to be clear to teacher and pupil alike. Kyriacou (1992: 114) clearly states that:

> Skilful assessment of pupils' progress in meeting the National Curriculum targets depends very much on how well assessment tasks are integrated within normal class work without disrupting or interfering unduly with the normal progress of learning.

This is the key to successful monitoring of progress by teachers.

Homework

Homework is increasingly becoming a high priority in all phases of education. As this is an influential practice, it is important to identify the uses and purpose of homework setting. Homework has many functions, some more pertinent than others, depending on the phase and age group of the pupils. However, pupils of all ages should be encouraged to take their learning home to explore with parents and peers. Homework can be thought of as:

- promoting autonomous learning;
- promoting investigative and research skills;
- consolidating and extending learning;
- extending and challenging understanding;
- encouraging study skills;
- providing opportunities for independent private study;
- encouraging parental involvement in learning;
- extending the school day;
- developing pupils' organizational skills;
- providing feedback on learning difficulties.

Homework tasks in all phases of education are important in providing feedback about pupil performance and how future lesson planning may be directed. Homework can be a useful mechanism for pupils to learn how to organize their own learning through a variety of skills, such as researching, collecting material, memorizing spellings or tables. Homework should not just focus on the learning of new material, the revision of prior learning for tests, or routine tasks to reinforce learning – homework should also be creative, investigative and motivating. As a teacher it is important to understand the purpose of homework, and why the chosen tasks are set. This applies equally to the pupils. Pupils must not only understand the task set, but they must also appreciate its value and the worth of completing the task. For this to happen all homework must be marked and incorporated into the pupils' future learning.

When setting homework consider the following carefully, especially when working with very young and immature pupils:

- give very *clear and simple instruction* as to what to do and how it should be presented;
- say when it is going to be collected or needs to be submitted – when, where and to whom are essential elements;
- show where it fits in to the overall learning taking place;
- say how it will be assessed, including the criteria that will be used;
- indicate where it fits into the National Curriculum levels of assessment.

It is important to remember that if pupils are to learn from the tasks that have been set, they have to engage with the material or questions given to them. Homework should be planned into a lesson; it should not be thought of as an add-on activity. It should be well thought out and be an extension to pupils' learning.

Task 7.6

- Identify and plan a creative homework task for a specific age group of pupils.
- Devise a marking framework for the homework task.
- Discuss this and the outcomes with your mentor.

Task 7.7

Discuss with your mentor how you can collect a variety of homework tasks that will motivate and promote learning in your phase or age group of pupils.

Statutory assessment

Chapter 2 gave a clear explanation of the National Curriculum. Here the role of assessment is explained within the National Curriculum framework. It is essential that you have a clear understanding of what the statutory requirements for assessment are within a given stage. Each stage has a series of assessments:

Foundation Stage: 5-year-olds, Foundation Stage Profile
Key Stage 1: 7-year-olds, NC Levels 1–3
Key Stage 2: 11-year-olds, NC levels 3–5
Key Stage 3: 14-year-olds, NC levels 3–8
Key Stage 4: 16-year-olds, GCSE

Teacher assessment contributes to the end of Key Stage assessment, and assessment of the core subjects – English, mathematics and science – is conducted through national tests.

Teacher assessment is through Attainment Target Level Descriptions. These provide an overview of the knowledge, skills and understanding required to meet each of the levels in the subject. In their assessment teachers identify what they consider to be a 'best fit' of their pupils' work to the National Curriculum levels. The Qualifications and Curriculum Authority (QCA) has produced many exemplars to help this process at each Key Stage and level for all subjects. Trainees should familiarize themselves with the QCA material and use it where appropriate in their planning and preparation of lessons and schemes of work.

Key features of the written tests are:

- test markers are appointed by external agencies, except for Foundation and KS1;
- external agencies are used for moderation and quality assurance procedures;

- there is an appeals procedure with respect to remarking;
- test results are reported to parents alongside the teacher assessment.

Foundation Stage: key features

Teachers have always informally assessed pupils on their entry to school. A formalized baseline assessment became a legal requirement for all 4–5-year olds from 1998. This assessment mechanism was replaced in 2003 by the Foundation Stage Profile that allows teachers to assess pupils across their first year at school in relation to national assessment scales.

The assessment scales have a direct relationship to the Curriculum Guidance for the Foundation Stage and are in the six areas of learning:

1. Personal, social and emotional development.
2. Communication, language and literacy.
3. Mathematical development.
4. Knowledge and understanding of the world.
5. Physical development.
6. Creative development.

Assessment is through normal classroom practice, including observation and questioning. It is based on the principle of assessment for learning. Teachers assess the pupils' current knowledge, skills and understanding in order to provide learning experiences that are relevant and that motivate the pupils.

Key Stages 1, 2 and 3: key features

Pupils are assessed as they complete each Key Stage of the National Curriculum. The assessments are twofold, through structured tasks and tests and through teacher assessment, and have equal status. At KS1 pupils complete tests and tasks in English and mathematics. Teacher assessments are made in English, mathematics and science. At KS2, English, mathematics and science are assessed through tasks and tests and through teacher assessment. At KS3, English, mathematics and science are assessed through tests and through teacher assessment.

The tasks are activities that must be carried out as specified in the QCA documents. These are led by the teacher. The tests are formal written assessments that are completed by the pupils. At KS2 and 3 the tests are timed. Optional materials are available for those working above or below the level of the tests.

Marking of the KS1 tests takes place in school and is moderated by the LEA. At KS2 and 3 the tests are marked and moderated externally and the results and test scripts are returned to the school for purposes of analysis.

Teacher assessment is undertaken by determining which Level Description 'best fits' the performance of each pupil in each Attainment Target. Teachers use the evidence they have collected across the year and Key Stage to decide the most appropriate level. Additional QCA test material is available in Years 3, 4, 5, 7 and 8 to support teachers in making their teacher assessment judgements. Although this material is optional it has been adopted for use by many schools.

Task 7.8

Look at the level descriptors for your subject. With your mentor discuss and identify the knowledge, skill and understanding required for a given topic that you will be teaching during your school-based experience.

Key features of GCSE

The General Certificate of Secondary Education (GCSE) exemplifies the work of Key Stage 4. The end of Key Stage 4 assessment is the externally taken examinations of the various GCSE exam boards. The main features of the GCSE system include:

- a balance between course work and final examinations; the percentage of course work taken into account varies from subject to subject;
- differentiation through tiered papers: mathematics has three tiers, most of the other subjects have two tiers, one that covers grades G-C and the other that covers grades D-A;
- an exceptional performance grade of A*.

GCSE course work

This part of the GCSE is based on teacher assessment and it is very important for teachers to understand their role in it. All course work should be within the ability and attainment of pupils, it should allow for creativity and individuality, and it should be educationally valid.

Task 7.9

Within your subject area explore the use and assessment of course work at GCSE level.

Teacher-based assessment

It has been stated earlier in this chapter that teachers are assessing pupils in a variety of ways all the time. But what is teacher-based assessment and how is it functional in the classroom at all phases of education? Teacher-based assessment can include:

- *Written assessments.* These can motivate pupils to study and learn in preparation for a formal test – these can be times tables, spelling, reading a short paragraph, fact tests, vocabulary or reasoning tests.
- *Observation-based assessments.* These look at pupil performance. Practical skills such as art, drama, experimentation, etc can all be assessed by the teacher.
- *Communication-based assessments.* Pupils reading aloud, speaking a foreign language, discussing and arguing about pre-researched work.

All assessment activities need to have purpose, clarity and a clear focus. There are several points that need to be considered prior to planning any assessment activity:

- Teacher-based assessment over a long period of time should be varied to cover a large range of learning outcomes.
- The assessment task should actually assess what was intended to be assessed.
- Assessment should relate to intended learning outcomes appropriate to the National Curriculum requirements or as part of a particular course of study.
- All assessment tasks should be fair by way of assessing work covered, so that pupils have the opportunity to perform well.

It is important to realize that the nature of the assessment activity will determine the teacher's action in actually marking the assessment. If the pupil is expected to read aloud, the teacher is expected to listen. If a pupil performs a practical task the teacher is expected to observe. Hence the teacher's role in this type of assessment activity is crucial. The responsibility of assessing lies with the teacher irrespective of whether it is in the primary or secondary sector of education. Each phase of education has its statutory demands and it is the responsibility of trainees, with the help of their mentor and university/college tutor, to understand and be able to implement them within a working classroom situation.

Task 7.10

- Develop a teacher-based assessment activity for a particular skill.
- Discuss this with your mentor.
- Attempt to conduct the assessment and evaluate your success.
- Reflect with your mentor.

If assessment tasks relate to individual pupils, the teacher's classroom management skills become essential. This is because, when a teacher focuses attention on one pupil rather than 'scanning' the classroom to make sure learning is taking place, the rest of the class needs to be kept on-task. When planning single pupil assessment activities consideration must be given to planning the nature of the task or tasks the rest of the class will be doing while you assess the individual pupil.

Essentials of teacher-based assessment

- Do not over-assess – quantity of assessment is no substitute for quality teaching and quality assessment.
- Plan work or topic areas thoroughly so that assessment becomes an integral part of the planning routine rather than an add-on activity.
- Spend time developing assessment strategies and techniques. Don't rush a design of a test: a bad test shows nothing; a good test helps both teacher and pupil.
- Incorporate National Curriculum requirements into the planning of assessment criteria.
- Get a second opinion – show colleagues and mentors the assessment procedures you intend using. A more distanced view can help you focus on what you actually want to assess, rather than what you think you are assessing.

Recording and reporting

As stated earlier, record keeping links monitoring and assessment with reporting. However, if this activity is to be completed efficiently and effectively some questions have to be addressed. Why do teachers keep records of pupils work, whom are they for, and what is their value?

A prime purpose of record keeping is to help monitor the progress of individual pupils and plan their future learning. Ofsted continually states the importance and need for teachers to keep good records of pupil progress. One of the many reasons for this is that they show that teachers have fulfilled their statutory responsibilities such as delivering the National Curriculum and monitoring pupils' progress through the framework of targets and level descriptors.

There are three main functions of record keeping, discussed below:

1. to monitor and plan ahead;
2. to inform others;
3. to demonstrate that these purposes are being properly followed.

Task 7.11

Investigate your school/department's record-keeping policy. Identify all the records and reports you are likely to be involved in throughout your placement.

Thinking about good and effective record keeping requires an understanding of the usefulness of records. There are two areas that need to be addressed: the detail/quantity of information to be recorded, and how the information is going to be used. Records that are very detailed, dense and incomprehensible have little chance of being used. Headington (2000) advises that records should be objective, succinct and purposeful.

The three main functions of good record keeping need to be recognized, understood and implemented throughout the trainees' teaching placement. Trainees should appreciate the importance of the three functions and monitor how they affect or change their practice.

To monitor and plan ahead

The type of information teachers collect and record should relate directly to learning objectives and so help the planning of future lessons and schemes of work. It should also help identify specific problems that individual pupils may have. Planning in this context requires teachers to build upon previous progress and ensure that they allow the pupil to progress in an adequate way by covering learning areas in breadth and depth. The trainees' own monitoring of pupil progress through their teaching placement should be given to the class teacher prior to leaving. These records will enable the class teacher to establish where the pupils are, the work they have covered and the nature of the progress the pupils have made. Passing on information is a key to monitoring the continuity and progression of learning.

The teachers' lesson plans and evaluations are a starting point for information gathering, followed closely by their monitoring and assessment records. All teachers keep a record book of some kind in which they record marks, grades, comments and scores. How the trainee uses this is key to accurate records and the monitoring of whole-class activities as well as individual pupil progress. Many approaches may be taken; an example is given in Table 7.1. Recording in this way provides a quick visual check on work completed, nature of the task, grade obtained, work outstanding through absence or incomplete work submitted, and targets to be met through future learning.

This example is a starting point. As trainees progress, recording skills will develop and become more refined. This will be reflected by including the levels they have reached as described by the National Curriculum assessment framework.

Table 7.1 Example of pupil work record

Take a double page from a standard record book for each class. List class names down the left-hand side. At the top of each column write the date and title of work set plus grading.

Pupil name	Date and title of task Grade/ID	Date and title of task Grade/ID	Date and title of task Grade/ID	Date and title of task Grade/ID	Analysis and targets
	2.4.03	10.4.03	18.4.03	26.4.03	Found difficulty with abstract terms
John	fractions 9/10	decimals 7/10	algebra 5/10	end of unit test 6/10	Link work with fractions

Task 7.12

Devise a record-keeping journal that shows your understanding and progress in recording pupils' attainment.

To inform others

Records are kept not only to monitor progress of individual pupils but to provide evidence and so enable the teacher to inform a variety of audiences as to the work, progress and problems encountered when teaching a whole class as well as the individual pupil. There are three main areas in reporting that the trainee needs to be aware of:

1. Reporting to parents.
2. Reporting to pupils.
3. Reporting to colleagues/departments/the whole school.

Each requires different skills and use of evidence, but each type of report has to be informed by and based on evidence.

Reporting to parents

The parent has a key role to play in a pupil's learning and development, so reporting to parents has to be effective, meaningful and coherent. Schools normally offer three routes to obtaining information about their pupils' progress: written reports, parents' evenings, and individual meetings with the class teacher or tutor. Written reports to parents must be provided at least once during each academic year. Reports should indicate the progress of the pupil against the curriculum followed and give targets for future development. At the end of each Key Stage reports must also include the results of the pupil's National Curriculum assessment, comparative data from the school and national data from the previous year.

Task 7.13

With your mentor discuss and examine the school's policy of reporting to parents. Examine examples as a way of understanding how your school reports progress to parents.

Task 7.14

Ask to help with a parents' evening. With your mentor prepare a series of reports for a set of pupils; they should show both academic and pastoral progress.

Reporting to pupils

Teachers report to pupils orally and in writing, both formally and informally, focusing on attainment and approach. They may smile, say, 'Well done' or write, 'A good analysis of the situation'. Pupils make greater sense of this feedback if they are involved in the assessment process and are given the opportunity to use assessment for learning.

If pupils know what they are to learn and can recognize when this is achieved they will become more motivated in their learning (Clarke, 2001). It is the responsibility of the teacher to involve the pupils by sharing learning objectives, discussing approaches and outcomes and working with them to develop and track targets for future learning.

Reporting to colleagues

This is a skill that trainees will need to develop throughout their teaching career. When on placement trainees will need to keep a close record of the curriculum covered, including topic areas, texts used, exact areas of the schemes of work covered, homework set, extra activities covered and assessment results. All this information will have to be passed to the class teacher when the placement has been completed. The information is an important record: it informs colleagues of problems that may have been encountered by pupils during the teaching of certain topics. The records should be specific, with examples of where and how the pupil or pupils encountered problems, the targets set, the action taken and the consequence of this. Trainees should appreciate that detailed records are also a means of monitoring their own practice in relation to pupils' learning successes or difficulties.

Summary

Monitoring and assessment takes place throughout primary and secondary schools in many different forms. Recording and reporting are essential means of tracking and analysing progress and informing others of the outcome of learning. Assessment *for* learning is essential to the formative development of teaching and learning. Assessment *of* learning enables progress to be measured and analysed at key points, to monitor pupil performance within and beyond the school.

References

Black, P and Wiliam, D (1995) *Inside the Black Box*, King's College, London

Clarke, S (2001) *Unlocking Formative Assessment*, Hodder and Stoughton, London

Daugherty, R (1995) *National Curriculum Assessment: A review of the policy 1987–1994*, Falmer Press, London

DES (1988) *National Curriculum Task Group on Assessment and Testing: A report*, DES, London

Department for Education and Employment (DfEE) (1998a) *Requirements for Courses of Initial Teacher Training*, Circular 4/98, HMSO, London

DfEE (1998b) *Baseline Assessment of Pupils Starting Primary School*, Circular 6/98, HMSO, London

Gipps, C (1994) *Beyond Testing: Towards a theory of educational assessment*, Falmer Press, London

Gipps, C and Stobart, G (1993) *Assessment: A teacher's guide to the issues*, Hodder and Stoughton, London

Headington, R (2000) *Monitoring, Assessment, Recording, Reporting and Accountability: Meeting the standards*, David Fulton, London

Kyriacou, C (1992) *Effective Teaching in Schools*, Simon & Schuster Education, Padstow

Sutton, R (1991) *Assessment: A framework for teachers*, Routledge, London

Task Group on Assessment and Testing (TGAT) (1988) *A Report*, DES, London

TTA (2002) *Qualifying to Teach*, DfES, London

8   Special Needs in the 'Mainstream'

Steve Alsop and Robin Luth

Introduction

Special Educational Needs (SEN) can be a highly emotive subject for both teachers and parents. Presently, over 90 per cent of pupils with SEN are educated in mainstream schools (Morris, 1998) and with the recent publication of the Government's Green Paper, *Excellence for All Children*, the commitment to further integration of children with significant sensory, cognitive and physical difficulties into ordinary classrooms is affirmed. It will be incumbent upon Local Educational Authorities (LEAs) to offer parents of a child with a special educational need a place in a mainstream school *before* other specialist placements are considered. Therefore, it is likely that a teacher entering the classroom for the first time will experience an increasingly complex environment, populated by many pupils exhibiting a variety of impediments, requiring a range of teaching styles and resources to ensure equality of opportunity and treatment.

Since the first edition of this book in 2000, much of the legislation surrounding the equality of opportunity and treatment in SEN has been heavily strengthened and given teeth. Hopefully this will ensure that those with a special educational need or specific disability cannot be unfairly treated by any part of the education system or suffer discrimination by any educational institution. The major legislative instruments that have been placed on the statute books since 1999 and have greatly influenced the present legal morphology of the education world are explained in the following paragraphs.

The Code of Practice on the Identification and Assessment of Special Educational Needs (DFE, 2001)

This is a heavily revised version of the previous Code of Practice that revolutionized the whole system of SEN in 1994. It truncates the five-stage model of identification into a shorter and, apparently, less bureaucratic three-stage model that places greater emphasis on the class teacher to identify and plan suitable material for an increasingly diverse cohort of students within the mainstream classroom.

This Code demarcates SEN as the responsibility of all teachers working within any school – not solely the responsibility of the Learning Support Department (LSD). The identification, assessment, planning and monitoring of pupils with SEN are therefore important skills to be learnt by any new teacher and ones that will assume greater importance as the philosophy of integration gains momentum.

The Disability Discrimination Act (Education Amendment 2001)

This Act makes it illegal to discriminate against or obstruct the rights of pupils with specific disabilities or impediments to access and fully participate in mainstream education unless it is reasonably proved that a school cannot meet the needs of a particular pupil. LEAs and schools are now having to do everything that is reasonable to limit such rejection, minded that it is open to legal challenge from a variety of parental and legal bodies. Both the LEA and school must be seen to act reasonably and within the law at all times to ensure that discrimination in terms of school admission, buildings access and curriculum provision does not take place as a result of a physical impairment, sensory difficulty or emotional impediment. The DDA has far-reaching consequences for schools and for the diversity of need in the student body for young teachers working in the emerging legal and pedagogic culture of our schools.

So how does a newly qualified teacher (NQT) gain the knowledge and understanding to cope with students with a complex and serious range of challenges that impede social, emotional and educational progress in the context of a busy and complex school environment? This chapter will attempt to provide helpful suggestions to teachers embarking upon their careers in an era which, paradoxically, is applying ever increasing egalitarian expectations to those whose training in SEN is at best minimal.

In essence, what follows is an introduction to a complex and multifaceted area. Our aim is to provide a clarification of the class teachers' role within the context of recent legislation and the new skills they need to acquire. We will examine the Code of Practice and outline how the process of identification and assessment is carried out by both the school and the LEA, and discuss the role and responsibilities of the class teacher, with suggestions for teaching strategies. We then propose a basic framework of approaches that will enable the class teacher to provide access to the school curriculum for all.

Objectives

By the end of this chapter, the trainee teacher will have:

- an awareness of the recent legislation in SEN (in particular, the Code of Practice);
- an understanding of how SEN operates in ordinary schools and the class teacher's role in SEN;
- an appreciation of the processes involved in the assessment of special needs;
- an awareness of ways of structuring lessons that are likely to succeed in meeting pupils' special needs.

Integration versus inclusion: semantics and process

The Warnock Report of 1978 and the subsequent 1981 Education Act placed a great deal of emphasis on the meaning of the word 'integration'. The term was the hopeful genesis for a new era of SEN provision that focused on the meeting of special educational needs in mainstream settings and saw the special needs students 'fitting' into mainstream school culture and adapting to the challenges such an experience would expose him or her to. Integration meant exactly that: the student would be integrated into existing curriculum structures, school routines and access philosophies that took little account of the actual needs of the SEN student.

The thrust of the legislation from 1994 onwards attempted a semantic change to emphasize the weaknesses inherent in a system that saw the philosophy of integration as a pivotal factor in creating a world of equity and opportunity for SEN students. The philosophy of 'inclusion' was coined to challenge the stable and passive culture that had been created by those whose preoccupation with the 'integration' led to a pretty conservative world that did little to challenge the institutional impediments placed before students with disability and SEN.

Inclusion was promoted as challenging the school or institution to change dramatically to accommodate the needs of the SEN student. The curriculum, timetabling and physical access to the building would all have to change in order to meet the needs of the pupil. In short, instead of the integrated student 'fitting' into the school, the philosophy of inclusion sees the school changing to 'fit' the needs of the student. Inclusion sees the school reflecting on its whole management process and organically adapting to the needs of a wide diversity of included students and constantly attempting to facilitate their educational, social and emotional development. Integration placed little burden on the school's existing policies or practices, negating its obligation to think about the challenges that social and educational change would inevitably bring.

What is a Special Educational Need?

All children have particular needs – some individuals will prefer some topics, teaching styles and learning approaches to others and all classrooms have a range of abilities. However, in the UK, the term 'special educational need' has a distinct definition. The DFE defines a child as having a special educational need if:

> He or she has a learning difficulty which calls for special educational provision to be made for him or her. A child has a learning difficulty if he or she:
>
> (a) has a significant greater difficulty in learning than the majority of children of the same age
> (b) has a disability which either prevents or hinders the child from making use of educational facilities of a kind provided for children of the same age in schools within the area of the local educational authority
> (c) is under five and falls within the definition at (a) or (b) above or would do if special educational provision was not made for the child. (DFE, 2001)

This style of comparative definition can be traced back to the Warnock Report of 1978 (DES, 1978) and the subsequent Education Act of 1981 (DES, 1981). Prior to these reports, special needs was seen as constituting only about 2 per cent of the school population – those, predominantly, educated in special schools, units or classes. The Warnock Report broadened the definition of SEN and highlighted the 20 per cent (the famous one in five) of all school pupils who may at some time or another be in need of some form of special provision. The 1981 Education Act brought about changes in SEN responsibilities and procedures. LEAs and school governors were required to make provision for SEN and parents were included in the assessment processes and had a right of appeal. The Act re-emphasized the two groups of special needs pupils: the larger group, the 20 per cent, who would have their learning requirements met within an ordinary provision, and the smaller subgroup of these pupils (about 2 per cent of pupils) whose needs require special provision, with the LEA obliged to provide a statement of their needs.

The range of special needs is extremely diverse and any one pupil can exhibit a combination of need in any educational setting. Their impact on the learning of the student and the learning of other students might also change over time and from classroom context to classroom context. The main special educational needs are:

1. cognitive and learning difficulties (including specific learning difficulties);
2. autistic spectrum difficulties;
3. social, emotional and behavioural difficulties;
4. sensory and physical difficulties;
5. communication and interaction difficulties.

Although these groups are useful as an overview, it is important to be cautious when generalizing about pupils' needs. It is inexact to assume that a pupil will fall into any one of these groups as he or she is likely to exhibit a combination of special needs. It is also inappropriate to assume that because a pupil has a learning difficulty, he or she may not be in the superior range of intelligence. For example, many pupils who exhibit Emotional and Behavioural Difficulties (EBD) are also formatively assessed to be in the high average or superior range of intelligence, as are students who present with specific learning difficulties in literacy acquisition (SPLD). Similarly, a student who may be described as having Moderate Learning Difficulties (MLD) may well evidence a variety of emotional and behavioural difficulties as a result of feelings of frustration and anger at not being able to complete classroom tasks. The labelling and categorization of students with SEN need very careful interpretation; nevertheless, the categories serve a purpose here for the identification and discussion of need.

1. Cognitive and learning difficulties

Students whose needs are best described in this category can exhibit a profound combination of complex physical and cognitive handicaps. Equally, they may just have difficulties with literacy and numeracy skills and present with little difficulties. This group also includes those students who evidence specific learning difficulties and present with dyslexia-type problems.

Specific learning difficulties

Students with SPLD present a frustrating deficit in spelling, writing or number skills. This is the appropriate name for the condition labelled 'dyslexia'. Many 'dyslexic' students are in the high average band of ability and are completely frustrated by their inability to grasp simple spelling patterns or number bonds. Research continues into the particular causal factors of SPLD, with retentive memory processing probably being to blame in the areas of aural and visual short-term memory. SPLD students need qualified teachers who understand the need for specially constructed teaching programmes. 'Dyscalculia' is now becoming a more useful term for 'mathematical dyslexia'. There are many students with SPLD in mainstream classrooms.

2. Autistic spectrum difficulties

Autistic pupils present a variety of social, emotional, behavioural and communication difficulties and many exhibit behavioural problems that preclude them from an inclusive education. However, some students with a condition named Asperger's Syndrome can progress very well in the inclusive, mainstream environment. Their intellectual skills are usually above average and they are well placed in the mainstream curriculum although they will exhibit varying degrees of social and emotional needs. Asperger's Syndrome has received recent attention because of the extraordinary talents of Stephen Wiltshire, the teenager who has the ability to visualize and depict buildings in fine detail.

3. Social, emotional and behavioural difficulties

With the current drive to include all students within mainstream settings, no other group is causing more controversy and debate in schools and universities. The term 'EBD' means many things to many people. People mostly relate to the 'behaviour' component of this group and visualize aggression, disruption, distraction and lesson-stopping aberrant behaviour from students who are rude, out of control and impossible to bargain with! They tend to forget that the 'emotional' component of the term describes a student whose emotional development may have been affected by terribly traumatic events or neuro-chemical conflicts that drive inappropriate behaviours in social contexts. Such students may have suffered multiple bereavement or physical or sexual abuse and are as challenged as any group in society. They are undoubtedly the most researched, with many books advocating many psychodynamic and behaviourist responses to their management needs at both a group and an individual level. There is no doubt that these students are difficult to teach, but they deserve as much empathy as any other child in need, if not more, as it can be hard to empathize with somebody who is intent on wrecking your lessons!

Trainee teachers are frequently frustrated when dealing with students deemed to have EBD. Good communication with more experienced colleagues and a whole-school behavioural management system go a long way to help sustain confidence in dealing with these students and in meeting their needs in a mainstream environment.

4. Sensory and physical difficulties

Pupils with varying degrees of physical, visual and hearing impairment are frequently placed in mainstream schools. They will usually be statemented or on the way to being correctly assessed and supported by specialist teachers working on a peripatetic basis. They should also have access to an array of specialist resources that enable and facilitate curriculum access.

It is important to consider carefully the physical learning environment for these pupils. For example, it is essential that you read the school records of all the pupils you teach to ensure that those children who wear audio aids or need glasses are correctly located in the classroom. Students with physical disability will need their access to the curriculum carefully planned to ensure that the school and classrooms are made fully accessible to wheelchair users. Remember when teaching those students with such difficulties that you see the student and not the wheelchair and don't generalize about disability and intellectual performance. Our experience suggests that those individuals with a degree of physical handicap in our mainstream schools won't let you! It is important that you recognize and understand the needs of these pupils as well as providing a suitable learning environment.

5. Communication and interaction difficulties

This category is new to the revamped Code but hugely deserves its place as it represents a group of children who may present as being difficult as a result of a combination of speech and language, neural organic or other medical, autistic-type difficulties that require further and complex medical analysis of their needs. Certainly the link between their early emotional and linguistic development has had a significant impact on their ability to learn and control their behaviour appropriately or interact with peers. It is not a coincidence that almost all children statemented for social, emotional and behavioural difficulties have a concomitant language problem of a significant and, largely, unresolved nature.

A note on those students defined as gifted and talented

These pupils are not defined as having a special educational need under current legislation; nevertheless, they pose a particular challenge in mainstream schooling.

It is the class teacher's responsibility to provide activities that extend the ability of these pupils, but recent research suggests that many of them are underachieving. A review by Her Majesty's Inspectorate (HMI, 1992), for instance, suggests that many exceptionally able pupils are 'insufficiently challenged' in many lessons. The phrase 'dumbing down' has been coined in the USA to refer to cases where teachers are found to provide activities that are beneath pupils' abilities. In some cases, these activities have been chosen to offset poor management techniques by keeping pupils occupied (McLaughlin, 1995). It is important as a trainee teacher that you identify pupils with exceptional ability in your subject and nurture their talents. You need to adapt the teaching and learning approaches in your classroom to cater for their advanced needs.

Task 8.1: An introduction to SEN in your classroom

Find out about the special needs of the classes you are going to teach. If possible, talk to the class teacher, form teacher and a member of the LSD. Ascertain the particular needs of the groups and any additional SEN support, if available. This information can be combined with your own experiences of observing the group. Find out if any pupils have special educational needs:

- What are these needs?
- Are any pupils statemented?
- Are there any pupils of exceptionally ability?

Observe and reflect upon how the class teacher (and any additional support) meets the needs of these pupils.

Identifying and assessing SEN

As a class teacher you have a key role in the identification of special needs. It is your responsibility to voice the initial concern regarding a pupil in your class in relation to his or her learning. The 1993 Education Act and its revisions in 1996 and 1998 and the subsequent revised Code provide a detailed analysis system for identifying, assessing, planning and monitoring SEN. The main thrust of this legislation places the school and its teachers at the forefront of the stage model that puts the school's internal procedures for identification and assessment in the first three stages and the LEA's procedures in the final stages of statementing students. The end result of this stage model is usually the issuing of a Statement of Special Educational Need for the pupil and of some extra resources that follow the pupil into his or her school. The first two stages of School Action and School Action Plus are of particular interest to the trainee teacher and for this reason we will consider them in more detail. It is important to emphasize that the model of the revised Code of Practice presented below is primarily concerned with the identification and assessment of a pupil who may be evidencing some form of learning, social, emotional, sensory or physical difficulty in the class. The result of such a process helps in the planning and monitoring of an educational programme which, in part, is individualized to help accommodate the needs of that pupil within your classroom.

School Action

School Action (SA) is the class teacher's responsibility and involves the initial registering of a concern about a pupil's learning. It is usually expressed by either a class teacher or a form tutor and so has great relevance to 'mainstream' teachers. It could be that the student has difficulty in basic skills or completing work, or evidences some emotional or sensory difficulty. In any case some form of help should be offered and this usually takes the form of an increase in differentiated worksheets or extra time given to complete tasks. The name of the student should be given to the school's Special Needs Co-ordinator (SENCO) who may decide to contact the parents. Inherent in the Code of Practice is that teachers will attempt to begin to meet the individual needs of the pupil within their own curriculum delivery and lesson planning.

School Action Plus

School Action Plus (School Action +, or SAP) is the classroom teacher and SENCO's responsibility. It also involves partnership work with a large body of other professional agencies and the LEA. In this stage an Individual Education Plan (IEP) is formulated. Concern is now increasing and the school SENCO becomes involved. The Co-ordinator will draw up an IEP, which describes in detail the type and depth of special needs and classroom strategies useful in meeting those needs. The SENCO will work alongside the class teacher, tutor, pastoral head of year and parents. Extra resources in the form of class-based support teaching are not usually available at this stage but the more detailed assessment does help with planning for that pupil's needs.

Statementing

This is principally the SENCO's responsibility, with the involvement of outside agencies. After a preview of the student's needs, the SENCO is concerned that there is a definite special educational need that requires further, detailed assessment. For this reason a range of external professionals may be asked to come into the school and help assess and identify those needs. Some assessments, for example by the student's GP or psychiatric services, may take place in the appropriate environment. The school's educational psychologist will undertake a proper assessment of the student's abilities. The SENCO will work closely with the class teachers and pastoral teachers to ensure that information is promulgated effectively. Parents are kept closely informed of the increasing level of concern about the pupil. Either the school SENCO or parent will ask that the LEA begin a formal assessment of the student's needs with the hope that the LEA will issue a Statement of Special Educational Need, which will bring some form of extra resource to the pupil. The LEA will usually ask for the following professional reports:

- school;
- parents;
- educational psychologist;
- medical;
- Social Services;
- other, e.g. speech therapist or physiotherapist.

Within 10 weeks the LEA must inform that parent whether it will issue a statement. If the decision is positive, the statement must be written and finalized within six months. Before 1994, it was perfectly possible for a student to enter a school at Year 7 and not receive the statement until he or she was in Year 10 or 11!

The LEA describes the needs in a statement and allocates extra money to the pupil. The school must then implement and provide the extra support the pupil requires. Usually this is in the form of a support teacher specializing in literacy development or behaviour, or it might be a piece of enabling equipment like a laptop computer, a hearing aid, or low vision equipment.

Task 8.2: Understanding the Code of Practice

The Code of Practice contains more detail about the procedures involved in the identification of SEN. Study the Code and make sure you are aware of your involvement and responsibilities, in particular, at School Action and School Action Plus. Consult with your mentor and ask if you can look at the Individual Education Plans for the pupils in your classes. You will need to use these when preparing your lesson.

Induction and SEN

From September 2003, NQTs have to demonstrate that they have passed certain competencies in order to be qualified practitioners. Many of these competencies have links to what is accepted good practice for teachers of any students, but some relate directly to students with SEN and have been developed to stimulate the process of inclusion as described earlier in this chapter. You will need to be fully acquainted with these competencies and demonstrate that both your theoretical knowledge and your actual practice reflect a good grounding in SEN.

The competencies involve confidence in dealing with a wide variety of SEN issues concerning identification, assessment, planning and monitoring students with SEN. There are also some relating directly to classroom management, dealing with behavioural issues and how cultural, emotional and social background can affect a student's capacity to learn. The competencies are divided into three groups and each one has specific skills listed relating to SEN.

The first concerns your professional practice and values in the relationships you build with other staff and the ethos of the school. It particularly mentions demonstrating an awareness and an appreciation of working with support staff and learning support assistants. It also sets out expectations that you demonstrate and value the communication process with parents and carers – especially crucial with parents of students with SEN.

Secondly, competencies are examined in relation to your knowledge of your subject and issues relating to the cognitive, emotional, social and cultural background of those you teach. An understanding of the main tenets involved in the Code of Practice is also listed in this section.

Finally, a section that relates directly to your competencies as a teacher examines your ability to plan and deliver lessons to pupils of varying abilities and, crucially, that potential is assessed. The actual competencies relate to your capacity to produce lesson content that meets the needs of a range of pupils and takes into account your understanding and practice of differentiation. It also seeks to test your competency in behavioural management and your knowledge of strategies that can be used to produce a good working climate in your classroom.

In order to facilitate your growth in the basic NQT competencies, we now move on to examine how you can best acquire an understanding of SEN in a school-based setting and offer advice on how best you can seek help in your first year. Further information on this can be found at www.teachers.net/professionaldevelopment/opportunities/nqt/induction.

SEN in your school

The arrangement for the education of special needs pupils varies between different LEAs and different schools. As a trainee teacher you are most likely to become involved with special needs as a consequence of your subject teaching and any form tutor responsibilities. All schools are required to have a SENCO and special needs policies, designed to support and meet the needs of both pupils and staff. The number of designated SEN staff will vary with the size and type of school as well as with the number of pupils on roll who have been identified as having special needs.

The SENCO will often participate in school INSET to clarify and improve the understanding of all issues relating to SEN within the mainstream spectrum. He or she will also distribute the paperwork that is used to identify, assess, plan and monitor the learning of all pupils with SEN. This might include, typically, the Special Needs Register, copies of IEPs and any relevant psychometric testing data. In some schools this paperwork is widely available to all staff; in other schools information is more restricted.

To provide an illustration of the institutional structure of SEN provision, in the following sections we document two indicative case schools. The first school is a large inner city comprehensive, the second is a one-form entry first school.

School 1: SEN in an inner city secondary mainstream school

Enford Grange is a large, inner city comprehensive with a diverse multicultural mix. It has 1,200 pupils on roll arranged as a five-form entry. There are 345 pupils on the Special Needs Register with 55 of those having a statement of SEN. Of those on the Register some 200 are at Stage 2 of the Code of Practice model and a further 96 are at either Stage 3 or Stage 4. Many of the pupils who exhibit Stage 1 difficulties are not formally identified and this presents challenges to the class teacher.

The school's LSD has three full-time teachers, including the SENCO who is head of the department, and two specialist SPLD staff plus seven learning support assistants who are on part-time contracts and deal solely with the needs of statemented pupils. The LSD operates a tripartite system of intervention to help meet the needs of the students on the special needs register:

1. In-class support. The supporting of statemented pupils with either teacher or learning support assistant by on-task focusing and the modification of materials.

2. Withdrawal in groups for reading development. Some 60 students in groups of 10 are withdrawn for a corrective reading scheme four times a week to boost deficits in the acquisition of literacy skills.
3. Individual withdrawal for severe SPLD.

Some students with severe difficulties and demonstrating little ability in the area of comprehension of written or spoken language are withdrawn for very intensive work to boost basic classroom skills. These students are withdrawn four times a week either individually or in groups of two.

The department can also draw on the expertise of various outside agencies that can offer specialist advice and materials for those students on the Register above Stage 3. These might typically include:

- educational psychologist (one visit every three weeks);
- educational social workers (one visit every three weeks);
- behavioural support teachers (as necessary);
- peripatetic teachers of the visually and hearing impaired (one visit per half term);
- referrals to child guidance clinics for students with severe behavioural problems;
- other satellite professionals including speech therapists, physiotherapists and occupational therapists.

The department primarily identifies and assesses pupils who may have a significant learning difficulty. It then promulgates that information to all other concerned staff within the school and advises on teaching strategies and materials to help meet the needs. Obviously with so many pupils on the Register, the response in meeting those needs must be whole-school and it is the responsibility of all teachers to plan and monitor effective curriculum resources for all pupils. It is probable that within the school, large departments such as the core NC departments nominate one teacher to act as the SALT (Subject Area Liaison Teacher) to liaise with the LSD.

School 2: special needs in a first school (ages 5–11)

The Cedars School is a one-form entry first school with 150 pupils (ages 4 – 7). There are 18 pupils on the Special Needs Register with three pupils having a statement of need – two for visual impairment and one for EBD. Six pupils are at Stage 2, and five at Stage 3/4 of the Code. Special needs is coordinated by the science coordinator who receives an additional scale point for the SEN responsibility. The SENCO is allocated two hours timetable relief per week, which takes place during school assembly. The school operates a policy of inclusion and the SENCO addresses the needs of pupils by:

1. liaising with staff, developing IEPs and providing any necessary INSET;
2. coordinating the classroom assistants (parent helpers); and
3. coordinating support from outside agencies.

The headteacher has used the revenue from the statemented pupils to employ three part-time helpers. Each class teacher has a regular meeting with the SENCO (two per term), usually after school, to review the progress of any pupils on the Register as well as discussing concerns about other pupils. The SENCO is in close liaison with the LEA and other outside agencies that may typically include:

- educational psychologists (two visits per term);
- educational social workers (two visits per term);
- behavioural support (once a week);
- medical and other health visitors (six visits per term);
- an LEA peripatetic teacher of the visually impaired (two visits a week);
- LEA reading recovery support (five lessons per week for maximum of 20 weeks).

Task 8.3: Special needs in your school

Find out about SEN in your school. How does your school compare with the case schools above? Acquire a copy of your school's special needs policy (and departmental policies if available). If possible, speak to a member of staff with responsibility for special needs. Find out about any pupils in your classes (or form group) with special needs and the support mechanisms that are available.

Special needs in your classroom

Under the 1981 and 1998 Education Acts, it is the responsibility of classroom teachers to provide access to the curriculum for all pupils:

It is part of the teacher's professional role to recognise and develop the potential of individual pupils. All pupils should be encouraged throughout their school career to reach out to the limit of their capabilities. This is a formidable challenge to any school since it means that the school's expectation of every pupil must relate to their individual gifts and talents. (DES, 1981)

As a trainee teacher it is your role to ensure equality of opportunity for all your students, at any stage in the Code of Practice, to access the National Curriculum. It is especially important that your curriculum planning for all students at School Action reflects an awareness and early amelioration of any problem you may feel a student evidences.

The key to promoting access to the curriculum is to consider individual needs and then structure the classroom environment to meet these needs. The more relevant information you can gather about the background and learning style of a pupil, the more you can plan effectively in preparing suitable curriculum resources for that pupil. It is essential that learning tasks are *differentiated* to match the needs of pupils. Differentiation is complex and is closely associated with varying cognitive tasks and outcomes, for example catering for children with different abilities and work rates. While this is essential, it is also important to consider learners' emotional, physical and sensory special needs as these will also require differentiated tasks. A well-designed teaching activity will offer a challenging learning experience that pupils can achieve and that will remove any obstacles to their learning. Such a learning experience must build upon the learners' prior knowledge, be emotionally engaging, and cater for any physical and sensory needs. Learners need to be able to progress at a rate governed by their cognitive ability and not be hindered by any other special needs.

A schematic representation of four stages in planning for SEN is shown in Table 8.1. Successful planning is best achieved through the identification of needs and clear learning objectives and using this information to provide differentiated lesson activities matched to the needs of the class and opportunities for clear assessment and feedback. With this approach, it should be possible to address the needs of all members of the class – including any with special needs. As noted by the National Curriculum Council (1989) 'What is good practice in relation to special needs is good practice for all.'

Task **8.4:** A focus on differentiation

Consider the particular cognitive, emotional, sensory and physical requirements of your subject area. In what ways can you differentiate your subject teaching to provide access for children with special educational needs?

Ways of improving access for SEN pupils

In this section we suggest some ways of improving access to the curriculum for pupils with special needs. As previously noted, individual pupils often have a combination of needs so it is essential that you consult with the LSD or SENCO to

Table 8.1 Key considerations when planning for SEN

Stages of Planning	Key Considerations
1. Identification of lesson learning aims and objectives	Consult the National Curriculum Programmes of Study and identify the lesson's learning aims and objectives. Select subject matter that builds upon or extends pupils' current understanding.
2. Identification of needs	Identify the cognitive, emotional, physical and sensory special needs of individuals in the class.
3. Planning for differentiated learning	Use the information gathered in the first two stages to select the most appropriate teaching and learning approaches to engage all in the curriculum. Consider:· • The teaching style (how best can my teaching approach cater for the needs of all class members?) • The vehicle for teaching (what lesson activities are best to convey my lesson aims?) • The context for the subject (how can I make the subject both relevant and interesting?) • The physical learning environment (how can I ensure that physical and sensory-impaired pupils have full access to my teaching?) • The social environment (how can I group pupils to create an effective learning environment?)
4. Assessment, monitoring and feedback of pupil performance	How can I ensure that all pupils feel a sense of achievement? How can I best assess the performance of all pupils? (Consult the NC Level Descriptions.) How can I provide feedback to encourage all? What are my indicators of a successful lesson?

be aware of pupils' needs. Some pupils will be accompanied in your lessons by a designated SEN in-class support. If support is available it is important that you fully utilize it. If possible, speak to the teacher in advance of the lesson and make long-term plans, and consider how you can work together to meet the needs of individuals and classes – their presence and role needs to be included in your lesson planning. Try to provide them with details of the lesson subject and structure prior to it – they will offer you invaluable advice. They will be able, for example, to give you feedback on the appropriateness of the language level of your worksheets and handouts.

The following is a list of strategies we have found useful in meeting special educational needs. The list is not designed to be a recipe or panacea, but rather a collection of key points that you could find helpful in your lesson planning. In the case of statemented pupils, it is particularly important that you consult with the SENCO.

Pupils with SPLD (language and literacy)

One of the basic prerequisites for learning is that the student can read and understand the language and the texts you are placing before him or her! However, research consistently suggests that teachers use texts and worksheets for reading ages far in advance of those of the students they teach (Jones and Charlton, 1996). It is not uncommon, for example, for some children at SA in the Code to be asked to read worksheets and books designed for reading ages three, four or five years in advance of their actual abilities. The process of taking meaning from such texts is too complex and only increases their feelings of frustration and low self-esteem. Such perpetuation of failure leads to an increase in the chances of behavioural problems developing in the lessons. If you can discover the reading ages of those students who present literacy problems in your lessons and plan work that is appropriate for their abilities, it is likely that they will learn more effectively and the chance of any major disruption occurring will decrease.

As a new entrant to good classroom practice, you must bear in mind that if students are off-task for any length of time this can lead to misconduct and be a distraction to other members of the class. It may be worth your while to develop your professional skills by asking your SENCO to check the readability of your lesson worksheets and OHTs. He or she can also show you how to use a simple, diagnostic reading and spelling test – it can be quickly administered and will help you immensely in catering for the individuals who may have significant or very significant reading deficits in your lessons. You are also then contributing to an increasingly professional assessment of those students who are concerning you.

The following strategies can be used to adjust the linguistic demands of your lessons and lesson materials:

- Reduce the length of paragraphs and sentences and simplify the language.
- Write sentences that are active rather than passive ('the dog ate the cat', rather than 'the cat was eaten by the dog') and avoid complex sentence structures (e.g. subordinate clauses).
- Present material in uncluttered format, with headings and subheadings, and use illustrations.
- Print hand-written worksheets or better still use word-processing facilities.

- Move from simpler to harder tasks and keep the learner active to maintain interest.
- Use numerical pointers to break up large sections of text. For instance, in a comprehension exercise, structure the reading with indicators of the nature of the task – 'Read lines 1 to 10 and answer questions 1, 2 and 3.'

Remember that simplified text will often be longer than the original text and any linguistic audits should be performed systematically rather than randomly.

Pupils with social, emotional and behaviour difficulties (including social and communicative disorders)

Pupils with emotional and behavioural problems may present with a variety of difficulties that range from very disrupting, challenging behaviours to silent and withdrawn behaviours which can mask immense emotional upset. Students who present difficulties in emotional health or aberrant behaviour do so for many and varied reasons and a great deal of input and skill are needed in meeting their special educational needs. Problems with concentration, distraction and intolerance to rules within the classroom are commonplace and help in dealing with such difficulties needs to be orchestrated within the school and involve the expertise of many outside agencies. Most schools will operate a system that utilizes a multidisciplinary team involving professionals from education, health and social services.

It must be remembered that some of the students who have EBD and present you with your greatest challenges in the classroom are also the most deserving in that their home environment and previous experiences are often the most adverse and difficult. In all cases, liaise with the school SENCO and your line manager as many of these students benefit from a whole-school response and your experiences of them will usually be duplicated throughout the school in other teachers' classrooms.

The following points will help you cope with students who present such difficulties:

- Set firm and explicitly clear boundaries on the behaviour you expect.
- Ensure that students can succeed in the work that you set.
- Be positive at all times, as praise lifts self-esteem.
- Be consistent in your responses to behaviour that is unacceptable. Remember to reprimand the action and not the child.
- Try to find some individual time with the pupils to develop a more helpful relationship with them and decrease the anxiety they may be feeling about you as a new teacher.

Pupils with sensory impairments

You need to be aware of any pupils in your classroom with visual and hearing impairments. It is particularly important to be aware of the degree of these impairments as this will directly affect the ability of the pupil to function in your lesson. Hearing or visual impairments will vary – for example, pupils can have selective hearing impairment and be more sensitive to some sound frequencies than others (if high frequencies are lost then the higher notes of consonants will be difficult to hear; if low frequencies are lost then pupils may experience difficulties with the lower frequency vowel sounds). There are several types of visual impairment, usually classified in terms of functioning, and include totally blind pupils, pupils who can see contrasts and pupils who have difficulties in focusing. It is likely that some pupils in your class will be colour blind and as a consequence may be unable to distinguish between reds and greens – this is an important factor to be borne in mind when using coloured worksheets or recording a colour change in a chemical reaction in science. When teaching children with hearing and visual impairment you need to consider the following.

For children with hearing impairment:

- Make sure any hearing aid is worn and is functioning properly.
- Wear any additional microphones or communicators provided by the pupil – these can improve communication greatly (and remember to return them at the end of the lesson).
- Make sure that the pupil is sitting in a position where he or she is facing you and can see you clearly; remember to speak directly to pupils as much as possible.
- Make sure a pupil is looking at you when you are speaking. If a pupil is lip-reading, speak normally but make sure you do not obstruct your mouth, and repeat what classmates say during any class discussions.
- Use visual support to emphasize the key teaching points; for example, use the board or OHT to provide an overview of the lesson or give a handout with the key lesson points at the start of the lesson.
- Try to improve the acoustics of the room, for example by changing the seating arrangements or installing curtains.

For children with visual impairment:

- Make sure the visually impaired pupil is sitting close to the board, and if there are any demonstrations ensure there is appropriate lighting available. (NB: take care as some pupils may be sensitive to bright lights.)
- Try to use specific and clear language, particularly when giving instructions, and don't rely on gestures or other visual cues when teaching. Use big, bold and colourful visual aids.
- Visually impaired pupils will need more time to complete tasks – note taking, etc. – because of their disability. Pupils should not be expected to share texts.

- Familiarize yourself with any specialist equipment needed and have a working knowledge of its function.
- Develop good liaison with specialist support staff so that worksheets and texts can be enlarged or modified to meet the needs of the pupil.

Pupils with physical impairments

When dealing with pupils with a physical disability it is important to consider the pupil and not just the disability. If you need to address the disability this should be done in the context of the pupil. Many pupils with physical disabilities will be state-mented, and it is essential that you either read the statement or discuss the particular needs with the SENCO. In all cases, the key is to provide access to the curriculum – pupils need to be presented with tasks that they can achieve.

Particular needs will vary depending on the disability. For example, for pupils with wheelchairs the following considerations are essential:

- Make sure that there is space to move around the classroom; consider the suit-ability of any emergency exits.
- Check work surfaces to see if they allow access and are at a suitable height. Is there sufficient space for pupils to work collaboratively in groups? Is there sufficient space for a helper?
- Will pupils require moving in and out of the wheelchair? If so, take care and use an appropriate lifting procedure – for both your own and the pupil's safety.

Task 8.5: The special educational needs of Terry and Carly

Case study 1. Terry

Terry is a Year 9 pupil who is causing you concern. He is at SA+ of the Code of Practice assessment procedures and has great difficulty in remaining on task for any length of time, is easily distracted by others in the room and is often mobile in any class which he attends. He is above average ability but is reading some three years behind his chronological age and is very sensitive about this issue. He has supportive parents who value education. Terry has significant needs as identified by the school SENCO, and as such he is one of 30 out of 50 SA+ pupils who receive a corrective reading programme. He is withdrawn four times a week from curriculum areas to receive help in reading. He is currently concentrating on developing better reading fluency and increasing his word attack skills in subject-specific language.

Imagine that Terry is a pupil in one of your classes:

- How can you best enable Terry to access your lessons and learning objectives?
- How can you best support the SEN teacher by increasing his linguistic skills?
- How can you best contain Terry's tendency to wander off-task and cause disruption?

Case study 2. Carly

Carly is a Year 5 statemented pupil who is visually impaired and has temper tantrums. She receives 15 hours a week of primary learning support assistant time and is visited every month by a peripatetic teacher of the visually impaired. She has tremendous difficulties with low vision and cannot read normal print. As a consequence, she has poor spatial awareness and difficulties with fine motor skills.

Imagine that Carly is a pupil in one of your classes and consider:

- How can you best enable Carly to access your lessons and learning objectives?
- How can you best support the SEN teacher by increasing Carly's spatial awareness and poor fine motor skills?

Final words of advice

When starting to teach it is easy to be overawed – you are concerned with your performance, your ability to explain your subject and how the pupils will respond to your teaching. Special needs at this stage can appear daunting. Schools are very busy institutions with much ongoing day-to-day business, but more experienced colleagues will always answer questions concerning students who are causing you difficulty or you suspect evidence significant problems in learning in your classroom. Developing good liaison skills with your mentor, other teachers, senior managers and parents will enable you to function as a better teacher and reduce the stress you may feel as a result of dealing with difficult students. So learn to talk to others in order to understand and gather information about pupils who worry you. Also, remember that one differentiated worksheet completed on a computer can be saved and amended so that you are developing a reservoir of materials that can be used again and again. Special needs pupils are often the most vulnerable pupils in school but they can also be the most rewarding to teach.

References and further reading

Department for Education (2001) *Code of Practice on the Identification and Assessment of Special Educational Needs* (revised edition of 1994 Code), TSO, Norwich

Department for Education and Science (1978) *Special Educational Needs. Report of the Committee of Enquiry into the Education of Children and Young People* (The Warnock Report), HMSO, London

Department for Education and Science (1981) *The School Curriculum,* HMSO, London

Dyson, A, Clarke, C, Skidmore, D and Millward, A (1997) *New Directions in Special Needs – Innovation in mainstream schools,* Cassell, London

Farrell, P (1997) *Teaching Pupils with Learning Difficulties,* Cassell, London

Hegarty, S (1993) *Meeting Special Needs in Ordinary Schools,* Cassell, London

Her Majesty's Inspectorate (1992) *The Education of Very Able Children in Mainstream Schools,* HMSO, London

Jones, K and Charlton (eds) (1996) *Overcoming Learning and Behaviour Difficulties – Partnership with pupils,* Routledge, London

McLaughlin, M (1995) 'Re-building Teacher Professionalism in the United States', paper presented at the Re-thinking UK Education: What Next conference, The Roehampton Institute, 5 April

Montgomery, D (1989) *Managing Behaviour Problems,* Hodder and Stoughton, London

Morris, E. (1998) In … and out of the mainstream, *Guardian Education,* 9 June

National Curriculum Council (1989) *Implementing the National Curriculum – Participation by pupils with special educational needs,* Circular No. 5, NCC, York

National Curriculum Council (1993) *Special Needs and the National Curriculum: Opportunity and challenge,* NCC, York

Smutny, J (ed.) (1998) *The Young Gifted Child – Potential and promise: An anthology,* Hampton Press, London

9   The Inspection Process

Gill Nicholls

This chapter introduces the inspection process by guiding the trainee through the inspection system and the implications of the inspection process on a school and trainees should they be involved in it through the course of their training. The trainee is taken through the requirements of an inspection, considering what is needed before, during and after an OFSTED inspection.

Objectives

By the end of this chapter the trainee will have an understanding of:

- the inspection process;
- the role of OFSTED;
- the nature and timeline of an inspection;
- the role of the school;
- the part played by a trainee/teacher in the inspection process.

Introduction

OFSTED has now been in the educational system for over 10 years. In that time it has been through many restructures, but it still causes worry and anxiety in schools. Increasingly OFSTED has taken into account the nature of the school and the community it serves, as well as the need to help schools improve and become more effective. Other aspects have not changed. Schools are still graded, but the mechanism by which such grading occurs has altered over the years. Schools now play a significant role in evaluating their strengths and weaknesses through the documentation required by OFSTED. The current requirements have been redesigned and can be found in OFSTED (2003a). The new framework becomes operational in September 2003.

The inspection system

The 2003 inspection framework reflects and incorporates recent policy developments in education and school inspection processes. Inspections will now:

- promote and draw from school self-evaluation;
- evaluate leadership and management at all levels in the school;
- recognize the increasing diversification of the curriculum in many schools;
- focus more on the inclusivity of the school and how well it meets the needs of the individual pupils;
- take greater account of the views of pupils, as well as parents and staff;
- recognize that an increasing number of schools provide for children and families beyond the school day. (OFSTED, 2003a, p1)

These requirements reflect changing educational policy demands and expectations of schools. Past literature suggests that OFSTED was and continues to be a demoralizing, time-consuming and negative experience (Boothroyd *et al*, 1996; Field, 1999; Field *et al*, 1998; Parsons, 1997). More recently schools have accepted that there are positive aspects to the inspection process, such as improved learning, leadership and educational environments. The challenge of OFSTED remains an experience often complained about. However, within the accountability and quality assurance argument the OFSTED inspection process is often thought of as providing schools with the opportunity to consider and experience external evaluation of the quality of learning, teaching, leadership and management that takes place within them, by offering analysis of strengths and weaknesses and priorities for improvement.

The Role of OFSTED

Much has been written about the role of OFSTED and how it has influenced the development of schools and educational practice (Hargreaves, 1995; Learmonth, 2002; Lonsdale and Parsons, 1997). Within the statutory framework of schools OFSTED has a very specific role of quality assurance. It is accountable to the Department for Education and Skills (DfES), parents and pupils. OFSTED also provides the government with advice based on evidence collected and analysed from the inspection process.

OFSTED's inspecting remit has over the last five years extended beyond primary and secondary schools to include Early Excellence Centres, further education colleges, initial teacher education, Connexions and youth work services and local authorities. OFSTED is also responsible for childcare and early years education.

OFSTED is guided by a set of principles that apply to all inspection activities. The principles are aimed at ensuring that:

- the findings of inspections contribute to IMPROVEMENT;
- the process of inspections promotes INCLUSION;
- inspection is carried out openly with those being inspected; and
- the findings of inspection are VALID, RELIABLE and CONSISTENT. (OFSTED, 2003b, p2)

OFSTED's very specific role requires it to have clear and well-defined parameters in which it works. It is very important that trainees understand both the context and the nature of the inspection process. If the trainees' school has recently undergone or is about to go through an inspection, it is important that they understand the implications of the process and its results and demands. Becoming familiar with the OFSTED framework is a good starting point for the trainee.

The OFSTED framework

The OFSTED framework, *Inspecting Schools,* outlines the inspection process in detail. The process is divided into four parts:

Part A, The purpose of School Inspection – this describes the basis of the inspection process and models as they apply to different types of schools.
Part B, Before the Inspection – this describes the actual inspection process, setting out the requirements of registered inspectors and inspection teams.
Part C, The Evaluation Schedule – this describes the evaluation schedule, which specifies what inspectors must consider in order to judge how effective the school is, and to explain why.
Part D, Quality Assurance – explains how the quality of inspections is assured. (OFSTED, 2003b, p1)

The purpose of school inspection

The law requires that all maintained schools be inspected on a regular basis. Normally OFSTED inspections follow a six-year cycle and are proportional to need, which means that the most effective schools have the greatest gap between inspections. All OFSTED reports on schools cover four distinct areas:

1. the educational standards achieved in the school;
2. the quality of education provided by the school;
3. the quality of leadership and management, including whether the financial resources made available to the school are managed efficiently;
4. the spiritual, moral, social and cultural development of pupils in the school.

Each of these four elements is covered by the evaluation schedule of the inspection process. The inspectors have to evaluate schools on the following aspects of the school's work:

- standards achieved;
- pupils' attitudes, values and personal development;
- teaching and learning;
- the quality of the curriculum;
- the care, guidance and support of pupils;
- partnership with parents, other schools and the community;
- leadership and management;
- the areas of learning, subjects and courses of the curriculum;
- other matters that HMCI may specify. (OFSTED, 2003b, p4)

Task 9.1

Examine your current school's last OFSTED report and identify the areas of strength and weakness recorded by OFSTED. Discuss with your mentor the school's action plan and approach to addressing the weaknesses and reinforcing the school's strengths.

What types of inspections?

The current framework (2003) suggests that all inspections will have generic and common elements and aspects, but that each school's individual or special features will be respected and taken account of. Currently the inspection system embraces one type of inspection for schools in each sector: primary, secondary and post-16. Each sector has specific areas of focus within the inspection system that reflect the needs, qualities and special features of that sector. Each sector has to produce information, evidence and materials that reflect the focus of the sector.

Primary school inspections

The OFSTED framework suggests that:

Primary inspections include the evaluation and reporting of standards achieved by pupils, the quality of teaching and learning, curriculum leadership, and any other factors that have a bearing on pupils' achievements in:

- the Foundation Stage, where appropriate and in Key Stages 1, 2 and 3 as applicable;
- English (including literacy across the curriculum), maths including numeracy, science, ICT and ICT capability across the curriculum and religious education (where inspected); and
- work seen in other subjects.' (OFSTED, 2003a, p5)

Secondary school inspections

These include the evaluation and reporting standards achieved by pupils, the quality of teaching and learning, curriculum leadership, and any other factors that have a bearing on pupils' achievement in:

- the National Curriculum subjects in Key Stages 2, 3 and 4, as applicable, and religious education (where it is inspected);
- at least one vocational course in Key Stage 4;
- work seen in as many other subjects and courses as possible; and
- where applicable, a sample of between four and 13 subjects or courses in the sixth form.

Before the inspection

For many, the period before an inspection is when the actual inspection is won or lost. OFSTED notifies schools six to 10 weeks before the planned inspection. This allows the school to organize, prepare and collect documentation in advance. The framework (OFSTED, 2003a, pp12–24) provides clear guidance and criteria by which teachers and schools will be assessed. The provision of accurate information related to the categories by which a school is judged provides the team of inspectors with a positive framework for assessment.

Schools need to be thoroughly prepared and this takes time and commitment from everyone, including trainee teachers. The inspectors will require the following from schools:

- Information related to the school, pupils, governing body and the school's self-evaluation document (see OFSTED framework, p9);
- access to the Web pages that contain the school's data;
- a copy of the school's current development or management plan;
- the school prospectus or brochure;
- the most recent LEA monitoring report on the school's progress against its targets;
- the school timetable;
- the plan of the school.

Clearly the preparation of documentation is the responsibility of all teachers. Additional material may well be required during the inspection, including attendance registers and samples of pupils' work, records and reports to parents.

When the Registered Inspector (RgI) meets the headteacher, a date and time for a pre-inspection meeting with the parents will be negotiated. All parents are sent a standard questionnaire, which is returned in confidence to the RgI. Following an analysis of the questionnaire and a summary of the meeting with parents (which no members of staff may attend, unless they have a child or children of their own in the school) the general consensus is shared with the headteacher. The RgI seeks, through the questionnaire and the meeting, parents' views on attainment and progress, the attitudes and values promoted by the school, communication with parents, help and guidance available to pupils, homework, behaviour and attendance, the role of parents, and the school's readiness to deal with suggestions and complaints.

The information collected by the RgI comprises the pre-inspection sections of a school's profile, which is then circulated to the full team of inspectors. Along with the school profile is a brief commentary and copies of documentation relating to individual inspectors' areas of responsibility.

Members of the inspection team scrutinize the documentation forwarded to them up to two weeks in advance of the inspection. Subject inspectors use the information to begin to build a bank of evidence under each of the categories to be reported upon, and formulate questions that will help to clarify concerns and issues. The subject inspector will also make a provisional observation schedule with the intention of observing all teachers of the subject, across the age and ability range. The timetable is provisional as events may overtake plans (see 'During the inspection', below).

The subject-related paperwork conveys many messages to the inspector. The inspector will begin to ascertain whether subject aims and objectives contribute to whole-school aims; if teachers appear adequately qualified and trained; and if examination results meet with national norms. Schemes of work will demonstrate if National Curriculum requirements are met and policies on differentiation, equal opportunities and assessment begin to provide evidence of effective teaching. Expectations and methodology help to paint a picture of the subject provision.

At this stage the documentation does not provide answers. It does, though, help the inspector to form an opinion and to formulate questions. It is during the inspection that answers should emerge. Good inspectors will base their judgements on a range of evidence. Inspection is intense work for inspectors too. The criticism that inspectors do not always appear to have read the paperwork provided by the school in advance (Boothroyd *et al*, 1996) is in fact to challenge the professionalism of the inspector. Inspectors are bound by a code of conduct and schools are monitoring inspectors' conduct throughout an inspection. Any complaint must be supported by evidence, and consequently teachers need to record any disquiet and concerns as they emerge.

During the inspection

During the week of inspection, inspectors are required to complete the gathering of evidence and to provide answers to the questions formulated beforehand. The framework (OFSTED, 2003a, pp18–20) provides clear guidance on how this procedure is conducted. The majority of the evidence is collected first-hand by:

- observing teaching and learning;
- talking to staff, pupils and others in the school;
- observing extracurricular activities and the way in which the school runs on a day-to-day basis;
- tracking school processes such as evaluation and performance management;
- analysing samples of pupils' current and recent work;
- joining meetings such as school council or management meetings, and observing management processes, such as monitoring of teaching directly;
- analysing documents provided by the school, including teachers' records of pupils and their progress; and
- analysing records relating to pupils with special educational plans, statements, annual reviews and transitional reviews. (OFSTED, 2003a, p18)

All the information is collated during the inspection on standard forms including evidence forms, inspector's records, and records of corporate judgements. These, together with any briefings, plans or instructions prepared by the RgI, form the evidence base of the inspection. They must be retained for 12 months following the end of the inspection.

Making judgements

The inspection team meet regularly throughout the process to share and review their findings. The RgI ensures that all procedures follow the evaluation schedule

Table 9.1 Inspectors' seven point scale (OFSTED, 2003a, p20)

Quality descriptor	Grade	Implications
Excellent: exceptional; outstanding; first-rate; very highly effective; very rapid (as in progress)	1	Worth disseminating beyond the school
Very good: well above average; highly effective; rapid	2	Worth sharing within the school
Good: above average; effective	3	Worth reinforcing and developing
Satisfactory: average; acceptable; sound; typical; expected	4	Adequate but scope for improvement
Unsatisfactory: below average; worse than expected; inadequate; slow; ineffective	5	Needs attention
Poor: well below average; very ineffective; much worse than expected; very slow	6	Needs urgent attention
Very poor: far worse than expected; extremely ineffective; extremely slow	7	Immediate radical change needed

laid down in the framework (OFSTED, 2003a, pp25–35). The overall judgements reflect all the evidence collated, considered and examined by the inspection team. At the end of the process the inspection team consider whether a school falls into any of four categories, which are: special measures, serious weaknesses, under-achieving, or has an adequate sixth form.

Inspectors have to make a wide-ranging set of judgements, which are summarized on a seven-point scale, shown in Table 9.1.

At the end of the inspection, oral feedback is given to the headteacher and staff.

Feedback

Informal feedback to teachers after lessons is much valued. The feedback by the subject inspector to the subject leader is often seen as anti-climactic. Inspectors are always guarded. After an intense few days of gathering data, inspectors must present their judgements. The oral report must not differ in tone from the final written report. The RgI encourages inspectors to exemplify good and bad practice. School staff may challenge factual details, but not the inspectors' judgement. The inspectors' role is not to provide advice, but simply to report. The outcome of all this is that the oral feedback is very often a monologue, presented in 'OFSTED speak'. The inspector is compelled to translate numerical gradings into words, generating what Field *et al* (1998) have called 'scalar statements'. It is not difficult to relate the gradings to terms such as 'excellent', 'very good', 'good', 'satisfactory', 'unsatisfactory', 'poor' and 'very poor'. The final feedback to the senior management team differs little in tone. Through lengthy discussion, inspection criteria have been graded by the RgI seeking the opinions of all inspections. The feedback is therefore formal and closely structured by the gradings given. The grades are not revealed, however.

There is no doubt that the inspection week is busy and stressful. Inspectors try not to increase the stress levels beyond the inevitable. Rarely do inspectors enter the staff room, for example, and the OFSTED code of conduct emphasizes the need for courtesy and understanding. Nevertheless, it would be naive to suggest that all stress can be avoided. The best news on offer is that teachers can be prepared to the extent that they know what to expect.

After the inspection

The completion of the inspection week is often met with a sense of anti-climax. Memories of the inspection for heads of subjects centre around the feedback, which is inevitably relayed to colleagues in relevant teams. The outcome of the inspection will lead to several possible actions. At worst, the school will be called a 'failing' school, and will then be placed under special measures. A detailed action plan is required, and the school will be re-inspected. Headteachers can be replaced and governing bodies required to resign. At the very worst, a school can be closed or the school can be taken over and run by an authority, until such time as it is felt to be back on course.

The usual procedure following the inspection is that after a period of five to six weeks the full report is produced by the RgI. A summary of the report is sent to all parents, and parents are informed that a copy of the full report is available from the school. The school may only charge for the cost of photocopying. The report is soon placed on the Internet (http://www.open.gov.uk/ofsted/ofsted/htm), and is therefore a public document. Schools use the report to issue a press release, which generally reflects the most positive aspects of the report. At school, the governors are responsible for the completion of an action plan, which serves as a response to the report. The action plan must be completed within 40 working days. Evidently, governors devolve responsibility to the headteacher, who consults with appropriate staff. Many schools – up to 19 per cent – employ a consultant to assist (Fidler *et al*, 1995). The consultant is often a member of the LEA support team, who has to read and interpret the report. Inspectors, whom many would judge to be in the best position to offer advice, are unsure as to whether they should do so. OFSTED inspections work on the principle that an audit is best performed by outsiders, and inspectors run the risk of breaking the code of conduct by engaging in consultation work.

The report

The report is the most lasting part of an inspection. OFSTED's (2000) guidance suggests that the report and the summary should:

- be clear to all its readers – the appropriate authority, parents, professionals and the wider public;
- concentrate on evaluating rather than describing what is seen;
- focus on the educational standards achieved and the factors which impact on standards and quality;
- use everyday language, not educational jargon, and be grammatically correct;
- be concrete and specific;
- use sub-headings and bullet points where they help to make the message clear;
- use telling examples drawn from the evidence base in order to make general-izations understandable and to illustrate what is meant by 'good' or 'poor';
- employ words and phrases that enliven the report and convey the individual character of the school.

Field *et al* (1998) have analysed the language of OFSTED reports, and the results do not match up to the list of objectives above. The vast majority of sentences are 'scalar' in that they are verbal representations of a numerical scale. The report notes the percentage of lessons that fall into the categories of 'very poor', 'poor', 'sound', 'good' and 'very good' – the original five-point scale. Terms such as these occur as often as once every 50 words in some reports. 'Qualitative' judgements – statements when the RgI attempts to explain the judgements through exemplifi-cation, noting causal factors and/or offering advice – are much more limited in number. The overall outcome is that the school's strengths and weaknesses are described. There are no suggestions to help the school remedy problems. Many commentators challenge the validity and reliability of the reports. The style of the report is that which measures output and performance. Maw (1996: 28) comments: 'validity and reliability cannot be subsequently checked for accuracy and fairness, because no record of events and observations exists in any other form other than evaluative'.

The report contains comments and judgements on each subject inspected and also on all aspects (see earlier) A copy of the report is sent to OFSTED, along with copies of the school profile (numerical gradings), subject profiles (numerical gradings), codes and grades from observation forms, and the headteacher's form. That which is sent to OFSTED forms part of a national database, providing evidence for the chief inspector. The policy of naming good and bad schools in the press is morally questionable, but difficult to negate on the grounds that the judgements are based on evidence. Little or no account is given to value-added issues. Performance is presented in terms of the relationship with national standards, and the report is the only publicly available document to support or challenge the judgement.

Action plan

Within 40 days the school has to produce an action plan, which must relate to the OFSTED report. Indeed the report contains 'key issues' and 'recommendations for action'. The task is not therefore onerous, albeit focusing on the negative shortly after the gruelling experience of an inspection. Lonsdale and Parsons (1997) discovered that three-quarters of issues contained within an action plan had already been identified by schools in advance of the inspection, and are contained within school development plans. Very often sensitive issues are 'to be kept under review', a tactic Lonsdale and Parsons see as fudging the issues. On the other hand, Lonsdale and Parsons also identify an 'empowering' report – one that can be used by the school as a lever with the LEA, as a means of prising out more resources. The action plan is therefore seen by some as a tool to implement plans that the school has wanted to introduce for some time.

On the whole 'action planning' is seen as positive, as a way of ensuring that inspections have an impact on schools and school development. Copies of action plans are sent to parents, thereby increasing the notion of accountability.

Conclusion

OFSTED inspections are now a part of school life. However, their purpose is clear and the procedures are transparent. The data generated is interesting, and teachers are required to understand how the information can be used to improve practice (TTA, 1998, 2002).

First it is important to know how to access a report. Any member of the public can ask for a copy from the school, for the price of photocopying. Copies are available on the Internet (http://www.open.gov.uk/ofsted/ofsted/htm), although users need Adobe Reader to download the files. For new teachers the reports can assist in forming a picture of the ethos and image of a school. The real use of the reports is wider-reaching than simply to absorb what they contain. Analysis of the headteacher's form and examination and test results gives a good picture of

Table 9.2 Table for locating information within the school

	Attainment	Progress	Attitudes, behaviour, personal development	Teaching	Curriculum and assessment	Spiritual moral, social, cultural	Leadership and management
Headteacher's form							
Subject handbook							
Subject development plan							
Internal assessment records							
Pupils' work							
Schemes of work							
Displays							
School curriculum model							
Timetable							
School policies							
Subject policies							
Extra curricular opportunities							
Inventory							
Records of subject expenditure							
Minutes of subject meetings							
Accounts of in service courses attended by subject staff							

the level of performance. Self-evaluation systems, resulting in detailed school and subject development plans, and value-added systems all help to provide a full picture of a school's life.

The OFSTED report is simply one document among many that help to drive up standards. Alone it serves little purpose. Nationally speaking, a common, standardized inspection system does allow for the comparison of schools, and the database does tend to throw up key issues. In this way the system is effective in that it provides the Secretary of State with an ongoing evaluation of educational policies. It is less the effectiveness of the policy which experts question, but the efficiency. Inevitably OFSTED's own question is thrown back at the system: is OFSTED value for money?

Task 9.2

Consider all the documentation available in school. How can the documentation generate evidence under each of the OFSTED categories?

- Use Table 9.2 to help you to locate information. Map out where you would expect to find details.
- Read the relevant information and note down how well you think the school provides for learners in each category.
- Read the school's OFSTED report, and compare your judgements to those of the inspection team.

References

Boothroyd, C et al (1996) A Better System of Inspection, OFSTIN, Hexham

Fidler, B, Earley, P and Ouston, J (1995) Ofsted School Inspections and Their Impact on School Development, a report of ECER/BERA Conference, September, Bath

Field, C (1999) The inspection process, in Learning to Teach, ed G Nicholls, Kogan Page, London

Field, C et al (1998) Ofsted inspection reports and the language of educational improvement, Evaluation and Research in Education, 11, pp 125–29

Hargreaves, D (1995) Inspection and school improvement, Cambridge Journal of Education, 25 (1), pp 117–25

Learmonth, J (2002) Inspection: What's in it for schools, RoutledgeFalmer, London

Lonsdale, P and Parsons, C (1997) Inspection and the school improvement hoax, in School Improvement After Inspection, ed P Earley, Paul Chapman, London

Maw, J (1996) The handbook for the inspection of schools: models, outcomes and effects, in *Ofsted Inspection: The early experience*, J Ouston, P Early and B Fidler, David Fulton, London

OFSTED (2000) *Guidance 2000*, TSO, Norwich

OFSTED (2003a) *Framework for Inspections*, TSO, Norwich

OFSTED (2003b) *Inspecting Schools*, TSO, Norwich

TTA (1998) *National Standards for Qualified Teacher Status*, Teacher Training Agency, London

TTA (2002) *Qualifying to Teach. Professional standards for Qualified Teacher Status and requirements for Initial Teacher Training*, TTA, London

10 Working with parents

Tricia David

The aim of this chapter is to introduce the trainee to the concepts and issues relating to 'working with parents'. It identifies the key role parents have to play in their children's education from nursery to post-16. Primarily the chapter deals with recent changes in legislation and how these affect the teacher and trainee. Issues such as learning from birth, educating the under-5s, transition points in schooling and teacher-parent partnerships are discussed. It is a key chapter in helping the trainee to acquire a rounded knowledge of working with parents.

Objectives

By the end of this chapter the trainee will have an understanding of:

- the need to work and closely liaise with parents;
- recent legislation affecting parents' rights;
- parent-teacher partnerships;
- transition points in schooling;
- growing and changing: life phases and transitions in learning.

Parents: the primary educators

Despite the fact that pioneers such as Margaret McMillan, who opened nurseries in highly disadvantaged areas of Bradford and London almost a century ago, promoted the view that parents needed to be informed about their children's health and about the education process, it was not until after the publication of the Plowden Report (CACE, 1967) that the key role and influence of parents and families began to be truly recognized by teachers and schools. A further catalyst had been the impact of the pre-school playgroup movement, founded in the early 1960s, since (usually) mothers who had been engaged in their children's early learning through participation in playgroup sessions and courses no longer accepted a role defined by teachers – outside the school premises and on the school's terms. They wanted to know what went on in classrooms, how their children were learning, and how they could help them at home. Further, some research carried out for the Plowden Report demonstrated the importance of parental influence on children's school attainment and when educational priority areas (EPAs – see publications by Eric Midwinter, eg, for further information) were set up to provide support for children and schools in areas of disadvantage, one key element was deemed to be the enrolment of parents as helpers in classrooms, as fund-raisers, and as members of supportive networks for other parents. In other words, parents gained recognition as the 'primary' educators of their children. However, the meanings and development of home–school partnerships have continued to be very mixed, and parents continue to feel sceptical about their ability to influence what happens in schools.

It was to be another 20 years before the then Secretary of State for Education, Kenneth Baker, in setting out his proposals for the very first UK National Curriculum in 1988, told parents at the Annual General Meeting Conference of the National Confederation of Parent Teacher Associations (NCPTA) that he was handing power over to them through his Education Reform Act. At that time, the assembled parent representatives shunned his proposal, saying they wanted partnerships not power. As has subsequently been observed, parents continue to have little power over the education system, so one might argue they were simply being delegated the role of 'policing' schools rather than actually engaging in decisions about what their children should be taught and how. In England at least, power over the content of the curriculum, and some might even argue pedagogy too, has become more centralized. Where others among our European partner countries are involving as wide a membership of the population as possible in debates about schooling, values and childhood (for example Spain and Sweden), we seem to have submitted to being told what must be done and how – as can be seen from the recent imposition of the literacy hour and arguments about whether or not this innovation is mandatory.

However, the ability to forge strong home-school links is clearly seen as an important attribute of well-trained teachers, particularly those qualified to work in the early years and primary sectors. Circular 4/98 (DfEE, 1998b) includes in the standards that must be met in order to be awarded Qualified Teacher Status (QTS) relating to phases 3–8 and 3–11, a requirement to:

demonstrate that they. . . have a knowledge of effective ways of working with parents and other carers (p 11);. . . manage, with support from an experienced specialist teacher if necessary, the work of parents and other adults in the classroom to enhance learning opportunities for pupils (p 14).

In addition all trainees for primary and secondary teaching must:

> demonstrate that they:. . .
>
> 1. recognize that learning takes place inside and outside the school context, and
> 2. understand the need to liaise effectively with parents and other carers and with agencies with responsibility for pupils' education and welfare. (p 16)

Thus it is no longer permissible to assume that knowledge of and some experience in working with parents can be left until newly qualified teachers have a few years' teaching under their belts and teachers in partnership schools will, according to Annex D Circular 4/98, be required to offer training appropriate to such demands.

Schools already have a statutory duty to:

- report to parents on their children's progress;
- enable parents to participate in the statementing process if their child is deemed to have special educational needs at that level and to inform parents of all decisions about the child's progress whatever the level of special educational need diagnosed (see Chapter 8 of this book and DfEE, 1994);
- ensure they have access to copies of inspection reports on the school, as well as other information documents about the school's policies and curriculum;
- hold an annual meeting at which parents may ask questions and make comments about the school's approaches.

Parents are also represented on each school's governing body. In the case of voluntary and private nursery settings, parents may be on a management committee, but this is not a statutory requirement. Thus all schools should be able to help trainees gain an understanding of the basic aspects of home-school liaison. However, what many headteachers, teachers and early childhood educators (ie those who work in the voluntary and private or independent pre-5 sector) have tried to do is to encourage partnerships with parents in a variety of ways, because they acknowledge the enhanced progress children can make when their parents are able to support their learning as a result of being well-informed. Additionally, close liaison between children's families and staff can help the teachers learn about children's existing knowledge and experiences, since each child's home will form the unique central core of an 'ecological niche' (Bronfenbrenner, 1979; Bronfenbrenner and Morris, 1998) in which that child's learning process will have begun. Parents and children co-construct their own worlds and their own meanings: parents are not a homogeneous group, even within a particular community. Each home will have its own culture and shared understandings and to teach appropriately, in ways that will ensure each child is able to access what is being taught, practitioners need to be able to see from the child's point of view, or as it is often put: 'to start where the child is'. Starting in a different 'place' will render teaching pointless, as learning is either boringly repeated or too difficult and off-putting.

In this chapter I will present information about the practices intended to support a child's entry into formal education and how parents can be key players throughout the child's educational career. I will use the term 'parent' to mean those adults with the major parental responsibility for a child, though it may be that several people, for example, grandparents, step-parents, carers, nannies and childminders share this role. Prior to the 1989 Children Act, parents were seen as having rights over their (birth) children, but this Act recognized children's rights by instituting the concept of parental responsibility and laying down the expectation that professionals (such as teachers and social workers) would always involve parents (those with parental responsibility) in decisions about their children, even in cases (now relatively less frequent) of children being taken into care, and work together to provide support for them, as the Act requires (see Chapter 8).

Making human sense: learning from birth

During the last 20 years we have begun to recognize the ways in which dependence upon (or collusion with?) developmental psychologists, whose methods caused the underestimation of what babies and young children are capable of achieving (Deloache and Brown, 1987), confirmed low expectations not only of small children themselves but of those who worked with and cared for them, at least in terms of their intellectual stimulation. The whole attitude to provision of nurseries as 'edu-care' settings demonstrated how unimportant the early years of life and learning were deemed to be. As a result parents who wish to or must continue employment outside the home after children are born continue to undergo crises and heartache as they attempt to ensure their children are happy, stimulated and safe with carers who will provide a continuous service. It seems strange that, were parents told when their children reached the age of 11 that their child would have to attend a number of different institutions year on year, they would be horrified. Yet this is accepted almost without question in relation to under-5s, exemplifying indoctrination to the effect that under-5s do not learn or do very much and so can be treated almost like parcels, being left to be 'minded'. However, we now know that during the first five years brain growth is at its most rapid and more is learnt during this phase of life than at any subsequent stage.

Babies' propensity for wanting to 'making sense' of the context in which they find themselves and their preparedness for language are factors which led contemporary researchers (eg Trevarthen, 1992) to conclude that human beings come into the world 'programmed' to be social learners. Children are learning from birth (and probably even before that). As educators we cannot afford to waste children's precious time before 5 by giving them meaningless tasks – or after 5 by failing to build on what they already know and can do. Children, like the other participants in the process (the parents, teachers and headteachers) bring to their admission to nursery and reception class a rich history of varying experiences (Barrett, 1986). The same is true of each successive transition. The more we can help all pupils use their previous learning to make sense of and exploit the next learning situation, the faster and more confident will be their settling-in and progress.

Educating under-5s

The new Labour Government, while adopting different strategies from the previous government for achieving the expansion of nursery education, has continued the push for every 4-year-old whose parents wish them to attend nursery to be offered a place. In fact, most 4-year-olds are found in the reception classes of primary schools in the academic year in which they become 5. Many such classes are on the one hand being seen as part of the expansion of 'nursery provision' but on the other many are still operating as if they are providing for older children, failing to ensure the kind of approaches, staffing ratios, space and equipment that would be available in a nursery. Parents at first reported that in some cases they were told that their child could not be guaranteed a place at the school of their choice if they did not transfer their child from a local nursery or play-group/pre-school to the reception class at the start of the academic year or term determined by the school. Others still find that schools impose a part-time regime on children who have already settled well in a nursery for full days.

Naturally children need a period of time to adjust to and become familiar with a new setting, but some schools have been overly rigid in imposing this pattern on families, sometimes creating great difficulties for working parents, particularly working mothers whose families may rely on their incomes. What happens to children during the rest of their day, and the difficulties faced by some parents because of school hours and lack of 'out of school' care facilities, have not generally been high on the agendas of schools because other demands (such as the curriculum, assessments, inspections and the mass of paperwork) have taken precedence.

The Government's directives to local authorities to set up nursery partnerships and early years forums, which should review both education and care provision in the area, are a positive move forward which will hopefully lead to greater coordination of services to suit both children and parents (DfEE, 1998a).

Meanwhile, most under 5s' services which are receiving funding under nursery partnership schemes are using the *Desirable Outcomes for Children's Learning* (SCAA, 1996 – currently being revised) as the basis of their curriculum planning. The six areas of learning delineated by the *Desirable Outcomes* are:

1. personal and social development;
2. language and literacy;
3. mathematics;
4. knowledge and understanding of the world;
5. physical development; and
6. creative development.

These 'areas' are thought more appropriate for thinking about young children's learning than 'subjects' in the National Curriculum, but they are linked to subjects and aspects of the curriculum for 5- to 16-year-olds in the *Desirable Outcomes* (SCAA, 1996).

Although the statements about the six areas detail 'goals for learning' at the time of entry to school (SCAA, 1996: 1) and the document itself indicates that 'compulsory education begins the term after the child's fifth birthday' (p 1), these same statements form the basis for assessments of children in their first term of reception class (when many are just 4) and the basis for the curriculum in most pre-school settings inspected according to regulations set up through the Nursery Education and Grant Maintained Schools Act 1996. Despite the fact that the *Desirable Outcomes* were not intended to be 'the curriculum', the latter is hardly surprising, since the criteria for nursery inspectors' judgements are breakdowns of the same statements (Ofsted, 1998a).

Having said that, the advantages of such documentation are that practitioners and parents can debate the *Desirable Outcomes* and appropriate pedagogy for achieving them, while the nursery inspection reports offer parents greater insight into the teaching and learning process in the early years than has been available in many institutions in the past. In addition, parents must be informed that a nursery inspection is to take place and the inspector must solicit the views of parents about the provision. In a section headed 'Common features of good practice', the *Desirable Outcomes* document states:

> Each setting has a statement, shared with parents. . . which outlines the aims, objectives and content of the curriculum, how it is taught and how children's progress and achievement are assessed, recorded and communicated to parents and the schools to which children will progress. . . Children's progress and future learning needs are assessed and recorded through frequent observation and are shared regularly with parents. (SCAA, 1996: 6)

Then in a section on 'Parents as partners' (SCAA, 1996: 7), effective home-nursery liaison is advocated and parents' knowledge and skills, as well as that of educators, are acknowledged. Staff in nursery settings are expected to recognize the parents' fundamental role in their children's education and to enter into partnerships based on mutual respect and shared responsibility.

So far, the main focus has been on the education of 4-year-olds during this first phase but developments for 3-year-olds are now in progress, as are better and more comprehensive care facilities for children under 14, which include plans for children from birth to 3. Further initiatives, such as 'SureStart' projects, are intended to promote early learning and to help parents encourage their children from babyhood.

Some key points need to be recognized:

- children are learning from birth, so all nursery partnerships will have to ensure that those who work with all young children are properly trained to provide for their learning in ways appropriate to their age/stage and cultural context;
- continuity in relationships and learning is an essential ingredient in the achievement of higher standards (Whitebrook *et al*, 1990), so parents need to be partners with educators and all involved need excellent lines of communication. Further, frequent changes of carer and educator will be counterproductive – nursery partnerships need to attempt to minimize the number of transitions during this phase and to ensure parents are enabled to act as the link persons with the best knowledge bases about their own children.

Parents as link: transition to primary school

There are few, if any, schools which do not now arrange several visits for children and their parents to familiarize them with the reception class and its staff in the term before children are admitted to primary schools. For some more fortunate children the transition from pre-school or home to primary school will be even smoother, since they may be attending an 'early years unit', where nursery and reception teachers work closely together and children aged 3, 4 and 5 spend part or all of the day together.

When this is not the case, parents too will be 'new' to a school and may have strong feelings evoked by memories of their own school days. For some these will not have been happy and successful, whereas for most adults who become teachers, school will have been a positive experience. That some parents are afraid to ask for help with their children's learning has been confirmed by government-sponsored research in which mothers from poorer families are found to understand the importance of a good education for their children but have little confidence in their own ability and feel too intimidated by schools and teachers to seek help. (The research was carried out by the National Campaign for Learning, a charity jointly funded by the DfEE and British Industry; Ghouri, 1998.) Thus, once again, teachers need to try to put themselves in the shoes of the other people – this time, parents.

Reiterating the principles set out in the *Desirable Outcomes* (SCAA, 1996) primary and secondary schools, like nurseries, need to consider whether their approach to parents is:

- welcoming;
- respectful;
- based on shared responsibility;
- explicit in its recognition of parents' role in their children's education;
- clear in demonstrating that dialogue is a two-way process;
- encouraging collaboration;
- using parents' and other family members' expertise to support learning in and out of school;
- ensuring parents are enabled to contribute to their children's achievements and assessments;
- stimulating and informing the continuation at home of learning begun at school.

From the school's point of view, it is also important parents gain accurate and fair information so that they may make informed decisions about choice of school (where that is possible). Sources of information include: other parents; inspection reports and league tables; and pre-school providers, so teachers, and especially head-teachers, need to think carefully about how these sources garner and interpret their information and how much they are able to influence the information passed on by providing evidence which is positive. In some areas, schools communicate to parents from linguistic minorities through interpreters of local minority community languages, either by recruiting teachers and support staff from those communities or by enlisting the support of 'experienced' bilingual parents and using media such as video with footage of school life, having voice-over in different languages.

Teachers must also be aware that some parents will be at pains to hide the fact that they are illiterate, so messages and information must be communicated verbally from staff to parents and through parent networks. The use of videos of school life, displays with photographs of learning activities and cartoon booklets for the children starting school (rather than printed), are all examples of strategies that are positive ways of engaging young children themselves as well as parents with such learning difficulties.

One of the most recent innovations to practice in reception classes is the QCA (Qualifications and Assessment Authority) baseline assessment scheme. Early years teachers have assessed young children's learning according to curriculum-related criteria for many years (see for example Tyler, 1979) in order to diagnose any learning difficulties and to plan for future learning. What is different about the QCA scheme is that assessments are largely focused on literacy and numeracy, with some items on personal and social development. The reasons for this are that a) literacy and numeracy are seen as paramount in the education process; and b) numeracy in particular is one of the few areas which is reliable in a statistical sense and which can be assessed on school entry and again at the end of Key Stage 1 in order to derive a 'value-added' score for a school – that is, how much progress the children have made while attending the school.

The problem with baseline assessment is that it may end up producing a top-down pressure on parents and pre-school educators, who in their turn may put pressure on young children to achieve high scores in a narrow test. Parents were already convinced their 4-year-olds needed more formal teaching in nursery (David, 1992) as a result of the testing at the end of Key Stage 1. Baseline assessment is likely to be similarly misinterpreted by parents unless educators and teachers convince them of the long-term benefits which are derived from a play-based, child-directed curriculum in the pre-school. Each year, the evidence from American High/Scope research indicates that such a curriculum has long-term advantages over formal, didactic teaching of such young children, in terms of their ultimate educational achievements, later emotional stability, employability and qualifications, avoidance of crime and teenage pregnancy (Sylva, 1998).

Parents' roles in (and out) of schools

It is of course easy to acknowledge in theory the importance of parental involvement in their children's education. In practice, some teachers find true partnerships more difficult to achieve. Perhaps one of the main difficulties for teachers arises out of the fact that all parents have themselves experienced schooling during their own childhood and they therefore bring with them a preconception of what a teacher should be like and what teaching and learning in school should entail. Similarly, most teachers come to the work with preconceptions based on their own experiences. Younger trainees may remember their parents being involved in their pre-school setting and primary school and maybe as representatives on a PTA committee. However, lack of life experience and confidence may mean that they are not ready to involve parents in certain types of partnership until they have been teaching for a while. Mature students who have children of their own may have been pre-school supervisors, classroom assistants, or voluntary helpers in such settings, so they may be much more confident about engaging parents in a variety of ways. However, what actually happens will also depend on the expectations of the headteacher and other senior staff and the level of support for new teachers and trainees in this respect. If senior teachers act as competent and assured role models in their interactions with parents, newly qualified teachers and students have much more chance of becoming competent and assured themselves.

In the past, it was suggested that our education system offers parents three types of involvement in schools:

1. school-focused (usually fund raising; membership of the governing body for some);
2. curriculum-focused (helping with homework; helping in the classroom);
3. parent-focused (parents are seen as the primary educators and are given support and knowledge by the school) (Torkington, 1986).

Certainly the efficacy of some types of parental involvement and some roles allocated to parents in the past have been questioned (see David, 1990; Edwards and Knight, 1994).

The publication of the *Parent's Charter* (DES, 1992) by the previous government (and note the position of the apostrophe indicating perhaps that each parent is a single entity) reiterated their new 'role' as the consumers of education – despite the fact that the children are supposedly the beneficiaries and despite a teaching force which was by and large unhappy and unfamiliar with the notion of education as a commodity.

Teachers need also to be aware of parents' previous experiences and understandings of the proper relationship between parents and teachers. For some, this will mean a relationship that is socially distant and quite formal (Bastiani, 1997). Further, teachers are paid to do work in school and some parents may resent being asked to take on roles as unpaid help. Suschitzky and Chapman (1998: 94) propose one thinks of two types of parental roles: one is active involvement as a helper or fund-raiser; the other a partner in children's learning. Edwards and Knight (1994) and Bastiani (1997) claim that parent-school relationships are determined by the aims of the school and will be evident in its ethos. So, for example, if dialogue with parents is claimed to be important, the school will have in place structures to ensure that sufficient time is allowed for such dialogues. It is in the ethos that one can also detect whether issues of power have been addressed. If parents are seen as people who have to be 'educated' because they are perceived to be deficient, rather than experts on their own children and on other areas of knowledge they may be able to share with the school, a form of cultural supremacy will be operating which may 'resonate of colonization and ultimately lead to alienation' (Edwards and Knight, 1994: 114).

If one makes a list of what we expect of a 'good parent' and then list alongside it what we expect of a 'good teacher', one often finds it is the emphases and intensity rather than the actual responsibilities which differ. As the US early years expert Lilian Katz has commented, parent-child relationships are 'hot' – because parents invest such a lot in their children in many, many ways, whereas teacher-child relationships are 'cooler', less intense, because a teacher must 'invest' in a larger number of children over a shorter period of time (Katz, cited in Pugh and De'Ath, 1989). Teachers who claim that the parents at their school are not interested in their children's education because they do not come into the school or attend parents' evenings might ponder this and ask themselves if there are invisible barriers preventing some parents entering the school and how they might remove them.

Perhaps most of all, teachers need to recognize the ways in which parents, particularly mothers, act as mediators of their children's learning about the external world. As Pollard remarks in the conclusion to his research study:

> the notion of 'parents as consumers' does not recognize the vital role that mothers and fathers play in supporting children's identities, self-confidence and learning. The danger is that it can create detachment and division. (Pollard with Filer, 1996: 308)

In a review of the inspections of voluntary and private nursery provision, Ofsted (1998b) claims from evidence of inspection reports that:

> In 72 per cent of institutions there are good links with parents and carers. . . Parents and carers in general, are encouraged to contribute to assessments of children by sharing observations of their children's learning at home. Encouraging parents to engage more with their children's education is an objective that should be given greater attention in many institutions. (Ofsted,1998b: 14)

Since it is in these earliest years that the pattern for home-school partnerships can be laid, it seems somewhat worrying that almost one-third of the early years settings inspected under this framework did not successfully engage parents. During the next 12 months (1998–1999) each local authority nursery partnership will be required to plan the ways in which a qualified teacher will be involved in every nursery receiving funding under the scheme. It seems urgent, therefore, that part of such a teacher's brief should be to ensure that training and support relating to parental involvement is offered, possibly encouraging pre-school playgroups with special expertise in the area to share this with their colleagues.

Growing and changing: life phases and transitions

As children move through the education system they are also entering different life phases. The period of 'middle childhood' relates well to what is now called Key Stage 2 and it is during this phase that children become even more peer-oriented and independent. Depending on how schools in an area are organized, it may be that some children change from one school to another during this phase and having been confident 'elder pupils' they suddenly find they are 'the babies' again. How the school handles this transition, whether it can be seen as a happy 'rite of passage' or a stressful jolt, will depend on more than just parents and teachers. Older children can be enlisted to 'mentor' new pupils and the hidden curriculum of a caring school can be reinforced by – again – 'standing in the new child's shoes'. Just as at the start of nursery and reception class, familiarization visits, videos and so on, can help, but it must be remembered that it is often the case that as the children get older the school premises get bigger and more complex, with more groups moving around and more opportunities for bullying. Ensuring parents and children know they can talk to sympathetic senior or pastoral staff if they have any anxieties is vitally important.

Teachers' partnerships with other adults

In Chapter 8 the teacher's responsibility relating to the Children Act 1989 is discussed. One aspect of dealing with inter-professional liaison which must be thought through concerns school records. Parents are entitled to access to their own child's records, with the exception of confidential records kept to log cases of suspected child abuse. School personnel need to be clear about who does have access to these records and how long they are to be kept after a case has been dropped. Some of the professionals with whom teachers will be liaising during child protection investigations have Codes of Conduct requiring them to maintain confidential records, meaning they cannot share all the information they hold. At present teachers have no such code, although it seems likely that the General Teaching Council could institute a professional code of ethics. Meanwhile, teachers need time to debate such issues and in training to be provided with models of appropriate professional conduct whereby information on children and their families is treated with great respect.

It is difficult to find sufficient time to include training in inter-professional liaison in Initial Teacher Education (ITE), but the standards (DfEE, 1998c) do require that NQTs qualifying for work with young children can demonstrate an understanding of the roles and responsibilities of other agencies and all must understand their responsibility to protect children from abuse. Information about the great range of roles and agencies involved in the care of young children can be found in David (1994) and in Solity and Bickler (1993). A useful assignment for trainees can be to investigate the role of a worker from a different type of setting or service and to focus on the areas of overlap – for example, if investigating the work of a speech therapist, the trainee could explore the ways in which speech therapists and teachers approach and provide for language development and how they can work together.

In particular trainees need to understand the roles and responsibilities of all those involved in the assessment and provision for children with special educational needs (see Chapter 8), especially the ways in which the child's parents should be supported and given a voice.

However, perhaps the most important area which requires attention during ITE is general training in teamwork, since this is at the root of all effective collaborations both within the classroom, where a teacher may work with a team including nursery nurses, classroom assistants, parent and governor volunteers, advisory teachers, a variety of students, tutors from FE and HE (to name but a few) and more widely. Similarly, whole-school teams include more than the class teachers, since kitchen, caretaking and cleaning staff, dinner and supervisory staff, as well as classroom assistants, peripatetic specialists, governors and others are also part of the team. This means that even in a small primary school the team can be larger than is obvious, so team leadership requires thought and training.

Rodd (1994) suggests that effective team leaders:

- use their personalities to lead by example, stimulating a team culture;
- are innovative, improve team morale and productivity, and so make things better;
- ensure constructive relationships are established and maintained;
- foster self-esteem and confidence in team members;
- coach team members to improve performance.

Rodd also lists the features characterizing such team leaders: adaptability; energy; people-orientation; quality consciousness; being united (they clarify common purpose and promote cooperation); entrepreneurship; being focused; and informality. These features are imbued with particular values and attitudes and moving teams on systematically, step by step, involves setting achievable goals; clarifying roles; building supportive relationships (including developing trust); encouraging active participation using the skills and talents of individual team members; and monitoring team effectiveness.

School teams and inter-professional teams set up to deal with particular events must however beware of building so strongly that they exclude the very people they are working for and with – the children and their parents, who should in any case be seen as team members too.

Beyond the standards

The standards for gaining Qualified Teacher Status provided in Circular 4/98 are the basic criteria with which all must comply. In developing parent partnerships, teachers and headteachers may go beyond these standards by challenging their own and trainees' assumptions about parents. Parents are not a homogeneous group yet it is likely they all need support in raising and educating their children at some time. Few now live among their extended families and the school can be the centre of their community network. As the African proverb has it – 'It takes a village to raise a child.'

Task 10.1

Obtain the school's policy document for dealing with parents and outside agencies. Discuss with your mentor the implications of these policies with special reference to your teaching phase.

Task 10.2

Establish what policies the school has for pupils in transition. This can be from reception to Key Stage 1, Key Stage 1 to Key Stage 2, Key Stage 2 to Key Stage 3, Key Stage 3 to Key Stage 4 or from GCSE to A level.

Discuss with your mentor how such transitions are dealt with, both from a parent/pupil perspective and as a member of staff.

References

Barrett, G (1986) *Starting school – An evaluation of the experience*, AMMA, London

Bastiani, J (1997) *Home-school Work in Multicultural Settings*, David Fulton, London

Bronfenbrenner, U (1979) *The Ecology of Human Development*, Harvard University Press, Cambridge, MA

Bronfenbrenner, U and Morris, P (1998) The ecology of developmental processes, in *The Handbook of Child Psychology Volume I: Theoretical models of human development*, ed W Damon, Wiley, New York, pp 993–1028

CACE (1967) *Children and their Primary Schools* (The Plowden Report), HMSO, London

David, T (1990) *Under Five – Under-educated?*, Open University Press, Milton Keynes

David, T (1992) What do parents in Britain and Belgium want their children to learn?, paper presented at the OMEP International Congress at the University of North Arizona, August

David, T (ed) (1994) *Working Together for Young Children: Multi-professionalism in action*, Routledge, London

Deloache, J S and Brown, A L (1987) The early emergence of planning skills in children, in *Making Sense*, ed J Bruner and H Haste, Cassell, London

Department for Education and Employment (DfEE) (1994) *The Code of Practice on the Identification and Assessment of Special Educational Needs*, DfEE, London

DfEE (1998a) *Excellence in Schools*, TSO, London

DfEE (1998b) *Requirements for Courses of Initial Teacher Training*, Circular 4/98, DfEE, London

DfEE (1998c) *Teaching: High status, high standards*, DfEE/TTA, London

Department for Education and Science (1992) *The Parent's Charter*, DES, London

Edwards, A and Knight, P (1994) *Effective Early Years Education*, Open University Press, Buckingham

Ghouri, N (1998) Mum's too afraid to ask, *Times Educational Supplement*, p 4, 4 September

Midwinter, E (1996) Simply switch the future, *TES, 7 June* (4171), p 22

Ofsted (1998a) *Guidance on the Inspection of Nursery Education Provision in the Private, Voluntary and Independent Sectors*, TSO, London

Ofsted (1998b) *The Quality of Education in Institutions Inspected under the Nursery Education Funding Arrangements*, Ofsted, London

Pollard, A with Filer, A (1996) *The Social World of Children's Learning*, Cassell, London

Pugh, G and De'Ath, E (1989) *Working Towards Partnership in the Early Years*, NCB, London

Rodd, J (1994) *Leadership in Early Childhood*, Open University Press, Buckingham

SCAA (1996) *Desirable Outcomes for Children's Learning on Entering Compulsory Education*, DfEE/SCAA, London

Solity, J E and Bickler, G J (1993) *Support Services: Issues for education, health and social services professionals*, Cassell, London

Suschitzky, W and Chapman, J (1998) *Valued Children, Informed Teaching*, Open University Press, Buckingham

Sylva, K (1998) Too formal too soon?, Keynote address, Islington Early Years Conference, 9 July

Torkington, K (1986) Involving parents in the primary curriculum, in *Involving Parents in the Primary Curriculum*, ed M Hughes, Exeter University Occasional Papers, Exeter

Trevarthen, C (1992) Infants' motives for speaking and thinking in the culture, in *The Dialogical Alternative*, ed A H Wold, Oxford University Press, Oxford

Tyler, S (1979) *Keele Pre-school Assessment Guide*, NFER, Slough

Whitebrook, M, Howes, C and Phillips, D (1990) *Who Cares? Child care teachers and the quality of care in America*, Childcare Employee Project, Oakland, CA

11   Professional values and practice

Gill Nicholls

The aim of this chapter is to examine the issues related to the professional values and practice of a trainee, and how they may be addressed and developed in school through their teaching practice and beyond through continual professional development. The trainee is introduced to the concept of the professional, what it is to be part of a profession and how these impact on gaining qualified teacher status (QTS).

Objectives

By the end of this chapter the trainee should have a clear understanding of:

- the values and practice of a trainee as found in Qualifying to Teach;
- what it is to be professional and part of a profession;
- establishing effective working relationships across the school;
- the importance of personal presentation and conduct;
- professional responsibilities in relation to school policies and practices;
- working with young people as pupils;
- the importance of informal learning through after-school activities;
- awareness of the role of school governors;
- personal learning and development;
- GTC requirements for professional values and practice.

Introduction

The aim of this chapter is to examine the issues related to the professional values and practice of a trainee teacher, and how they may be addressed and developed in school through their teaching practice and beyond through continual professional development.

Becoming a teacher requires many skills and attributes, as suggested in Chapter 1. Towards the end of the initial training period, more emphasis will be put on the professional values and practice made by the teaching profession and particularly the GTC. These fall into two distinct areas. The first relates to professional duties such as pay and conditions of employment, legal liabilities relating to race, sex and health education, safety and the Children's Act of 1989. The second area relates to professional issues directly related to the trainees' day-to-day responsibilities and commitments. These are clearly stated by the GTC:

1. young people as pupils;
2. teachers as colleagues;
3. other professionals, governors and interested people;
4. parents and carers;
5. the school context;
6. learning and development.

These six areas are discussed in this chapter.

The training process requires in-depth understanding of the nature of the world the initial teacher trainee is entering and developing in. It requires taking on considerable responsibility and professionalism. What are the implications of these on the trainee? What is meant by being a professional and demonstrating professionalism in the work of the teacher?

It is important to establish what is required by a professional and the implication this has for a new teacher.

The six areas identified by the GTC need to be considered in the context of the school and the teaching environment in order to help trainees understand their commitment and responsibility to the teaching profession. It requires trainees and newly qualified teachers (NQTs) to:

- reach a certain standard and competence in both training and knowledge base;
- continually develop their classroom skills as well as refine the nature of their professional judgements;
- have high personal standards of achievement, involvement and reflection as a means of becoming an effective teacher;
- have a clear understanding of professional practice.

These areas span the whole of teachers' professional education, whether trainees or experienced teachers. For initial teacher trainees, it is essential to understand how these affect their development. The DFES standards for the award of QTS and the GTC Professional standards relate to the six areas identified above. Each area of professionalism in pactice will be considered.

Teacher colleagues: establishing effective working relationships across the school

Establishing successful working relationships within schools is essential to good training and future long-term development. Every teacher is a member of several different groups and teams within a school. These include year teams, subject departments, sport groups, peer groups and academic groups as well as friendship groups. Teaching can often be a lonely profession, so it is important for the trainee to become involved within the school by becoming a member of one or more groups of people.

Working with colleagues, whether formally or informally, is an essential part of training and becoming a professional. The GTC states that 'teachers support their colleagues in achieving the highest professional standards ... They all respect confidentiality where appropriate. These aspects require understanding of working within a community.' As an individual within a group it is important to know what contribution can be made, and the value of that contribution. The nature of an individual's interaction within a group falls into five main categories:

1. sharing in common activities;
2. promoting a cause or idea;
3. gaining power or status;
4. establishing friendships and gaining a sense of belonging;
5. understanding that working in groups is part of one's job.

Working together with other teachers is a skill that develops and grows with time.

Trainees and NQTs can and should make an important contribution to any established groups. They bring with them new and fresh ideas, frequently challenging traditional approaches. These types of challenges are good for the group and the development of those involved. For the new teacher it is a case of trying to understand when to make suggestions and when it is better to be seen but not heard. It is important that NQTs realize they do have a voice both within their institution and within the community in which they work. It is essential that they learn how to use that voice effectively. Mentors should help and support NQTs and trainees to develop these skills. Working at group relationships is a very important part of the trainee's training and personal development.

The importance of personal presentation and conduct

Personal presentation and conduct have a considerable impact on the way teachers are perceived and develop. Raymond *et al* (1992) suggest that:

the link between personal and professional dispositions makes it important for teachers to have opportunities to examine their own personal commitments, histories and teaching styles. Discovering and making explicit the roots of their commitments, understanding the personal grounds that underlie their professional work, being clearer about the types of educational contexts … assist in the process of teacher development.

This description applies to all levels of professional development. What is important for trainees is to understand the impact personal presentation and conduct may have on the way their teaching develops. It is about recognizing the importance of being professional, and understanding the needs of pupils and colleagues alike. This is a large responsibility when starting out on a teaching career.

Being professional starts with the way trainees present themselves to the teaching community and school as a whole. It reflects the commitment and views the trainee holds regarding education, teaching and learning. It is important that trainees are aware of the school ethos and code of dress, as well as the nature of conduct expected by the headteacher of the staff generally. They need to familiarize themselves with the working practices and principles of the school, such as starting times, staff room rules, expectations about playground duty and duties in general, register taking and accessibility to senior staff such as the headteacher. All these will reflect your style and approach to the teaching profession.

It is also essential that trainees realize and appreciate that they will be a role model for pupils, irrespective of the pupils' age. Even the very youngest pupil will observe the way a teacher dresses, talks, looks and reacts. Personal presentation at this level is a starting point to development.

The way in which trainees conduct themselves is equally important to the nature of being a professional teacher. Joining a group of established professional teachers is not always easy. Trainees should be prepared to integrate into the life of the staff room and the school. Becoming part of the group may take time, but understanding the dynamics of that group and where one can slot in is part of the trainee's professional development as a teacher.

Professional personal conduct is not restricted to the staff room or in front of the senior management: it stretches into the classroom. It is essential that the trainees' conduct in the classroom is nothing less than professional. Mutual respect is the key to success. Pupils will judge teachers on their behaviour and interpersonal skills. If a teacher continually shouts at the pupils, the pupils will undoubtedly respond in a similar manner, causing a noisy and disruptive classroom; if the teacher is continually late to lessons, the teacher cannot expect pupils to be on time. These are the key elements to be aware of and there is a need to consciously develop good practice throughout the teaching placement and beyond. Courtesy and respect for colleagues and pupils constitutes good professional conduct.

The school context: understanding professional responsibilities in relation to school policies and practice

All teachers and trainees have professional responsibilities, which will vary from school to school. However, trainees need to be aware of the types of responsibilities that exist within the education system, and particularly those that are expected of them throughout their training placements. These can be divided into two types of responsibilities: professional and contractual.

Professional responsibilities

Professional responsibilities can be divided into two sections: those that deal with young people as pupils and those that deal with personal learning and development. Professional responsibility is about maintaining the highest quality of work a teacher is capable of. This will include lesson planning and preparation, marking of pupils' work, reporting and recording pupils' work, as well as considering the staff they work alongside and who are involved in the trainees' school based training. It is the trainees' professional responsibility to explore and find out about the school's policies and how they directly affect their work as a teacher in the school. The trainee needs to be aware of the school's policies on assessment, discipline, bullying, pastoral care, special educational needs, after-school activities and school uniform. In order to gain QTS trainees have to take responsibility as professional teachers to familiarize themselves with the nature of these policies and how they are implemented within the school.

Young people as pupils

The Code of Professional Values and Practice from the GTC states that:

> Teachers have insight into the learning needs of young people. They use professional judgement to meet those needs and to choose the best ways of motivating pupils to success. They use assessment to inform and guide their work. Teachers will have high expectations for all pupils, helping them progress regardless of their personal circumstances and different needs and backgrounds.

These statements put the pupil at the centre of teacher professionalism, by ensuring that teachers understand that students need to learn through a variety of methods and learning environments. As a trainee you will be expected to learn, understand and incorporate these values into your everyday working practices.

Learning and development

Personal development and continual professional development are very important aspects of any teacher's career. Learning and development is a lifelong activity. As a professional you should come to understand your own learning needs and how best these can be developed. The Code of Professional Values and Practice clearly states that:

> Teachers entering the profession in England have been trained to a ... standard that has prepared them for the rigours and realities of the classroom ... understand that maintaining and developing their skills, knowledge, and expertise ... achieving success. They take responsibility for their own continual professional development, through the opportunities available to them, to make sure ... the best and most relevant education. Teachers continually reflect on their own ... to improve their skills and deepen their knowledge.

Chapter 12 will help you achieve the requirements of the above expectation. Continual professional development spans a variety of activities and learning experiences. Trainees and NQTs should ask for and expect support for these activities from their schools and their individual mentors.

Contractual responsibilities

Teachers have a variety of contractual responsibilities and duties. The trainees' contractual duties will be negotiated between the university/college, the school and the individual trainee. When qualified those who choose to be employed in state schools in England or Wales will be governed by the DfEE's *School Teachers' Pay and Conditions* document (1998b). This is issued under the School Teachers' Pay and Conditions Act of 1991. They will also be subject to statutory responsibilities and duties. These have been established by the government through legislation; the main features are set down in the *Ofsted Handbook for Inspection, Part 6. The Statutory Basis for Education* (1997). Trainees will be involved with a considerable number of legislative areas; the most important at this stage of development include:

- pupils' spiritual, moral, social and cultural development;
- behaviour and discipline;
- attendance;
- subjects of the curriculum and other curriculum provision;
- assessment, recording, and reporting;
- equality of opportunity;
- provision of SEN;
- teaching and non-teaching staff;
- resources for learning.

It is important to understand the context in which these issues are assessed and developed within a school, whether it be through direct professional development or through school-defined policies. All schools are subject to Ofsted inspections and trainees will be responsible for the pupils they teach. It is therefore in the trainees' interest to have a working knowledge of these issues. The training period is a key time to investigate, explore and consider the effect legislative procedures can have on an individuals' professional development.

In addition to this as a trainee and a teacher there are legal responsibilities arising from the following legislation and guidance:

- the Race Relations Act 1976;
- the Sex Discrimination Act 1975;
- Sections 7 and 8 of the Health and Safety at Work etc Act 1974;
- teachers' common law duty to ensure that pupils are healthy and safe on school premises and when leading activities off the school site, such as educational visits, school outings or field trips;
- what is reasonable for the purposes of safeguarding or promoting children's welfare (Section 3(5) of the Children Act 1989);
- the role of the education service in protecting children from abuse (currently set out in DfEE Circular 10/95;
- appropriate physical contact with pupils (currently set out in DfEE Circular 10/95);
- appropriate physical restraint of pupils (Section 4 of the Education Act 1997 and DfEE Circular 9/94);
- detention of pupils on disciplinary grounds (Section 5 of the Education Act 1997);
- the progression from SCAA's *Desirable Outcomes for Children's Learning on Entering Compulsory Education* to KS1, the progression from KS1 to KS2 and from KS2 to KS3.

These are the Acts and recommendations of which trainees need a working knowledge and understanding. During trainees' periods in school they should with the help of their mentors and senior staff familiarize themselves with the basic issues related to these Acts.

Task 11.1

Select one of the above Acts or sections of an Act and identify the central issues of concern. Discuss these with your mentor and reflect on the impact they may have on your present and future practice.

The importance of informal learning through after-school activities

Recent legislation has raised awareness of the need to keep pupils occupied in learning after school hours. Schools have risen to this challenge in a variety of ways, by introducing homework clubs, and discipline-based activities that encourage the learning of science and maths in less formal settings. There is an increased need for trainees and teachers to understand the importance of such informal and community-based learning for pupils. The fact that learning takes place inside and outside the school context, and that parents and carers have an equally important role to play in that learning, needs to be accepted and understood by trainee teachers.

Chapter 10 gives a clear explanation of the implications of working with parents.

All schools are involved in the process of information exchange, whether it be between pastoral and academic staff, parents or members of external agencies such as the social services. Each has a procedure and this may well be different in every school. The important point is that trainees should acquaint themselves with the procedures in place. They need to know what to do with information that is gathered about the pupils in the school. Systems that are in place need to be adhered to and respected.

There are many areas of a child's life that are brought into school. It is easy to forget once inside the classroom the impact life outside of school may have on a pupil. Taking the register is a good way of getting to know your pupils. Absence notes are more than an administrative procedure: they can give considerable insight into a child's life outside of school.

Task 11.2

Consider the following absence note, then discuss with your mentor the various options you have for dealing with such a situation:

> James will be absent from school for the next week. I am going into hospital next week for surgery, and as I have no one to look after the younger children, James will have to take over.

Yours sincerely,
Gill Brown

How a teacher reacts to a pupil in such a situation, or any sensitive situation is crucial. Awareness of home situations is a very important part of a teacher's role. As a teacher you convey powerful messages to your pupils, their parents and colleagues, all of which can affect future relationships. Trainees often come across situations such as pupils' suffering a bereavement in the family, or a break-up of the family home. In such cases trainees should always seek expert help from their mentor or senior teachers, and at the same time watch and learn from the way they deal with the potential problems and passing of information.

In learning the art and craft of dealing with moral and social issues that may affect a pupil's progress, speak to the pastoral head of the placement school. Become aware of how to deal with potentially sensitive areas and which of the agencies can or should be used to help pupils.

After-school activities are another means by which pupils learn, whether it is being involved in school sports, play, music or a chess club – they all form a vital part of education. Being a trainee teacher is an ideal opportunity to gain an understanding of the importance of the learning that takes place in 'informal settings'. These are very powerful learning zones and can profoundly influence a child's development. A good example here is that of the child who has excellent computer skills and can gain information easily and actively from the Internet.

Task 11.3

Identify areas of informal learning that a group of pupils in one of your classes are involved in. Reflect on their responses and identify how this may affect your teaching.

Working with other professionals, governors and interested people

Schools have working relationships with an ever-increasing number of interested people including governors, national agencies, industry and local communities. As trainees and NQTs you come to recognize and understand that pupils develop differently and require different levels of support during their time in school. Working in partnership with outside agencies and interested parties is often a key aspect of ensuring a successful learning experience for pupils in your school. It is therefore essential that as a trainee or NQT you are aware of the nature and extent to which your school works with outside agencies and other interested parties.

Awareness of the role of school governors

As a trainee teacher it is unlikely that you will have any real contact with school governors. It is however a requirement to understand what their role is and how they operate within the school structure.

There are different types of governors within any governing body, including teacher governors, parent governors, nominated governors, and co-opted governors. The headteacher can choose whether or not to be on the governing body, but has the right to attend meetings in any case. Minutes are taken at all governor meetings and are available for inspection by any interested party. Teacher governors are elected within the school by ballot, and are there to represent the interests of the teachers and to relay back to the staff decisions etc from the governing body.

Parent governors are nominated and elected by parents, usually by ballot. Parent governors are very important as they represent all the parents of the school. Their role is to bring parent-related issues and problems to the attention of the governing body. Their opinions are crucial as it is their children who are at the school.

Nominated governors are usually nominated by political parties through the LEA. Their role is to give an overall perspective to school governance. Usually, major political parties are represented.

Finally, co-opted governors are chosen to fill gaps in the expertise of the school's governing body.

Following the 1988 Education Act governors have had an increasingly important role to play in the running of schools, both primary and secondary. The roles and responsibilities of school governors are wide and varying and include:

- school policies on issues such as sex education, uniform, special educational needs, the curriculum, budgets, appointment of staff, and health and safety aspects of the school generally;

- maintaining relationships with staff in the school, parents, the community and the LEA;
- helping to maintain good standards within the school.

Governors can and often do delegate a great deal of these responsibilities to the headteacher, who in turn regularly reports to the governing body. Governors' roles within schools can vary: some schools allocate governors to departments, while others appoint governors to particular areas within the school, for example special educational needs or the curriculum. Whichever approach schools take, governors generally work with the staff with the aim of giving pupils the best learning opportunities possible within the school. Governors are not paid members of staff, yet they hold considerable power and are now trained to fulfil their duties. A key person is the chair of governors. Some governing bodies take a high-profile approach to governance. They will be seen around the school, visiting classrooms and being actively involved in day-to-day school issues. Others take a more discreet approach to their work and appear to be in the background. Whichever approach is adopted governors' policy decisions can have a considerable effect on teaching practices and learning outcomes in schools. All trainees should be aware of the role the governing body has in their placement school.

A significant function of the governing body is to regulate the conduct and discipline of staff, and to dismiss where necessary. All governors' roles and responsibilities are covered by regulations and codes of conduct. These can be obtained from the professional teaching bodies.

Task 11.4

Identify the variety of agencies and outside partnerships that your school is involved in. Try to understand the contribution these external bodies make to your school and the possible positive effect it may have on the pupils.

References

Department for Education and Employment (DfEE) (1994) *The Education of Children with Emotional and Behavioural Difficulties*, Circular 9/94, DfEE, London

DfEE (1995) *Protecting Children from Abuse: The role of the educational service*, Circular 10/95, DfEE, London

DfEE (1997) *High Status, High Standards: Requirements for courses of initial teacher training*, Circular 10/97, DfEE, London

DfEE (1998a) *Requirements for Courses of Initial Teacher Training*, Circular 4/98, DfEE, London

DfEE (1998b) *School Teachers' Pay and Conditions* document, TSO, London

Fullan, M and Hargreaves, A (1995) *Developing Planning for School Improvement*, Cassell, London

Ofsted (1997) *Handbook for the Inspection of Schools: The statutory basis for education*, Ofsted, London

Raymond, D *et al* (1992) Contexts for teacher development: insights from teachers' stories, in *Understanding Teacher Development*, ed A Hargreaves and M Fullan, Cassell, London

SCAA (1997) *Desirable Outcomes for Children's Learning on Entering Compulsory Education*, SCAA, London

TTA (2002) *Qualifying to Teach. Professional standards for Qualified Teacher Status and requirements for Initial Teacher Training*, TTA, London

12 Continuing professional development

Carol Morgan and Peter Neil

This chapter aims to inform the trainee of two distinct areas within professional development. The first section deals with applying for a teaching position, constructing a CV and preparation for interview. The second deals with the concept of professional development from both a personal and institutional point of view. Trainees are directed to construct their own action plan for future development and will link into the performance management programme in your first school. You will need to balance these personal needs with the developments envisaged by your school (in its School Development Plan), where certain aims and priorities may already have been identified.

Objectives

By the end of this chapter the trainee will have a clear understanding of:

- the need to apply for and secure a first teaching position;
- how to apply for a teaching position;
- how to construct a CV and prepare for interviews;
- how to prepare for performance management;
- different kinds of CPD;
- different sources of CPD.

Applying for and securing your first teaching post

Securing your first teaching position will be one of the most important steps in your teaching career. As such it needs careful planning and preparation. You will need to consider several issues prior to application. These may well include:

- *Where you want to work.* You may want to return to your home area, or you may wish to remain in the area that you have trained in. What you must realize is that the more flexible you are the more opportunity there is for employment.
- *What age range you want to teach.* You may wish to teach only a particular Key Stage; this will restrict the types of vacancies you can apply for.
- *What type of school you want to teach in.* You may wish to teach in a primary, middle, or secondary school; equally important to you may be your desire to teach in a denominational school. These types of decisions will direct you where to look for teaching positions.
- *Where teaching jobs are advertised.* The majority of teaching positions are advertised in the *Times Educational Supplement*, which is published every Friday. *The Guardian* also has a comprehensive job section, published every Tuesday. For those who wish to teach in specific schools, teaching positions are also advertised in religious and ethnic newspapers, such as the *Jewish Chronicle, Catholic Herald, Universe, Methodist Recorder, Asian Times* and *The Voice*. The Catholic Education Service also produces a weekly vacancy sheet. Most Local Education Authorities (LEAs) produce lists of vacancies that are sent directly to schools and departments of education in higher education institutions.
- *What information is available to help applicants.* There are several sources available, including *First Teaching Appointments Procedures*, published by the Association of Graduate Careers Advisory Service (AGCAS). The teaching unions also publish useful information that will help to produce a solid application.
- How to register. In England and Wales you will need to obtain your DfES number; you will also have to register with the General Teaching Council in the respective country. In Scotland you will have to register with the General Teaching Council for Scotland and in Northern Ireland with the Department of Education.

The application process

The first thing to note with applications is that if you are thinking of applying for a job in Scotland or Northern Ireland the procedures are different. Further information for such applications can be obtained from GTC in Scotland or from the Department of Education in Northern Ireland (the GTC (NI) from 2004). Full details of the role of the General Teaching Councils and the services and publications they provide can be found at the relevant Web site: England: www.gtce.org.uk, Scotland: www.gtcs.org.uk, Wales: www.gtcw.org.uk, and Northern Ireland (not yet available): www.deni.gov.uk. Within England and Wales applications can be specific to schools or open to LEAs. Open applications allow you to apply directly to the LEA asking them to consider you for a suitable teaching position. If you are thinking of applying in this way, or seeking to be considered for what some LEAs call 'teacher pools', your letter of application needs to state clearly the type of school you wish to teach in, the locality within the local authority area in which you wish to teach, your subject preference and subsidiary teaching subjects. These types of opportunities are becoming rare. More frequently schools advertise their own teaching vacancies in the publications mentioned above. In these circumstances specific applications need to be made directly to the school.

Read the advertisement for any job carefully to ensure that you meet the criteria. A distinction is usually made between essential and desirable qualifications/experience or qualities. For example, if it states that 'experience of teaching Advanced level is essential' and you do not possess such experience, it is not worth your while applying for the job. The legislation makes it quite clear that applicants shortlisted for jobs must possess all the essential qualifications/experience at the time of applying. If, on the other hand, it states that 'experience of teaching A-level is desirable', you may apply even if you do not meet the requirements. The advertisement will also contain details of how to apply. Some schools or LEAs produce application forms that should be completed in detail. Others require a letter and/or CV. If the advertisement does not state otherwise, you can submit a short letter and detailed CV or, alternatively, a detailed letter and summary CV. If it asks for letters of application only, make sure you put as much detail in the letter as possible, highlighting aspects of your application that make you the most suitable person for that job.

With specific applications schools may suggest you visit them prior to application. It is good practice to take up such an offer. The merits of doing this are twofold: it suggests to the prospective school that you are genuinely interested in the school, and it gives you the opportunity to see the school in working conditions. The thing to remember on these types of visits is that there is no such thing as a truly informal contact with a school prior to application. The school is observing you just as you are viewing the school. Where it is not clear whether pre-visits are encouraged or if you are unsure as to the procedure regarding visiting the school, telephone the school secretary to find out what is expected. The following paragraphs will help you prepare a letter of application and a CV.

Letter of application

Your letter of application and application forms are often the first point of contact between you and the school you have chosen to apply to. It is important to realize that if your application is not read you stand very little chance of being selected for interview. Many applications are rejected immediately due to:

- poor presentation – illegibility, typing errors, too much information on one page;
- spelling mistakes – these include the name of the headteacher and the school, poor grammar, general spelling mistakes, careless use of English;

- failing to address points stated in the job description – the main issue here is answering questions inappropriately or not addressing issues at all.

The letter of application is where you market yourself: it is your way of telling the headteacher and governors what you can offer the school. You are ultimately trying to persuade them to interview you.

A good letter of application takes time and planning. You need to research the school and find out what it is actually looking for in a newly qualified teacher (NQT) in your chosen subject and age range. You will also need a well constructed and formatted CV. Allow yourself plenty of time to structure your letter of application and your CV. These are vital to your success in securing an interview.

Applications for teaching positions are mainly in one of two formats: that specified by the LEA or that specified by individual schools. Some LEAs have set application forms which require careful completion; these are often accompanied by a statement of support and your CV. Applications direct to a school often require a letter of application and your CV. Make sure you are clear about the type and format your application has to take. Most important here is to be positive and enthusiastic in your writing. Focus on what you think makes you a good teacher and suitable for the particular position you are applying for. Unless otherwise requested in the job advertisement, it is better to word-process your letter of application and your CV. Do not write an essay: aim to be concise but informative.

Neumark (1996) provides the following advice on letters of application. They should:

- be no longer than two A4 sheets;
- be specific to the job advertised;
- be word-processed;
- contain short snappy paragraphs;
- contain details of referees;
- refer to practical experience.

Preparing your CV

Your CV should present the basic information that would normally be incorporated in a standard application form. The following details should appear on your CV:

- Name.
- DfES number.
- Date of birth.
- Marital status.
- Schools and colleges attended. Give information about your schooling post-11.

- Qualifications. List these starting with your GCSEs and A levels, followed by your university education/courses and degree. PGCE students should include information on the content and class of degree.
- Other qualifications. These may be sport, music, first aid, etc.
- Teaching experience. Give details of your teaching practice schools, including names and dates of attendance. You may wish to include here any teaching you have been involved in outside of your specific training, such as coaching a sport, teaching English as a foreign language, reading schemes in adult education, helping in play groups or nursery schooling.
- Other work experience. Give concise details of any previous work experience you have had. This is particularly important if you have changed career.
- Interests and activities. This section should tell the school something about you and your personal interests. Don't just list them – indicate their relevance to teaching and being a teacher, for instance youth club leader, scouting or guiding.
- Other information and additional skills. Give details of any specific qualifications you may have obtained, for example computing expertise, musical qualifications, driving licence, foreign languages, being bilingual.
- Referees. Choose your referees with care. In a first job it is expected that one of your referees is from the college or institution in which you have trained. The second referee is ideally the headteacher or head of department from one of the teaching institutions in which you have been training.

Even if you have a standard CV that you have used before, it is worthwhile really trying to get the flavour of the school/institution you are applying to and adapting your information accordingly. One headteacher said that he looks for a personal rather than a standard approach when sifting through applications: 'Is the personal statement full of fashionable phrases, or are there sparks of originality? Has the writer lots of personal interests and a real passion for education?'(Kent, 2001). Manning (2002) has some useful tips on personal statements:

- use the same heading system as the one in the job specification;
- provide evidence for statements;
- use positive language;
- avoid jargon;
- be proactive;
- include relevant information;
- be specific, concise and neat;
- check grammar and spelling.

It may be helpful to ask someone else to read through the personal statement and it will certainly be useful to complete a draft version early and then re-read it, checking spelling and that all the detail has been provided that has been asked for. It is likely that you will be sent an equal opportunities monitoring form so this will need to be completed and returned. You may also need a covering letter. This is usually brief. Finally, it is useful to photocopy the final version of your application and take this with you to the interview.

Task 12.1

Draft a CV and a letter of application. Discuss it with a senior member of your school, or your personal tutor at college. Taking account of their comments, reconstruct your application and CV.

This task will help you to be prepared for any vacancy that arises.

If your application meets the criteria, you will be selected to attend interview; usually candidates are given about seven days' notice for this.

Preparing for the interview

As a general preparation tactic it will be worthwhile re-reading the information pack sent to you; checking the school Web site if there is one; checking DfES and TTA Web sites; and reading the *Times Educational Supplement* so that you are up to date with the latest information on educational matters.

The interview is crucial to obtaining a teaching job. The interview is where you need to convince the headteacher and governing body that you are the right candidate for the job. You should have briefed yourself about the school, its catchment area, its Ofsted report, the standards achieved in the school, its sporting and after-school activities, its overall ethos, and parental involvement. This type of information will help you answer interview questions appropriately. It will also help you ask questions of the panel regarding aspects of the school you wish to know about.

The interview

Make sure you know how to get to the school and arrive in good time. At the interview itself there are likely to be between two and five people present, with an interview lasting 15 to 45 minutes. A common arrangement is for candidates to join the interviewers seated round a table (Smith and Langston, 1999). A 'WASP' format is usual:

- **W**elcoming;
- **A**cquiring (pressure questions to elicit information);
- **S**upplying (open questions to allow personal input);
- **P**arting (closing the interview).

Again it will be worthwhile practising dealing with pressure questions (with a colleague) and preparing answers to likely open questions.

There will be an opportunity for you to ask questions of the interview panel. Here it will be worthwhile carefully scrutinizing school information (documents and the Web site) to see if there are any areas that you would like to know more about. There may also have been comments or questions from the panel that have raised queries in your mind. It will be a matter of personal judgement as to how challenging you wish your questions to be or indeed whether you ask anything at all. It is worth thinking about what personal light your questions throw on yourself – what conclusions the panel would be reading about you from the questions – and balancing this against a genuine desire for information.

Very good advice for an interview is to 'be yourself'. It is important that the school or institution you are applying to wants to appoint someone who has your qualities: a question of matching. However, it is also sensible to present yourself in the best possible light: personal appearance and eye contact are important. One head comments: 'I note how a candidate comes into my room… Does she seem nervous, over-confident or relaxed but alert?' (Kent, 2001). Another acting head-teacher notes that: 'judgements are made within 30 seconds of anyone arriving in the room…We make instant assessments on the basis of what people look like' (Hardacre, 2002). You will be under scrutiny the whole time you are at the school whether you are talking informally to other teachers, doing a presentation, answering interview questions, or talking to the other candidates.

Post-interview decisions

After the interview you may be asked to stay to hear the panel's decision, or candidates may be sent home and contacted there. If you have been successful and you wish to accept, you will be expected to confirm your decision quickly and in writing. If you are unsuccessful you are likely to be given some instructive feedback about your application and interview performance. This feedback can be immensely helpful in preparing for subsequent applications. It is useful to remember if you have been unsuccessful that there may have been small margins of choice in the final decision, that the lack of match between yourself and the post might have meant an unsatisfactory outcome if you *had* been accepted, and that the interview itself can be a useful learning experience. You are now also legally entitled to see information that has been collected about you. The Employment

Practice Data Protection Code gives people access to employment and interview records as well as access to references once these have been received. More details can be found on www.dataprotection.gov.uk.

Applying for a promoted post

When you have been working for a few years, you will want to apply for a promoted post, either in your present school or in another institution. Much of what has been said about the application procedure and interviews in the earlier sections is still relevant but there are some additional considerations:

- the greater emotional demands attached to possible promotion in your own school;
- if selected for interview you may need to adopt a stance or language that is different from what you currently use;
- if successful in obtaining the post your existing relationship with colleagues is likely to change;
- if you are unsuccessful others will know of your lack of promotion and you will then be working with the person who was successful.

Smith and Langston (1999) remind us that, 'no matter how relaxed the surroundings or familiar the people both interviewees and panels participate in a stressful, and for candidates, competitive situation that can give rise to inconsistent behaviour and flawed judgements' (p112).

Professional development

This section introduces the concept of continuing professional development (CPD) and shows how trainee teachers can take responsibility for the early development of their professional career, bearing in mind possible future directions. The first year of this professional development will be covered by an induction programme in your first school and this aspect is covered in more detail in the chapter that follows.

The arrangements governing CPD will differ according to the part of the UK in which you are working (see Neil and Morgan, 2003). The principles are very much standard throughout the country but the specific details may differ. It would be advisable to consult the Web site of the GTC in the relevant jurisdiction and also the DfES and TTA sites to find out what specific requirements are currently in vogue.

Government requirements and support

There is a strong focus on personal responsibility for CPD in the DfEE strategy document *Learning and Teaching* (2001b, p21): 'Alongside an entitlement to professional development all teachers would also have **a duty to take responsibility for their own professional development**' (emphasis in the original).

You will already have prepared a career entry profile (CEP) during your training year (this is described in greater detail below). The government also recommends that you keep a personal log or portfolio of your achievements – a Professional Development Record (PDR) that can be used for interview and review purposes and also as a planning document (DfES, 2001). Further details can be found on www.dfes.gov.uk/teachers/professional_development. In other words the reflective process you have developed during your teacher training year, where you evaluate your own performance and set targets, is seen as the first step in a career-long progression of similar reflection and evaluation.

The government has put in place support for your induction year (this is described in more detail in the next chapter); there are also several more support mechanisms to aid your professional development after this first year:

1.   a programme of early professional development;
2.   funding opportunities;
3.   statutory requirements for schools.

1. Early professional development

A pilot scheme was introduced in a sample of schools (with evaluation from September 2001) to support early professional development for teachers in their second and third year of training. At the time of writing no information was available on the progress of this £25 million funded scheme.

2. Funding opportunities

Several opportunities for funded CPD are being offered to teachers who have been in post for several years: Best Practice Research Scholarships (BPRS) to fund a piece of personal research; professional bursaries to fund costs of travel or research; and six-week sabbaticals where cover is paid for in school. There are some restrictions attached to these funding opportunities and at the time of writing they are envisaged as lasting until 2005. These opportunities are worth bearing in mind as you plan your own professional development. Other smaller schemes (for science, RE and language teachers) also exist and these too merit investigation (details can be found in Neil and Morgan, 2002).

3. Statutory requirements for schools

Schools are required to institute professional development arrangements for their staff linked to a performance management scheme (DfEE 2001b, pp20–21), and where appropriate to link this to improved levels of pay (DfES 2001, p74). Recommendations to OFSTED also include identifying within schools the appropriateness of professional development programmes for the identified needs of the school staff (DfEE, 2001b, p21).

Preparing for performance management/appraisal

You will be used to being appraised and to setting future targets from activities in your teacher-training course and in your induction year. The government has now envisaged a much firmer structure and this will continue after your induction year. One aspect that you may wish to consider is that you can have more input into your own CPD by carefully reviewing your own personal strengths and needs.

What is professional development?

Professional development is about enhancing and extending your knowledge, pedagogy and experience. It is a way of enhancing your effectiveness as a teacher, gaining promotion and developing a career. This can be achieved by considering your starting point and where you want to go in the future. Professional development involves self-review, target setting and individual planning. Most NQTs will start from their career entry profiles (CEPs) (see Chapter 11). You will have completed a CEP by the end of your training period. The CEP will have concentrated on four specific areas of competence:

1. subject knowledge and understanding;
2. planning, teaching, and class management;
3. monitoring, assessment, recording, reporting and accountability;
4. other professional requirements.

Your first school will expect to see development in all areas of competence from your CEP. What you need to appreciate is that it is your responsibility, with the help of your school, to be involved in professional development.

Your CEP is the starting point of your planning for future development. Evaluating your situation is key. Consider the following points when discussing or planning your future needs:

- What areas of development arise from my CEP?
- What other areas do I want to develop?
- What is my preferred style of learning?
- What personal areas do I want to develop to help my career path, eg pastoral, curriculum, or administrative?
- What do I want from my appraisal in terms of specifying development needs?

Kinds of professional development

There can, then, be several ways of developing yourself personally and professionally and It can be helpful to think of these in terms of the different roles that you can play in school. These can be described as:

- communicator;
- subject expert;
- subject teacher;
- classroom manager;
- pastoral tutor;
- administrator;
- team member;
- manager of other teachers;
- school member;
- representative (of the school);
- researcher;
- deliverer of government initiatives.

Sometimes these roles will overlap and coincide and at other times there may be some tension in terms of what you wish to or are able to develop. It will be helpful to talk through your choices with your line manager at school.

Sources of personal development

It is worth considering the many ways to pursue your professional development. These include:

- private reading;
- private or group research;
- in-school activities;
- outside speakers in school;
- off-site courses;
- networking with other schools.

Sometimes activities will be arranged in schools for the statutory five annual non-contact days when schools should be offering or arranging for CPD. These may take the form of outside speakers or in-school arrangements and these may be referred to as INSET (In-Service Education and Training). Your school may also have networking arrangements with other schools or have a well-established action research programme (where you critically evaluate your own practice) that you can join. In other cases you may wish to seek out your own sources of professional development through libraries or journals, or by contacting outside organizations (universities or colleges). In all cases it will be useful to consider both your personal goals and targets (perhaps an area of your own subject expertise or finding out more about a particular educational matter such as dealing effectively with special needs), and those areas prioritized by both the government (literacy and numeracy in primary schools, for example) and your own school.

Much is made in government documentation of being able to show that your professional development has an impact on pupil performance (DfEE, 2001a, 2001b) but it may be that this is difficult to prove in some areas of professional development. Here again you will need to consult with your colleagues and senior management in school.

Task 12.2

Consider your final reflections from teaching and determine what you feel your developmental needs are, both immediate and long-term. Set yourself some targets. These can be taken to your new job for discussion.

References

Craft, A (1996) *Continuing Professional Development*, Routledge, London

Department for Education and Employment (DfEE) (1997) *High Status, High Standards: Requirements for courses of initial teacher training*, Circular 10/97, DfEE, London

DfEE (2001a) *Good Value CPD: A code of practice for providers of professional development for teachers*, DfEE, London

DfEE (2001b) *Learning and Teaching; A strategy for professional development*, DfEE 0071/2001, DfEE, London

Department for Education and Science (DfES) (1969) Black Papers, HMSO, London

DfES (2001) *Schools Achieving Success*, TSO, Norwich

Hardacre, M (2002) We'll let you know, *Times Educational Supplement*, 7 June

Kent, M (2001) Unknown quantities, *Times Educational Supplement*, 12 January

Manning, J (2002) Be realistic about… your personal statement, *Times Educational Supplement*, 19 April

Neil, P and Morgan, C (2003) *Continuing Professional Development: From induction to senior management*, Kogan Page, London

Neumark, V (1996) What makes you the perfect candidate?, *Times Educational Supplement*, 12 January

Smith, A and Langston, A (1999) *Managing Staff in Early Years Settings*, Routledge, London

13 Induction for Newly Qualified Teachers

James Williams

Since May 1999 all newly qualified teachers (NQTs) who wish to teach in the state maintained sector are required to complete an induction year. Induction is an important first stage in your professional development as a teacher. Since its introduction, NQTs have benefited from a reduced timetable in their first year of teaching and a proper introduction to the profession. Over 99 per cent of NQTs who complete their induction year are successful. This chapter aims to focus your mind on the requirements, expectations and statutory demands of being a newly qualified teacher.

Objectives

By the end of this chapter you should have an understanding of:

- what it means to be an NQT;
- the aims and objectives of the induction period;
- the roles and responsibilities of those involved in induction;
- the induction standards;
- what is meant by unsatisfactory progress and the implications of failure.

An overview of induction

Gaining qualified teacher status is really the start of your professional development as a teacher. It is analogous to learning to drive: QTS has a theoretical and practical element, but just like driving you are not an experienced, advanced driver as soon as you pass your test. There are many teaching situations of which you will have little to no experience. In the same way that some driving schools offer post-test driving experience of motorways, the induction period is designed to ensure that you are fully prepared for taking on all the responsibilities of a full-time teacher.

The government's 1997 White Paper, *Excellence in Schools* (DfEE, 1997), outlined its commitment to providing training and support for new teachers. With the publication of the government's Green Paper in 1998, this support was further strengthened. It established the professional development to which all teachers have a right:

> The government will provide the necessary funding to guarantee all new teachers a reduced teaching load and a programme of support to ensure that they have the time to consolidate and improve their performance. (DfEE, 1998, para 120)

The induction year is neither new nor unwelcome within the profession. There used to be a probationary year for teachers, which was abolished in 1992 because it was felt that it was not a quality experience for new teachers. As a mechanism for support and continued professional development it mostly failed to deliver, and its abolition did not encounter much opposition. It is now appreciated that a quality induction programme is crucial to the recognition of teaching as a valuable and valued profession. In other professions, such as law and medicine, a professional approach to induction enhances those professions. The induction year must be viewed as a similar process for teaching.

Induction for NQTs wishing to teach in the state maintained sector is statutory and all schools have a duty to deliver a quality induction programme, except pupil referral units or schools on special measures (ie designated as having serious weaknesses after OFSTED inspection); under normal circumstances these schools are not permitted to employ NQTs. Private schools that do not follow the National Curriculum or that do not have an agreement to provide induction are not obliged to offer induction.

Once initial teacher training has been successfully completed trainees have their details registered by the General Teaching Council (GTC) for the country in which they trained – England, Scotland or Wales. These councils are responsible for maintaining registers of qualified teachers and continued registration will depend on successful completion of the induction period. The consequences of failing the induction period are severe. You will not be registered with the GTC and, therefore, will be unable to take up a post on the qualified pay scale in a state maintained school. Induction is not statutory for work in the private sector, though teachers moving from the private to the state sector who have not completed induction and who qualified after 7 May 1999 will be required to do so. Many private schools do now offer induction and teachers who move straight into employment in private schools after gaining QTS should opt to complete induction if it is offered so as to avoid having to do this later on should they move into the state sector. Induction in the private sector is overseen by the Independent Schools Council Teacher Induction Panel (ISCTIP) or by agreement with an LEA (appropriate body, or AB). The standards for induction in private schools offering induction are the same as those in the state sector.

Failing induction is a rare occurrence. Since induction became mandatory in May 1999 there have been 56,263 NQTs who have passed their induction, and only 94 who have failed (data provided by the GTCE 5/12/02) a failure rate of only 0.2 per cent. For those who do fail, there is an appeals procedure.

Induction is not a requirement for the following categories of teachers:

- teachers who obtained QTS on or before 7 May 1999;
- a person who is employed for a period of less than one term as a supply teacher (but be aware that an NQT can only work on short supply periods for five terms after the date of their first employment as a supply teacher);
- teachers who have successfully completed induction or probation in Scotland, Northern Ireland, Wales, the Isle of Man, Guernsey, Jersey or Gibraltar;
- a teacher employed on the GTP training route until they are awarded QTS, at which time the induction period applies;
- an instructor without QTS, employed while no suitable qualified teacher is available;
- a teacher trained overseas (employed up to a maximum of four years);
- a teacher trained overseas who is assessed for QTS and induction simultaneously;
- teachers from the European Economic Area (EEA).

Entitlements for NQTs

When NQTs are employed and undertaking induction, their employer must ensure that the job is suitable and appropriate for an NQT. You should expect your teaching timetable to be a maximum of 90 per cent of a normal teaching load, ie 90 per cent of the normal teaching load of a fully experienced teacher carrying no extra responsibilities that entitles them to non-contact time. The 10 per cent reduction must be used in connection with the induction and not be regularly used to cover other, absent teachers.

In addition, the job to which an NQT has been appointed must:

- not demand teaching outside the age range and subject(s) for which the NQT has been trained;
- not present the NQT on a day-to-day basis with acute or especially demanding discipline problems;

- involve regular teaching of the same class(es);
- involve similar planning, teaching and assessment processes to those in which teachers working in substantive posts in the school are engaged; and
- not involve additional non-teaching responsibilities without the provision of appropriate preparation and support. (DfES, 2001, para 28)

As an NQT you will receive a lot of help and advice from your school. Before taking up your post you should receive your timetable, the arrangements that have been made to support you during the year, a broad timetable for meetings (observations will be sorted out nearer the time), what the arrangements are for reporting, and the name of the contact person responsible for NQTs from the AB. You will also receive information about your entitlements to sickness pay (and maternity rights for female employees) and you should be given information on the school policies and a contract of employment and job description. Much of this information is often found in a staff handbook.

The aims of the induction period

The DfES issues guidance to schools on the arrangements that must be made for the induction of NQTs (DfES, 2001). These arrangements also set out the aims for the induction period, which are to:

- build upon the knowledge and understanding developed through initial teacher training, ie the standards attained as set out in the document *Qualifying to Teach* (TTA, 2002);
- provide a foundation for long-term continuing professional development (CPD);
- build upon the areas of development identified in the NQT's Career Entry and Development Profile (CEDP);
- ensure proper support is offered to NQTs making unsatisfactory progress;
- put in place rigorous assessment procedures for the induction year.

In order to fulfil these aims, it is important that the roles and responsibilities of those involved in an NQT's induction period are set out.

Roles and responsibilities during induction

Various bodies and individuals will have particular roles and responsibilities during the induction period. Successful induction will require all concerned to carry out their role professionally. The headteacher, the induction tutor, the NQT, the LEA (the AB) and the school's governing body all have a part to play in ensuring successful induction. Tables 13.1 to 13.5 summarize the roles and responsibilities of the various bodies and individuals involved in setting up, monitoring, assessing and reporting upon the induction of NQTs.

Table 13.1   The roles and responsibilities of the headteacher during NQT induction

Headteacher

Role	*Responsibility*
• To designate staff responsibilities	• To prepare staff for their roles during the induction period • To assign staff to act as induction tutors for each NQT in the school
• To develop the induction programme	• To ensure that an appropriate induction programme related to the NQT's CEDP is available
• To agree the NQT's timetable	• To ensure that the NQT's timetable is no more than 90 per cent of a substantive teacher's full timetable
• To provide rigorous and fair assessment of NQTs	• To ensure that induction tutors' assessment is fair and rigorous
• To provide independent assessment of NQTs failing to make satisfactory progress	• To observe the teaching of any NQT deemed to be at risk
• To collate assessment meeting reports	• To ensure that reports of any assessment meetings are forwarded to the appropriate body
• To make recommendations to the appropriate bodies	• To inform the appropriate body of any NQT who satisfactorily completes the induction period • To inform the appropriate body of any NQT who fails to satisfactorily complete the induction period
• To maintain NQT records	• To liaise with other schools and obtain/pass on records of NQTs who move jobs during the induction period • To liaise with other schools/appropriate bodies where NQTs are employed part-time
• To inform the governing body of induction arrangements/progress	• To ensure that governing bodies are aware of the induction programme and the progress of any NQTs

Table 13.2   The roles and responsibilities of the induction tutor during NQT induction

Induction tutor

Role	*Responsibility*

• Day-to-day monitoring and support	• To implement the school's induction programme
	• To act as a source of advice
	• To observe NQT's teaching
	• To report and feedback on observations to:
	  – the NQT
	  – the headteacher (where appropriate)

• Be trained for the role of induction tutor	• To attend INSET deemed necessary by the headteacher
• Apply induction assessment criteria	• To be familiar with induction assessment requirements • To apply induction assessment criteria rigorously and fairly
• Implement the NQT's CEDP action plan	• To translate the NQT's CEDP action plan into an achievable programme given the circumstances present within the school
• To enable full and proper support	• To ensure that there is an appropriate breadth of experience for the NQT • To arrange for additional support and experience outside the NQT's school if necessary
• Record keeping	• To maintain accurate records of the NQT's progress
• Assessment activity recording	• To ensure that assessments of NQTs are undertaken according to induction guidelines and keep formal records of their outcome

Headteachers have a responsibility for ensuring that a high quality induction programme is available for all NQTs employed by their school. This includes a number of management-specific issues such as preparing experienced staff for their role as an induction tutor, ensuring a fair yet rigorous assessment of NQTs, and other more administrative issues such as notifying the AB of when NQTs join and leave the staff of their school. The main role of the headteacher is to make a recommendation to the AB as to whether or not an NQT has successfully passed the induction year.

The induction tutor's role in supporting and monitoring the work of NQTs is vital. It is clear from the summary of their roles and responsibilities as set out in Table 13.2 that they must be accessible and approachable. In most cases, particularly in large primary schools or in secondary schools, the induction tutor will often be

Table 13.3 The roles and responsibilities of the NQT during induction

Newly qualified teacher

Role	Responsibility
• Take part in the induction programme	• To actively participate and monitor own work in relation to the induction standards
• Aid target setting	• To use the CEDP to negotiate short, medium and long-term targets for professional development
• Monitor the support, assessment and guidance given	• To raise professional concerns over the induction programme if necessary through the appropriate channels
• Understand the purposes of induction and the standards related to them	• To be familiar with the induction standards and the programme for induction

the NQT's line manager. In practice this will mean a head of department in a secondary school, perhaps a deputy head or subject coordinator in a large primary. In the case of a school with a small complement, the headteacher may be the only suitable person to take on this role.

The governing body has a responsibility for overseeing the establishment of induction within the school and for maintaining it. The appropriate body will usually be the LEA, or in the case of private schools, the ISCTIP.

NQTs have a duty to participate fully in the induction process and to monitor their own progress in meeting the induction standards. Should NQTs feel that the induction programme is not meeting their needs it is their responsibility to make this known to the headteacher.

Induction will last for a minimum of three terms and may, under exceptional circumstances only, be extended. This does not have to be a continuous period and it does not have to be all undertaken within the same school.

The monitoring and support programme

NQTs should be provided with an induction programme by their school that is to a large extent tailored to their individual needs. These needs will be directly related to the NQT's CEDP. The CEDP is intended to provide a series of transition points from trainee to teacher. The first stage, completed towards the end of training, will identify a trainee's strengths and areas for further development. It will be the areas for further development that will form the basis of the first year programme.

Table 13.4   The roles and responsibilities of the appropriate body during NQT induction

The appropriate body

Role	*Responsibility*
• Maintain a list of NQTs for whom it acts as the appropriate body	• To collect information from headteachers of NQTs employed and the term of induction that applies • To maintain a list of supply NQTs who are employed for a minimum of one term or more
• Liaison with other appropriate bodies	• To exchange details of NQTs employed part-time in more than one appropriate body's area
• Identify a named contact	• To ensure that a named contact is made known to schools and induction tutors with whom issues about provision can be raised
• Decide on satisfactory completion of induction	• To act on the recommendation of the headteacher as to satisfactory completion of induction • To act on advice that NQTs are not making satisfactory progress and respond to the headteacher's notification of this • In exceptional circumstances, to offer an extension to the induction period • Where there is disagreement between the headteacher's decision and the evidence produced to support this, to reject the headteacher's decision and substitute its own
• Liaison with the relevant General Teaching Council (GTC) and DfEE	• To inform the relevant GTC of those NQTs who have satisfactorily completed induction • To inform the Secretary of State for Education of those who satisfactorily complete induction • To inform the NQT of whether or not it accepts the headteacher's recommendation • To inform NQTs of the post-induction process • To maintain records until the relevant GTC informs them that NQTs are included on the register of qualified teachers
• Quality assurance	• To ensure that induction programmes are appropriate and of high quality • To ensure that headteachers and governing bodies are aware of their roles and responsibilities • To consult with headteachers and others on the form that quality assurance should take • To provide advice and guidance on how schools may meet the induction guidance arrangements

Table 13.5 The roles and responsibilities of the governing body during NQT induction

The governing body

Role	Responsibility
• Oversee induction arrangements	• To ensure that appropriate and adequate induction programmes are available in their school
• Liaison with the appropriate body	• To seek guidance on the nature, range and appropriateness of induction arrangements for NQTs
• Oversee the roles of individuals with responsibility for induction	• To seek guidance on the extent and nature of the roles of individuals responsible for the induction of NQTs

An evaluation of the effectiveness of the induction period carried out by Totterdell *et al* (2001, 2002) provides us with good evidence for the success of well-planned induction. It concluded that the majority of schools give consistent and individualized support. They also found that induction had provided an appropriate bridge between initial training and full-time work. The report also highlighted some concerns, mainly a lack of consistency in delivering the 10 per cent reduction in timetable commitments and a lack of opportunity for the NQT to meet regularly with the induction tutor.

Observation of the NQT's day-to-day work must be carried out regularly. In order for observation to be of benefit it must be clearly targeted. During the ITT programme, trainees will have benefited from observation by their school-based mentors – many of whom may also be induction tutors – and, in many cases these observations are moderated by the ITT institutions that provide support and training for mentors. Targeted observations, where the observer and the trainee, or in the case of induction the NQT, have discussed in advance the nature and the focus of the observation, eg class management, differentiation, formative assessment of pupils, etc, lead to the most productive evaluations of a teacher's work. Over the induction year, observation may be made by a wide variety of individuals apart from the induction tutor – senior school staff, staff with specific responsibilities such as subject coordinators, year heads, LEA advisory staff or advanced skills teachers (ASTs).

During their training, teachers frequently observe experienced staff to see good teaching in practice. Once qualified, it is a frequent complaint that these opportunities diminish substantially. The induction programme goes some way to remedying this situation by encouraging collaborative work with experienced staff. In small schools this could be a problem. Schools are encouraged to allow NQTs to observe teachers in other schools, such as beacon schools, which may have been identified as demonstrating effective practice.

The professional review of progress during your induction year will be ongoing. Your CEDP sets out a suggested plan for the induction year and what should happen and when (see Figure 13.1). It is important that you are clear about what the structure of the year is and that you actively monitor progress at each point. A series of support materials are designed to help you reflect and review progress during your induction year and you should be proactive in using these with your induction tutor (TTA, 2003a, b, c and d).

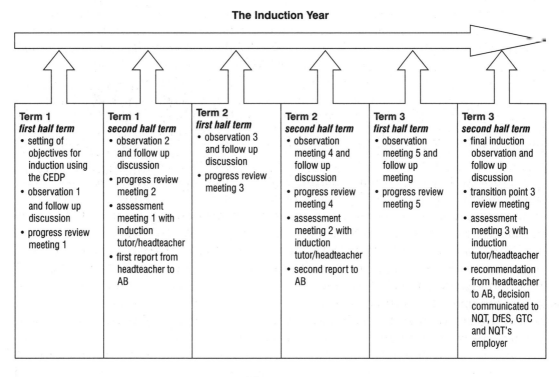

The Induction Year

Term 1 *first half term*	Term 1 *second half term*	Term 2 *first half term*	Term 2 *second half term*	Term 3 *first half term*	Term 3 *second half term*
• setting of objectives for induction using the CEDP • observation 1 and follow up discussion • progress review meeting 1	• observation 2 and follow up discussion • progress review meeting 2 • assessment meeting 1 with induction tutor/headteacher • first report from headteacher to AB	• observation 3 and follow up discussion • progress review meeting 3	• observation meeting 4 and follow up discussion • progress review meeting 4 • assessment meeting 2 with induction tutor/headteacher • second report to AB	• observation meeting 5 and follow up meeting • progress review meeting 5	• final induction observation and follow up discussion • transition point 3 review meeting • assessment meeting 3 with induction tutor/headteacher • recommendation from headteacher to AB, decision communicated to NQT, DfES, GTC and NQT's employer

Figure 13.1

A key part of professional development is access to high quality in-service training (INSET); NQTs should access this as part of their induction year. Many ABs have generic training for NQTs in their schools and many schools encourage NQTs to sign up for appropriate commercially provided INSET.

The induction standards

New induction standards apply from 1 September 2003 (see the appendix to this chapter). It is these standards that apply to any NQTs starting their induction period on or after that date. In order to pass the induction year an NQT must meet all of the induction standards and continue to meet the standards for the award of QTS, consistently and with increasing professional competence.

The induction standards are divided into three sections, *Professional values and Practice*, *Knowledge and Understanding* and *Teaching*. These complement the standards for QTS and, indeed, the new induction standards show how they relate to the standards for QTS. During the induction year the NQT, induction tutor and headteacher must gather evidence on the NQT's progress. That evidence will come from a variety of sources, such as long, medium and short-term lesson plans, how the NQT deploys support staff and teaching assistants, reports written on pupils, attendance and performance at parent evenings, etc. Starting a professional development portfolio in your induction year would be a good way of managing the collection of evidence needed to support your assessment. Chapter 12 gives more in-depth advice about continuing professional development, but the following list contains suggestions of things that may be included in your portfolio (TTA, 2003d; Williams, 2003):

- your medium-term and short-term curriculum planning;
- targets you set for your pupils and their progress towards meeting them;
- individual education plans that you have helped prepare and review;
- evidence from your self-review and evaluations of lessons you have taught;
- pupils' work you have assessed;
- reports to parents and carers;
- feedback from parents and carers (be aware of confidentiality issues);
- records of observations of your teaching;
- reflections on the range of professional development opportunities you have accessed;
- reflections on the lessons you have observed;
- evaluation of your professional development, including its impact on pupils' learning;
- learning logs you have maintained;
- reflection on the ways in which you have promoted creativity within your current post in school;
- evaluation of your contribution to collaborative working within your school, and your contribution to the work of the school beyond the classes you teach.

Unsatisfactory progress

The vast majority of NQTs who complete induction are successful. Schools must identify those NQTs who are not making satisfactory progress as soon as possible so that early action and intervention can take place to support the NQT. In most cases this identification should take place before the first formal assessment meeting in the first term. Any concerns over progress must be communicated to all those with responsibility for the NQT as quickly as possible. A report must be written that identifies the weaknesses, the evidence for those weaknesses, the support planned for the NQT and the agreed objectives set in relation to the requirements for the satisfactory completion of induction (DfES, 2001, para 71).

Unsatisfactory progress should not remain unrecognized until the final term. In all cases where NQTs are judged to be making unsatisfactory progress they should be observed by the headteacher (unless he or she is also the induction tutor) and they should also review the evidence. Where a headteacher is also an induction tutor, a third party should review the evidence and observe the NQT. After this assessment, concerns must be given in writing to the NQT and all of this should be communicated to the AB.

If any NQTs feel that the proper support is not being given or that the induction procedures are not being adhered to, they may in the first instance take this up with the headteacher. If they subsequently feel that their concerns are not being addressed, they may approach the named contact at the AB. All NQTs should be told who the named contact for their school is. There are only two circumstances in which the induction period can be extended beyond three terms: first, when an NQT has sustained a period of illness resulting in more than 30 days off work; second, when an NQT is on maternity leave, where a final assessment is made when she returns to work.

After final assessment a headteacher has 10 working days to communicate his or her decision to the AB. If that decision is to fail an NQT, then there is a right of appeal. Appeals are made to the AB, which can uphold the appeal, dismiss the appeal, or grant an extension period for as long as it sees fit.

Conclusion

Support for NQTs and attention to their continuing professional development were long overdue. The consequences of failure are severe, but with the rigorous assessment of trainee teachers now in place, NQTs are well placed to complete induction successfully. The CEDP sets out a series of transition points from trainee, to NQT, to teacher. After induction teachers embark on performance management, which aims to develop the skills of professional teachers and provide access to higher levels of pay and give opportunities for enhanced performance. To gain Advanced Skills Teacher status, teachers must develop and maintain a professional development portfolio. Induction is the first step in a continuum that is set to provide a challenge for entrants to the teaching profession that sees teaching as a true profession and not just another job.

Appendix: The induction standards

In order to complete the induction period satisfactorily, a newly qualified teacher must demonstrate all of the following.

Professional values and practice

They continue to meet the requirements of the Professional Values and Practice section of the Standards for the Award of QTS, and build on these. Specifically, they:

Seek and use opportunities to work collaboratively with colleagues to raise standards by sharing effective practice in the school.

Knowledge and understanding

They continue to meet the requirements of the Knowledge and Understanding section of the Standards for the Award of QTS, and build on these. Specifically, they:

Show a commitment to their professional development by:

- identifying areas in which they need to improve their professional knowledge, understanding and practice in order to teach more effectively in their current post, and
- with support, taking steps to address these needs.

Teaching

They continue to meet the requirements of the Teaching section of the Standards for the Award of QTS, and build on these by demonstrating increasing responsibility and professional competence in their teaching and when working with other adults, including parents.

Specifically, they:

Plan effectively to meet the needs of pupils in their classes with special educational needs, with or without statements, and, in consultation with the SENCO, contribute to the preparation, implementation, monitoring and review of individual education plans or the equivalent.

Liaise effectively with parents or carers on pupils' progress and achievements.

Work effectively as part of a team and, as appropriate to the post in which they are completing induction, liaise with, deploy, and guide the work of other adults who support pupils' learning.

Secure a standard of behaviour that enables pupils to learn, and act to pre-empt and deal with inappropriate behaviour in the context of the behaviour policy of the school.

References

DfEE (1997) *Excellence in Schools*, TSO, Norwich

DfEE (1998) *Teachers: Meeting the challenge of change*, DfEE, London

DfES (2001) *The Induction Period for Newly Qualified Teachers*, Circular 582/2001 DfES, London

Teacher Training Agency (TTA) (2002) *Qualifying to Teach: Professional standards for qualified teacher status and requirements for initial teacher training*, TTA, London

TTA (2003a) *Recording Reflections and Discussions*, TTA, London

TTA (2003b) *Writing Induction Action Plans and Reviewing Progress*, TTA, London

TTA (2003c) *For NQTs Who Move Schools During Their Induction Period*, TTA, London

TTA (2003d) *Maintaining a Professional Portfolio*, TTA, London

Totterdell, M, Heilbronn, R, Bubb, S and Jones, C (2001) *Evaluation of the Effectiveness of the Statutory Arrangements for the Induction of Newly Qualified Teachers: Final report*, December, Institute of Education, London

Totterdell, M, Heilbronn, R, Bubb, S and Jones, C (2002) *Evaluation of the Effectiveness of the Statutory Arrangements for the Induction of Newly Qualified Teachers*, DfES Brief No. 338, May

Williams, J (2003) Prepare to promote yourself, *TES, First Appointments*, 9 May, p14

Glossary: Common Education Abbreviations

AB	Appropriate Body
AST	Advanced Skills Teacher
ATL	Association of Teachers and Lecturers
BA	Bachelor of Arts
BEd	Bachelor of Education
BSc	Bachelor of Science
CEDP	Career Entry and Development Profile
CPD	Continuing Professional Development
CTC	City Technology College
DfEE	Department for Education and Employment
DfES	Department for Education and Skills
EdD	Education Doctorate
FEFC	Further Education Funding Council
GCSE	General Certificate of Secondary Education
GTCE	General Teaching Council (for England)
GTCS	General Teaching Council (for Scotland)
GTCW	General Teaching Council (for Wales)
HEFCE	Higher Education Funding Council for England
HEI	Higher Education Institution
HMI	Her Majesty's Inspectorate
ICT	Information and Communications Technology
IEP	Individual Education Plan
INSET	In-Service Education and Training
ISCTIP	Independent Schools Council Teacher Induction Panel
ITE	Initial Teacher Education
ITT	Initial Teacher Training
KS	Key Stage
LEA	Local Education Authority
LGA	Local Government Association
LPSH	Leadership Programme for Serving Headteachers
MEd/MA	Master of Education/Master of Arts

NAHT	National Association of Head Teachers
NPQH	National Professional Qualification for Headship
NQT	Newly Qualified Teacher
NASUWT	National Association of Schoolmasters Union of Women Teachers
NUT	National Union of Teachers
OFSTED	Office for Standards in Education
PAT	Professional Association of Teachers
PEIY	Project on the Evaluation of the Induction Year
PGCE	Postgraduate Certificate in Education
QA	Quality Assurance
QCA	Qualifications and Curriculum Authority
QTS	Qualified Teacher Status
SCITT	School-Centred Initial Teacher Training
SEN	Special Educational Needs
SENCO	Special Educational Needs Coordinator
SFC	Sixth Form College
SMART	Specific, Measurable, Achievable, Relevant, Time-bound
TES	Times Educational Supplement
TIAC	Teacher Induction Appeal Committee
TTA	Teacher Training Agency

Index

numbers in **bold type** refer to figures/tables

disapplication 36; flexibility 6, 31, 32, 36–7; foundation stage 6, 147, 197; foundation subjects 27; ICT 69–73; independence from 7; information on learning 35–6; key skills 35; learning objectives 21; lesson plans 37, **38**; level descriptors **29**, 30, 38; new look 31; pedagogy 41; phased introduction 26; programmes of study (PoS) 27, **29**, 31; progression, pupil 39–40; purposes 27; revision 21–2, 26, 39, 40; revolutionary nature 23; schemes of work 37, 38; SEN 169; statutory framework 31–2, 33; study tasks 26, 31, 32, 33, 38, 40, 41; subjects **32**, 36; teaching requirements 33–5; topic approach 38; whole-school planning policies 37–8 *see also* curriculum; Key Stages

The National Curriculum 5–16: A Consultation Document (DES, 1987) 25

National Curriculum Council 26, 170

National Grid for Learning (NGfL) 66, 68

Neil, P. 220–332

networking, teachers 230, 231

Neumark, V. 223

Newell, S. 132

newly qualified teachers (NQTs) 2; induction *see* induction for newly qualified teachers (NQTs); and special measures schools 234 *see also* trainees

Nicholls, Gill 1–2, 178–91, 208–19

non-maintained schools 8

norm-referencing 138

number application *see* numeracy

numeracy 40; developing pupils 35; hour 26, 59; and learning 59–60, **64**

Nursery Education and Grant Maintained Schools Act (1996) 197

nursery: inspection 197; partnerships 196–7, 198 *see also* foundation stage; pre-school learning

NVQ 31 *see also* GNVQ

objectives, learning 15, 16

objectives model 96, 99, 100, **101**; ability differentiation 106, **107**; evaluation procedures 106–8; lesson structure 105–6; modification 108; preparation 108–9; selection of learning material 105; specifying objectives 103–5 *see also* lesson planning

observation, assessment 142, 149

Office for Standards in Education (OFSTED) **5**, 178–9; accountability 179; framework 180–1; ICT use assessment 90; lesson evaluation 95, 112; parental involvement 202; principles 180; professional development 229; Registered Inspector (RgI) 183; reports, accessing 188; role 179–80; scalar statements **185**, 187 *see also* inspection

Ofsted Handbook for Inspection, Part 6. The Statutory Basis for Education (1997) 213

open-mindedness, teachers 19

Opportunity and excellence (DES, 2002) 37

paradigms, learning *see* learning paradigms

parental choice *see* choice

parents/carers, role 192–207; classroom helpers 193; as consumers 202; curriculum-focused involvement 201; *Desirable Outcomes for Children's Learning* (SCAA, 1996) 197–8, 199; fund raising 193; governing body representative 194; home background, influence 194–5, 196, 198–9; home-school partnerships/liaison 193, 194, 199,